Uptalk

'Uptalk' is commonly used to refer to rising intonation at the end of declarative sentences, or (to put it more simply) the **tendency for people to make statements that sound like questions**, a phenomenon that has received wide exposure and commentary in the media. How and where did it originate? Who are the most frequent 'uptalkers'? How much does it vary according to the speaker's age, gender and regional dialect? Is it found in other languages as well as English? These and other questions are the subject of this fascinating book. The first comprehensive analysis of 'uptalk', it examines its historical origins, geographical spread and social influences. Paul Warren also looks at the media's coverage of the phenomenon, including the tension between the public's perception and the views of experts.

Informed by a wealth of research findings, *Uptalk* will be welcomed by those working in linguistics, as well as anyone interested in the way we talk today.

PAUL WARREN is on the Editorial Board of *Language and Speech*, and is past editor of *Te Reo*, the journal of the Linguistic Society of New Zealand. He belongs to various professional organisations, including the International Phonetic Association, and is a founding member of the Association for Laboratory Phonology. Paul is an Associate Professor in the School of Linguistics and Applied Language Studies at Victoria University of Wellington.

Uptalk

The Phenomenon of Rising Intonation

Paul Warren

School of Linguistics and Applied Language Studies

Victoria University of Wellington

CAMBRIDGE
UNIVERSITY PRESS

University Printing House, Cambridge CB2 8BS, United Kingdom

Cambridge University Press is part of the University of Cambridge.

It furthers the University's mission by disseminating knowledge in the pursuit of education, learning and research at the highest international levels of excellence.

www.cambridge.org
Information on this title: www.cambridge.org/9781107560840

© Paul Warren 2016

First published 2016

Printed in the United Kingdom by Clays, St Ives plc

A catalogue record for this publication is available from the British Library

Library of Congress Cataloguing in Publication data
Warren, Paul, 1966–
Uptalk : the phenomenon of rising intonation / Paul Warren, School of Linguistics and Applied Language Studies, Victoria University of Wellington.
    pages   cm
Includes bibliographical references and index.
ISBN 978-1-107-12385-4 (hardback) – ISBN 978-1-107-56084-0 (pbk)
1. Intonation (Phonetics)   2. Phonetics.   I. Title.
P222.W37   2015
414'.6–dc23   2015023047

ISBN 978-1-107-12385-4 Hardback
ISBN 978-1-107-56084-0 Paperback

To Liz, Matthew and Chris.
In loving memory of two non-uptalkers, Bunny (1927–2011) and Brian (1937–2015), caring, inspiring and generous father and father-in-law.

Contents

Figures

Tables

Preface

This book provides an overview of a rising form of intonation, widely but not universally known as *uptalk*. This label refers to a rather innovative use of rising intonation on declarative utterances. Uptalk has become a topic of public discussion and of linguistic research in the latter part of the twentieth century, and is now frequently encountered in a range of varieties of English, as well as in other languages. The focus in this book will be primarily on English, and will include discussion of varieties of English, since these vary in the nature of their intonation patterns and in the shape and role of uptalk in their intonational inventory. It will nevertheless also include discussion of uptalk in languages other than English.

Uptalk is perceptually salient because although rising intonation is typically (and somewhat naively) associated with questions rather than statements in English, uptalk is the use of rising intonation in contexts where questions would not usually be expected. This salience means that it has received considerable attention, both from expert researchers and from the general public. Media commentary on uptalk has been highly speculative and often condemnatory, associating uptalk with uncertainty and insecurity among younger speakers, who are the more typical users of this form of intonation, and blaming the increasing incidence of uptalk on the influence of youth culture and in some cases even specifically on Australian soap operas. However, we will see that the meanings conveyed by uptalk intonation are more complex than a simple association of rises with questions, that the interpretation of uptalk depends on social factors as well as linguistic ones, and that uptalk plays an important role in tracking the listener's comprehension and in maintaining a constructive relationship between conversational partners.

Twenty-five years ago, an early review of uptalk-type intonation in Australian English (Guy and Vonwiller, 1989) posed three questions that were current in the debate at that time: What does this form of intonation mean? Is it changing and spreading? Who uses it? These questions remain relevant today, along with many others that have emerged since in both public debate and scientific research. The current overview therefore aims to bring together in one place some of the extensive discussion of the forms (Chapter 2) and functions

(Chapter 3) of this intonational phenomenon; to highlight and comment on the range of English varieties in which it is found (Chapter 4); to discuss its historical and geographic spread (Chapter 5); to review the social and textual factors that influence its use (Chapter 6); to describe how it is perceived, as revealed both in media commentary (Chapter 7) and in experimental research (Chapter 8); and to note also the incidence of uptalk in languages other than English (Chapter 9). Finally (Chapter 10), a few remarks about methodological issues help to explain some of the differences between results reported by different researchers and act as a guide for future uptalk research.

My aim in writing this book has been to bring together these different strands of linguistic research and public perception in an attempt to provide a coherent account of the origins, distribution, nature and use of that 'rising inflection at the end of each sentence, which makes every remark sound like a whiny question' (Fergus, 1997).

Acknowledgements

Many colleagues and collaborators have contributed to my interest in and understanding of intonation, and of uptalk in particular. I would especially like to thank Nicola Daly and Dave Britain for their contributions to our study of intonation in New Zealand English, and Janet Fletcher for discussions of intonational issues in both New Zealand and Australian English. I am also grateful to Sasha Calhoun for her close reading of and feedback on portions of the text.

Symbols and abbreviations

Stress (symbol placed before stressed syllable)
'   primary
ˌ   secondary
Nuclear tones (symbol placed before accented syllable)
\   high-fall
ˎ   low-fall
/   high-rise
ˏ   low-rise
∨   fall-rise
∧   rise-fall
>   level
Global tunes (also used in this text for nuclear tones where the height of the tone is not crucial)
↗   rising
↘   falling
H   high tone
L   low tone
*   pitch accent
-      phrase accent
%   boundary tone

Abbreviations

AQI	Australian Question(ing) Intonation
ERB	equivalent rectangular bandwidth
F0	fundamental frequency
HRT	high-rise/rising tone/tune/terminal
HRTD	high-rise/rising terminal declarative
Hz	Hertz (cycles per second)
ToBI	Tones and Break Indices
UNB	Urban Northern British
WHQ	wh-question
YNQ	yes–no question

1   Introduction – why 'uptalk'?

Before engaging in a detailed discussion of the forms and functions of uptalk, it is important to provide an outline description of what is meant by uptalk and to motivate why this book refers to this phenomenon as 'uptalk'. In addition, this chapter provides some background information on intonational analysis more generally, as well as introducing some of the methodological issues that will be expanded on in a later chapter.

1.1   Defining uptalk

It would seem that uptalk needs a new publicity agent. It has been referred to as an 'irritating verbal tic' (Marsh, 2006) and a 'real credibility killer' (DiResta, 2010). If you are a speaker who uses uptalk, then you sound 'as if you don't know your own mind and would like someone else to make it up for you' (Parkin, 2005), or that you have 'lost your own sense of power' (Edenson, 1996). You may also suffer from a crisis of identity, since an utterance with uptalk 'sounds like a question posed by an Australian' (Adams, 2009), but may also indicate that you are 'really a central Canadian' (Watson, 2000) or are someone who has 'tinges of California upspeak curling the edges of his sentences' (Hoad, 2005). These comments give a flavour of the opinions expressed in the popular press about this intonational feature, but they also indicate that discussion of this phenomenon is widespread. As we will see in Chapter 7, these opinions have tended to be negative, largely condemning the use of uptalk and often providing strong advice that it should be avoided if you want to speak properly.

The term 'uptalk' is not (yet) listed in the *Oxford English Dictionary* or the *Merriam-Webster Dictionary*, not even in their online versions (www.oed.com and www.merriam-webster.com. All online dictionary entries discussed in this section were accessed on 6 November 2014). However, the online resource Oxford Dictionaries calls uptalk 'A manner of speaking in which declarative sentences are uttered with rising intonation at the end, as if they were questions' (www.oxforddictionaries.com), while Dictionary.com defines it as 'a rise in pitch at the end usually of a declarative sentence, especially if habitual: often represented in writing by a question mark' (http://dictionary.reference.com) and the Urban Dictionary as a 'way of speaking that puts an upward inflection on the last word of a statement that makes it sound like a question when it's not. (Common among teens and surfers)' (www.urbandictionary.com). Objections can be raised with each of these definitions. To take just one point from each definition in turn: even if we disregard uptalk, rising intonation is not only found on questions, and not all questions are marked by intonation (see further discussion in Section 2.1); question marks may of course be used to mark uptalk in written texts (supernumerary question marks are mentioned in this context in Section 5.5), but they are of little use as a guide in dealing with what is largely a spoken phenomenon; and while uptalk is frequently found on the last word of a statement, it often begins earlier in the utterance. Nevertheless, these definitions are of interest in that they highlight the general location and nature of the intonation pattern (rising intonation at the end of a declarative sentence, see Chapter 2) at the same time as they comment on the speaker groups likely to use it (young people, and from 'surfers' one might infer Californians – see Chapters 4 and 6). Dictionary.com highlights that uptalk is 'habitual', i.e., there is a tendency for certain speakers to use it more regularly than others (see Chapter 6 for discussion of which types of speakers these may be), and the definition from the Urban Dictionary importantly acknowledges that while uptalk utterances might sound like questions, they are not (see Chapter 3).

As we will see elsewhere in this book, linguists have typically taken a more objective, descriptive view of uptalk than the characterisations found in the media, trying to gain a better understanding of who does it, why they do it and what it is really like. However, as pointed out by Di Gioacchino and Crook Jessop (2010: 2), 'the use of variable descriptions of uptalk by researchers makes it difficult to assign a concrete and stable definition'. As a working definition, uptalk is taken in this book to be

a marked rising intonation pattern found at the ends of intonation units realised on declarative utterances, and which serves primarily to check comprehension or to seek feedback.

This definition provides a lot of leeway, but at the same time constrains the possible scope of uptalk. The leeway is necessary because, as we will see in later discussion, the shape of uptalk is variable and quite possibly differs from one variety of English to another. Hence it would be too restrictive to define the shape of uptalk, as has been done, as a rise that climbs to at least 40 per cent above the voice pitch level found at the starting point of the rise (Guy et al., 1986). Not only would that exclude many uptalk rises with smaller relative pitch changes, but it would also require us to include other rises of 40 per cent

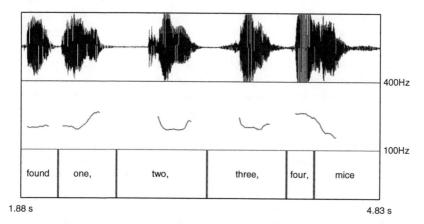

Figure 1.1 Speech wave, pitch track and text grid for a list utterance (female speaker of New Zealand English).

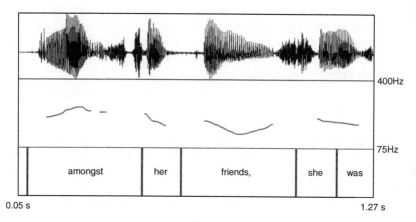

Figure 1.2 Speech wave, pitch track and text grid for the beginning of a two-clause utterance (female speaker of New Zealand English).

or more that most researchers would not consider to be uptalk. The use of the term 'marked' in the definition is intended, however, to indicate that the uptalk rise is not the same as other more expected rises. That is, the focus of this book is not on rising intonation in general, although discussion of other types of rise will inevitably be necessary as part of the process of narrowing in on uptalk. These other types of rise include the continuation rise at the end of each of a set of listed items apart from the final one, as in Figure 1.1 or at the end of an introductory adverbial clause, as in Figure 1.2. Each of these figures shows the recorded speech wave, the pitch track extracted from the speech data, and a text grid segmenting the utterance into words. The pitch track shows the fundamental frequency (F0) of the voice, which is the main acoustic correlate of the perceived pitch of the speaker's voice. This type of representation of speech recordings will be used throughout this book. The figures have been generated using the Praat software package (Boersma and Weenink, 2014).

It would be wrong to take the term 'marked' in the definition above to reflect a judgement that uptalk is peculiar. While this is clearly the view of many critics, and while it may be the case that uptalk is unusual or infrequent in some varieties of English, the discussion in this book should make it clear that for many speakers and speaker groups, uptalk is a perfectly usual and useful means of communicating a particular meaning, and as the Dictionary.com definition points out, uptalk can be habitual.

As regards the functions of uptalk, one meaning that uptalk is not intended to convey, or at least not directly or in the usual sense that is given by critics, is that of a question. Later discussion (in Chapter 3) will show that the meanings conveyed by uptalk may nevertheless be indirectly related to questions; for example, as a means of inviting the listener to engage in the conversation or as a check that she is still following what the speaker is saying. Defining uptalk as a rising intonation realised on a declarative utterance attempts to make it clear that these rises are not directly asking questions, and adding some broad functions in the definition reinforces this.

1.2   Labels

Given the comments cited above, and those foreshadowed for discussion in Chapter 7, it may seem surprising that I have decided to use the term *uptalk* in this book, rather than choosing a less negatively loaded label or indeed one that entails a more rigorous linguistic definition of the phenomenon. However, it is partly because *uptalk* is a label that is in the broader public domain that it can function as a useful and largely theory-neutral cover term. The sample of media coverage presented in more detail in Chapter 7 shows that the term *uptalk* is commonly used in the northern hemisphere (both in North America and in the United Kingdom), and is also known (but not as widely used) in the southern hemisphere (especially in Australia and New Zealand).

Some of the less flattering labels for uptalk, such as the 'moronic interrogative' (Robinson, 2010), can be found in media outcry about the phenomenon. In this section, however, our focus will be on the labels used in the linguistic literature. There are plenty of alternative terms to *uptalk*. Some of the differences in usage are geographic, reflecting the fact that the descriptions are of patterns of intonation that have arisen quasi-independently in different regions. Some differences, however, result from attempts to characterise particular aspects of the tunes in question. These differences are more problematic – do the labels reflect the specific focus of the researcher, or regional differences in how these tunes are realised by different speech communities, or do they mean that different phenomena are being referred to? That is, do they reveal more fundamental, systemic differences between varieties of English with respect to the tonal inventories that can be called upon?

One of the earliest and most widespread labels is *HRT*, which variously stands for *high-rise tone* or *high-rising tone* (e.g., McGregor, 1979; Guy and Vonwiller, 1989; Dineen, 1992; Steele, 1996; Shobbrook and House, 2003; Fletcher et al., 2005; Kiesling, 2005), *high-rising tune* (McGregor, 2005) and *high-rise terminal* or *high-rising terminal* (Meyerhoff, 1991; Britain, 1992; Ainsworth, 1994; Rehner and Legate, 1996; Borgen, 2000; Tennant and Rampersaud, 2000; Wolff, 2000; Spindler, 2003; Ueki, 2005; del Giudice, 2006; Stanton, 2006; Webb, 2008). An additional variant is found in the label *HRTD* or *high-rise* (or *rising*) *terminal declarative* (Allan, 1984, 1986; Meyerhoff, 1992), making it clear that the reference is to a rising tune used on declarative utterances. This is reflected also in Webb's (2008) use of the phrase 'declarative HRT' alongside 'question HRT'.

Although the references just listed include a few studies of British, US American and Canadian English, as well as Japanese, the HRT terms are predominantly used in Australia and New Zealand, with the *terminal* labels (rather than *tone* or *tune*) more frequent in New Zealand. HRT is clearly associated with Australia and New Zealand by Burchfield (1994: 559) in the glossary of linguistic terms that he provides for *The Cambridge History of the English Language*, where he defines it as 'a distinctive rise in intonation at the end of declarative statements, a characteristic feature of Australian and New Zealand English'.

Note however that the HRT label is sometimes deliberately avoided because of confusion with 'hormone replacement therapy', which is a more frequent 'hit' on an internet search. There is also some confusion when the search term is 'high-rise terminal', returning the occasional discussion of a new airport building.

A label often used in Australia, and consequently in attempts to 'blame' this intonation on Australians (e.g., Fry, 2001), is *Australian question(ing) intonation*, or AQI. In a newspaper discussion, the similar term *Australian interrogative intonation* has also been used (Beachcomber, 2012). Originally coined by Bryant (1980), the AQI label has also been used by Guy and his colleagues (Guy et al., 1986; Guy and Vonwiller, 1989). In explaining their choice of the use of the term AQI over HRT, Guy and Vonwiller (1989: 21) acknowledge that AQI is misleading because the intonation form that is being referred to neither creates questions nor is it limited to Australia, but they nevertheless use it as a 'convenient cover term for the full complex of rising intonation in a declarative syntactic frame with a particular meaning, in contradistinction with HRT, which describes only the intonational contour'. Another term that invokes the notion of question is Maekawa's (2012: 1304) *quasi-question*, a 'Japanese counterpart of uptalk'.

Keeping our focus on the same geographic region as AQI, we find the term *Antipodean Rise* (and indeed 'idiotic-sounding antipodean rise', Beachcomber, 2012), where 'Antipodean' is being used with a common northern hemisphere perspective, i.e., referring specifically to Australia and New Zealand.

A similar term to *uptalk*, but less widespread in usage, is *upspeak*, which is frequently found in discussions centring on the United Kingdom (Bradford, 1996, 1997) and on Canada (Talla Sando, 2009), but is not generally encountered in other regions.

The term *uptalk* itself was introduced by James Gorman in 1993 in a language column in the *New York Times* (Gorman, 1993a). Gorman, a journalism lecturer at New York University, was originally commenting on the English of his young female students. The linguist Mark Liberman, in his *Language Log*, agrees that the label *uptalk* is more appropriate, and explains why *HRT* is not an ideal term for the phenomenon (Liberman, 2006b, 2008d). In particular, he argues that definitions that describe HRT as a rise that must start high in the speaker's range before going even higher are based on contested ideas about a qualitative distinction between low-rises (i.e., rises starting low in the speaker's pitch range) and high-rises, and are therefore too limiting (Liberman, 2006b). This would also be an argument against adopting Tench's term *raised rising* or *raised rise* (Tench, 2003, 2014).

While some geographical variants of uptalk may indeed have the phonetic characteristics of being high and rising, it is by no means certain that this is the case in all regions. For example, in their study of Californian English, Tomlinson and Fox Tree (2011: 58, fn1) prefer the term *uptalk* 'because it encompasses rising pitch starting from both the lower and upper parts of a speaker's pitch range, not just the upper part as historically understood with the label high rise terminals'. For Australian English, Fletcher et al. (2002b: 301) point out that 'the phenomenon of uptalk goes beyond the simple high rise'. They find that low-onset high-rises are predominantly associated with statements, action directives or instructions, whereas high-onset high-rises are found with tag questions or information requests. Furthermore, Fletcher (2005) uses *uptalk* to refer not just to simple rises but also to complex/compound contours such as the 'expanded' range fall-rise.

It might seem that a term such as *declarative rise* might match the observations that the contours under discussion are rising in a very general sense (and not always high-rises) and that they are found on declarative rather than on interrogative utterances. However, this term is not adequate because it also covers a type of rise used in urban northern Britain (hence also the term *UNB rises*), where rises are found on statements but with different meanings from those involved in uptalk. In many commentaries, uptalk and UNB rises are confused with one another, despite evidence showing that they are different (see further discussion in Chapter 2).

In summary, *uptalk* may – at least linguistically speaking – be a more neutral label.

1.3   The forms and functions of intonation

In order to provide a framework in which the nature of uptalk might be better understood, this section considers both the forms and functions of intonation. To do this, I first provide a summary of two main approaches that have been taken to the transcription and analysis of intonation, before then considering key elements in the study of the uses to which intonation is put by speakers.

1.3.1   Traditions of intonational transcription and analysis

There are a number of systems for the transcription and analysis of intonation. Two main streams have developed for English – a holistic or tune-based system and a compositional, tone- or target-based system. The tune-based system has its origins in work carried out by British researchers in the middle of the twentieth century (O'Connor and Arnold, 1961; Halliday, 1967; Crystal, 1969) and is often referred to as the British tradition. It treats intonation as a system of tunes or pitch movements. The tone or target-based system has evolved from work in the United States (Pike, 1945; Trager and Smith, 1951), and has its most recent incarnation in the ToBI (Tones and Break Indices) system developed by Pierrehumbert and colleagues (Pierrehumbert, 1980; Silverman et al., 1992; Beckman et al., 2005). Target-based systems analyse intonation as a sequence of pitch targets, with the tunes arising through the movement of pitch from one target to the next.

Both of these traditions work on the basis that there are accented syllables. These are syllables that are stressed and that additionally carry pitch marking. Stressed syllables in English are lexically determined; that is, each content word has its own characteristic stress pattern. So for instance '*publish* has two syllables, of which the first is stressed (marked by ' preceding the stressed syllable), and while *en'gage* also has two syllables, it is the second that is stressed. Longer words can have multiple stresses, of which one will be the main or primary stress and the others are secondary stresses (marked by ‚), as in ‚*disser'tation*. Syllables that carry stress (primary or secondary) tend to be longer and to have fuller vowels than unstressed syllables, which are generally weaker and have shorter or reduced vowels and may have no vowel at all but a syllabic consonant, as in many pronunciations of the second syllables of '*bottle* or '*button*. When words are used in utterance contexts, some

(a)   (b)

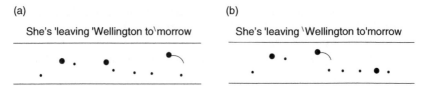

Figure 1.3 'Tadpole' drawings of two statement utterances in English.

of the stressed syllables are also accented, i.e., have pitch prominence. This highlights the words containing those syllables in the utterance context, perhaps because they convey novel or contrastive information. A further important aspect of intonational analysis is phrasing, i.e., the grouping of words or syllables into intonational units. One such unit is the intonational phrase (also referred to, especially in the British tradition, as the tone unit or tone group). The intonational phrase may contain multiple accented syllables, but typically one of these is more prominent than the others. This is referred to as the nuclear accent (or just nucleus, or 'tonic' in the British tradition). It is most frequently the final accented syllable in the utterance, and is for that reason sometimes known as the terminal accent (hence high-rising terminal).

With these characteristics in mind, we can now briefly summarise the British and American traditions of intonational analysis. Figure 1.3 shows what are known as 'tadpole' diagrams, in this case schematically representing the intonation of two utterances containing the same words. Such diagrams are frequently found in descriptions using the British tradition, although the properties they represent are relevant in all intonational analyses. They are impressionistic, rather than an objectively accurate representation of the speaker's utterance. The horizontal lines show the upper and lower reaches of the speaker's pitch range. The dots represent the syllables of the utterance, with larger dots indicating the stressed syllables. The vertical position of the dot indicates the relative pitch height of the syllable. If a dot has a trailing tail (making it look like a tadpole, hence the label 'tadpole' diagram) then the latter shows the direction of any pitch movement starting on that syllable. This is the nuclear accent. In addition, the text above the tadpole diagrams has been annotated with stress marks as well as with marks indicating falling pitch movement (`).

In both of the diagrams in Figure 1.3 the stressed syllables are the first syllable of *leaving*, the first syllable of *Wellington* and the second syllable of *tomorrow*. In (a) the nuclear pitch accent is on *tomorrow*, and in (b) it is on *Wellington*. In both cases the pitch falls from that accent and remains low throughout the remainder of the utterance. The step up in pitch from a low pitched unstressed syllable on *she's* to the first syllable of *leaving* contributes to the perception of a pitch accent on *leaving*.

(a)　　　　　　　　　　　　　　　　　　(b)

She's 'leaving ／Wellington to'morrow?　　She's 'leaving ／Wellington? | to′morrow?

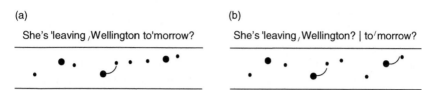

Figure 1.4 'Tadpole' drawings of two question utterances in English.

In the British tradition of intonation analysis, the *tune* is the overall pattern of intonation within the intonational phrase, and is largely determined by the pitch movement associated with the nuclear accent. In both of the examples in Figure 1.3 the tune is falling. Further key terms in the British tradition are *tonicity*, which refers to the location of the nuclear accent, and *tonality*, which is the amount of material that is included in the intonational phrase. The two utterances in Figure 1.3 show a contrast in tonicity – the falling nuclear accent (shown by ˋ before the accented syllable in the text above the diagram) is earlier in the right-hand diagram than in left-hand one. This may reflect a difference in focus – when the nuclear accent is on the final accentable (stressed) syllable, then focus is either broad, i.e., nothing in particular is being drawn to the listener's attention, or it is specifically on the final element, i.e., it is important that it is *tomorrow* that she is leaving. When the accent is earlier – for example, on *Wellington* in Figure 1.3 (b) – then there is narrow focus; the speaker is in this instance perhaps keen to convey that it is Wellington that the person is leaving. The portion of the utterance before the nuclear accent can include further accented syllables, as in both the examples in Figure 1.3. The stretch from the first of these accented syllables up to but not including the nuclear accent is referred to as the head (*leaving Wellington to-* and *leaving* in (a) and (b) respectively in Figure 1.3). The head can be preceded by unaccented syllables, which constitute the pre-head. The portion after the nucleus is the tail.

In the examples in Figure 1.4, the words being uttered are identical to those in Figure 1.3, but the tunes are rising, reflecting the fact that in these examples questions are being asked. The rises are marked on the text above the diagrams before the syllable on which the rise starts (with ／ or ′ for low- and high-rises respectively). We will discuss question types in more detail in Chapter 2, but the questions in these examples are often referred to as 'echo' questions, possibly repeating back something that another speaker has said, as a way of checking for understanding. The two diagrams in Figure 1.4 differ from one another in tonality or phrasing, in that (b) contains two intonational phrases, with the boundary between them marked by the vertical line symbol | in the text. This phrasing in (b) might correspond to the speaker's desire to question or to check two elements, i.e., that it is Wellington that she is leaving and that this is happening tomorrow. Only the first of these would be intended in the utterance shown in (a), which is a question form corresponding to the second statement in Figure 1.3.

There are three primary criteria used in defining types of nuclear tones in English, with the options for each varying somewhat between varieties. These are: the movement of pitch in and from the nucleus, which can be falling, rising or level; the relative pitch location of the beginning part of the movement, which can be high or low; and any further changes of pitch direction that might take place after the first nuclear movement (giving us complex movements such as rise-fall and fall-rise). There are a number of different descriptions of English nuclear tones, each with different categories. One description of British English (Cruttenden, 1986, 1997) lists seven main nuclear types which are distinguished on the basis of what they can mean, while their forms are defined using the above criteria. These are high-fall (ˋ), low-fall (ˎ), high-rise (ˊ), low-rise (ˏ), fall-rise (˅), rise-fall (˄) and level (˃). Some of these symbols have already been introduced in this text; others will appear below. In addition, the ↗ and ↘ symbols will be used to show general rising and falling intonation, including over nuclear accents, especially where it is not crucial whether the fall or rise is a high one or a low one.

As an example of different intonational meanings conveyed by falling nuclear accents, it is argued that while a fall on declaratives shows finality or completeness, different types of fall show different meanings, often quite nuanced. For instance, low falls tend to show that the speaker is uninterested or unexcited, while high falls show more interest and involvement. A rise-fall can also show finality, but in addition it can convey either that the speaker is impressed, as in the following example. (Note that the symbol ˄ indicates a rise-fall movement over the following syllable(s), the vertical bar indicates the boundaries between intonational phrases and the material in parentheses is the preceding context for the utterance.)

(1)   (He got an A+) ˄Did he! | In Lin ˄guistics, | ˄too!

or that the speaker is challenging the listener:

(2)   (I don't like to keep reminding him) But you 'damn well ˄ought to!

Early analyses within the American tradition of describing intonation in terms of pitch levels characterised falling and rising patterns such as those illustrated above in terms of a sequence of different pitch heights. More recent developments within this tradition use just two underlying pitch levels, high (H) and low (L), with further levels resulting from phonetic interpolation between pitch targets and from the effects of combining sequences of pitch targets. This use of H and L is found for instance in the influential ToBI framework, which also reflects insights deriving from earlier work within autosegmental phonology and especially from Bruce's (1977) analysis of word accents in Swedish.

Bruce's insight was that certain properties of these accents, particularly differences in how they are realised when produced in isolation and when produced in non-nuclear position in sentence contexts, could be better explained if the word accent itself is separated from aspects of intonation that are more properly part of the utterance. Pierrehumbert (1980, 2000) built this separation of lexical and phrasal aspects of intonation into her description of the intonation of English, which distinguishes pitch accents that are associated with (some of the) stressed syllables of the words in an utterance from phrase-level tones. Nuclear accents (falls, rises and so on) in the British tradition are the result of the combination of pitch accents and phrasal tones.

The key aspects of Pierrehumbert's system, and the basis of the pitch annotation in the ToBI analysis system, are the following. Pitch accents are marked by *, and can be high (H*) or low (L*), where H and L should be taken to indicate relative rather than absolute pitch height. Pierrehumbert's system also allows bitonal pitch accents; for example, which can be either early aligned L*+H or late aligned L+H*. The extent to which these are retained in descriptions of English depends on the variety being described, as well as on the analyst. Note that the use of only two levels is a marked departure from earlier four-level systems (Pike, 1945; Trager and Smith, 1951). Pierrehumbert comments that further levels result from specific tonal sequences (so that, for instance, certain tonal targets are phonetically 'downstepped', i.e., realised at a lower pitch level than preceding tonal targets, indicated by !H* for a downstepped high pitch accent), meaning that more than two abstract levels are unnecessary (e.g., Pierrehumbert and Hirschberg, 1990: 283).

In addition to pitch accents, there are two types of edge tones that are found at the boundaries of two types of intonational units. These units are intonational phrases and intermediate phrases. An intonational phrase contains at least one intermediate phrase, and so there are some intermediate phrases that finish within an intonational phrase and some that finish at the same point as an intonational phrase. Phrase accents mark the end of the intermediate phrase, and follow the last pitch accent of the phrase. Again they can be H or L, and are transcribed by means of a following -, i.e., H- or L-. (Phrase accents can also be downstepped, and like the downstepped pitch accents these are marked by a preceding '!', as in !H-.) The phrase accent in effect controls the pitch contour from the last pitch accent to the end of the intermediate phrase. A well-formed intermediate phrase has at least one pitch accent and just one phrase accent. Boundary tones mark the end of an intonational phrase, following a phrase accent. These are annotated with % and can be high (H%) or low (L%), although some systems also permit a 'neutral' boundary tone 0% (e.g., Grabe, 1998). A well-formed intonational phrase has all the properties of an intermediate phrase but also has a boundary tone. Since the end of an intonational phrase is also the end of an intermediate phrase, there are four

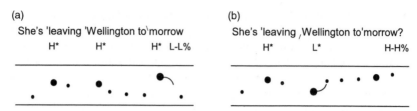

(a)

She's 'leaving 'Wellington to\morrow

    H*   H*   H* L-L%

(b)

She's 'leaving ˌWellington to'morrow?

    H*   L*   H-H%

Figure 1.5 'Tadpole' drawings of two utterances in English, with ToBI transcription.

combinations of phrase accents and boundary tones that are possible at the end of an intonational phrase: L-L%, H-L%, L-H% and H-H%. Note that since H and L are relative terms, a 'low' boundary need not, for instance, indicate a fall, but can show a flat, non-rising pitch at the end of a phrase.

The tune of a phrase can be defined by its sequence of pitch accent(s), phrase accent(s) and boundary tone; a typical statement intonation with a final fall is represented as H* L-L%, and a rising question contour is L* H-H%. The utterances in Figure 1.3 (a) and Figure 1.4 (b) are repeated in Figure 1.5 with ToBI transcriptions added below the utterance text.

This system of pitch accents and boundary tones allows the same inventory of pitch accents (H*, L*, L+H*, etc.) to be found in the nucleus and in other positions in the utterance. The difference between nuclear and non-nuclear accents results from the combination of the accent with the boundary tones in the former case. By contrast, in the British tradition (O'Connor and Arnold, 1961), this difference is shown through a structural contrast between the nucleus and the head.

A further key observation is that pitch accents are not properties of words (stress patterns are properties of words), but are pragmatic morphemes co-produced with words. Pierrehumbert (2000: 20) suggests that pitch accents happen to be aligned with prominent elements of words (stressed syllables) because of a general process of entrainment (cf. the synchronisation of patting your head and rubbing your stomach). This alignment may be language and even variety-specific, at least in its details (see Warren, 2005b, for New Zealand English).

In addition, Pierrehumbert and Hirschberg (1990) suggest an inventory of possible intonational patterns for (American) English, as shown in Figure 1.6. These are schematic drawings; the phonetic realisation of a contour involves interpolation between targets, contextual dependencies such as a typical pattern of declination (lowering in the pitch range) over a series of pitch accents, the speaker's choice of pitch range, and so on. Ladd (2008: 91) gives a table of equivalences between the American and British traditions, and these have also been reflected in Figure 1.6. Note that some of the correspondences might

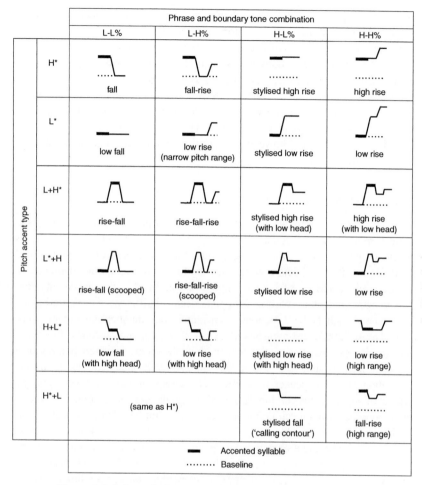

Figure 1.6 Schematic inventory of pitch accent, phrase tone and boundary tone combinations (based on Pierrehumbert and Hirschberg, 1990, Figures 14.13 and 14.14, with addition of British nuclear tone equivalents based on Ladd, 2008: 91).

seem peculiar – for example, the schematic for the stylised high-rise (H* H-L%) appears to show no rising movement. However, given the general tendency for pitch to fall over an utterance (a phenomenon known as declination), and listeners' expectations of such a fall, the high plateau corresponding to the H-L% sequence gives the perception of a rise. In addition, a process of catathesis, or downstep, tends to occur after the bitonal pitch accents (Pierrehumbert and Hirschberg, 1990: 280) so that the subsequent boundary tone combinations are lower in the speaker's pitch range than might otherwise be expected, as can be seen for instance in the schematic for L+H* H-L%.

Given the British and American traditions, it is possible to describe uptalk either as a specific pitch contour (as in the label 'high-rising terminal') or in terms of tonal targets (e.g., a H% boundary tone, or a H-H% combination of phrase accent and boundary tone). Both can be found in the research literature. From the labels in the figure we might conjecture that 'high rising terminals' could include the sequences H* H-L%, H* H-H%, L+H* H-L%, or L+H* H-H%. As we will see, however, descriptions of 'uptalk' also include other sequences than these.

1.3.2   Functional analyses

Any description of intonation needs to include not just an analysis of the possible forms of tunes or tonal sequences but also an account of the functions or meanings involved. This is no less true of uptalk than of other intonational features, and these aspects of uptalk will be further discussed in Chapter 3.

A key characteristic of intonation, and one that makes its analysis at times problematic (and, as we will see for uptalk, leads to differences of interpretation by listeners), is that it has functions and meanings on a number of different levels. Thus House (2006) distinguishes indexical, linguistic and discourse functions. *Indexical* properties of intonation tells us about the speaker, such as their regional or social background, their sex or their age. As with other features of speech, intonation varies by speaker, most obviously perhaps in terms of the pitch ranges typical of adults versus children and of adult females versus adult males, but also on a more individual level. Different speech communities also show differences in their intonation patterns. *Linguistic* functions include indicating whether an utterance is a statement or a question, placing an element in the utterance into focus, marking structure through phrasing and so on. The *discourse* functions of intonation involve the management of an interaction, such as holding or ceding the floor, or signalling inclusion of the listener in the conversation.

There are also affective, attitudinal or paralinguistic functions of intonation. That is, speakers can use intonational features as part of the expression of joy, surprise, excitement, boredom and so on. These attitudinal meanings are indicated primarily through pitch height or through the extent of a pitch movement, rather than being associated with particular contours. They are expressed simultaneously with other functions, as indicated, for example, by Bolinger (1972: 28) when he says that as well as marking finality or completeness, a falling intonation pattern can show the degree of conclusiveness by the extent of the fall – the deeper the fall, the more conclusive a statement is perceived to be.

The use of intonation to simultaneously convey different functions can make the analysis of intonational meaning complex and even problematic. Ideally, an

Table 1.1 *Closed and open meanings associated with falling and rising intonation (Cruttenden, 1981:81).*

Closed (falling)	Open (rising)
Reinforcing	Limiting
Statement	Question
Finality	Continuity
Closed-listing	Open-listing
Conducive	Non-conducive
Statement	Statement with reservations
Dogmatic	Conciliatory

analysis of intonation should 'dissociate the delimitative use of pitch and associated features from their affective and focusing uses' (Local et al., 1986: 433), but this is often quite difficult to achieve, and sometimes not even attempted. McLemore (1991: 1) points out that taking a single perspective, for example, looking at intonation from just one of the viewpoints of grammatical function, information structure, interaction or emotion, will be incomplete because 'the form itself is not divided up in a way that neatly corresponds to these distinctions in function'.

A number of researchers have attempted to provide a more unified account of the range of meanings conveyed by intonation by seeking to identify universal aspects of intonational meaning that might then be expressed at a number of levels. For example, at a very general level, it has often been claimed that low or falling intonation shows finality or closure, while high or rising intonation shows openness (e.g., Halliday, 1966; Bolinger, 1978; Cruttenden, 1981, 1995). Cruttenden (1995) suggests that a good test for the strength of this general tendency would be to imagine saying 'certainly' or 'possibly' in response to a question – the former would most likely be said with a fall and the latter with a rise. There is an alignment here of lexical and intonational meaning, i.e., of the meanings of the words and of the typical intonation patterns with which they would be realised in the given context. Earlier, Cruttenden (1981), commenting that the study of what intonation 'means' has focused on one or more of grammar, attitude or discourse, suggests that intonation operates with meanings that are at a higher level of abstraction than any of these. He groups together a range of meanings associated with falling tones, which he subsumes under a cover term 'closed', and a corresponding set of 'open' meanings associated with rises, as shown in Table 1.1.

In his discussion of the relationships between different types of meanings, Cruttenden points out (1981: 87) that a requirement for a meaning on one level can overrule a requirement on another level. As an example, he claims that if a speaker needs to convey an attitudinal meaning then this will overrule a required grammatical usage. So the fall at the end of the first intonation group in (4) is used by the speaker to convey assertiveness and this overrules the expectation of a continuation rise (a grammatical usage), as in (3).

(3) I went to the ˌstation | and caught the ˈtrain
(4) I went to the ˈstation | and caught the ˈtrain

One way in which intonation patterns have been linked to universal notions of meaning has been to invoke a biological code: 'of the parts of the human vocal system that are used linguistically, intonation responds more closely than any other to states of the organism' (Bolinger, 1978: 474). Thus Ohala (1983) refers to the Frequency Code, an extension to human communication of a phenomenon that has been observed in avian and mammalian communication, particularly in contexts in which some sort of challenge is involved. Typically, aggressive or dominant birds or mammals involved in such situations use lower pitch than more submissive participants. The biological aspect of this is that lower pitch indicates a larger individual. In many species, including humans, the distinction between lower and higher pitch range corresponds to a biological distinction. In the human case, this includes differences between male and female adults and differences in age. For example, the human adult male larynx is almost twice the size of the adult female larynx, and as a consequence produces a lower pitch range. In addition, the adult male larynx is lower in the throat, so that the male vocal tract is longer than that of females, resulting in lower resonances (i.e., in phonetic terms, formant frequency values) for vowels and other sounds, again suggesting a larger individual.

To the Frequency Code, Gussenhoven (2002) adds the Effort Code and the Production Code as further biological dimensions that relate to intonation. The Effort Code relates to increases in precision of articulation that result from putting more effort into speaking. This greater effort can also result in wider pitch movements. The Production Code is connected with the general observation that speakers tend to expend more effort at the beginning of an utterance than at the end. Biologically, this relates to the fact that subglottal air pressure is higher at the start of an utterance (just after a breath has been taken) than at the end. This results in the typical declination patterns, i.e., falls in intonation across an utterance, that are observed in most languages.

Importantly, not only can these three codes be linked more or less directly to biological determining factors such as those outlined above, but also they can be exploited for effect, by birds and mammals through their songs and calls, by humans in their intonation patterns. In human communication in particular, the effects of the biological determinants have been brought under control, so that a speaker can create the effect even when the biological conditions may not be present. For example, the wider pitch ranges that result from more effort are typically linked with the notion of emphasis, but a speaker can choose to use a wider pitch range, to mark emphasis, without necessarily expending greater effort.

Gussenhoven (2002) shows how the three codes (Frequency, Effort, Production) are each potentially linked to three areas of meaning: affective, informational and grammatical (see also Bolinger, 1964: 843–844, for similar comments). For example, the affective meanings associated with the Frequency Code include not only those most directly related to the avian and mammalian use of this code, i.e., dominance and submissiveness, but also further meanings associated with high pitch, such as friendliness, politeness, vulnerability or protectiveness, and with low pitch, such as aggression or scathingness. These are often also associated with feminine and masculine values respectively, again reflecting the biological determinants. Informational values associated with the Frequency Code include uncertainty versus certainty (for high versus low pitch), which is linked to the distinction between questioning and asserting. This last distinction is grammaticalised in most languages, with rises for questions and falls for statements.

Affective uses of the Effort Code include the use of extended pitch ranges to indicate surprise, pleasantness and helpfulness (Gussenhoven relates the latter in particular to child-directed speech with its dramatic sing-song intonation patterns), while some studies have found expanded range to be associated with anger. Informational meaning is conveyed through the Effort Code by the use of wider pitch for emphasis and/or for informational salience. This code is grammaticalised in the use of pitch accents to mark contrast and focus in many languages.

As far as the Production Code is concerned, Gussenhoven notes that there are informational meanings that can be linked to the natural tendency for utterances to start on higher pitch and end on lower pitch. Some of these meanings have become grammaticalised. As examples of this he notes how high versus low beginnings of utterance units correspond with new versus old topics, and how high endings relate to continuation (contrasting with the expectation of a fall to a low pitch at the end of a production unit), and how low endings mark the end of a turn in a conversation.

Gussenhoven points out that the same intonation patterns can convey different meanings, such as those listed by Cruttenden (1981) and repeated above in Table 1.1, and that these meanings can in some cases relate to different codes. For example, a rise can have an interrogative meaning, which relates to the Frequency Code, or a continuation meaning, which relates to the Production Code. The possibility of such multiple meanings will be important when we come to discuss the interpretation of uptalk. Note that Hirschberg (2002) suggests a supplement to Gussenhoven's analysis, involving the use of the conversational implicatures developed by Grice (1975) to help make a link between the biological codes and spoken communication; for example, a 'Maxim of

Pitch' might require the speaker to match rises and falls in pitch to the degree of confidence they wish to convey.

McLemore (1991) criticises some of the polarisation that has taken place in different intonational analyses, which have seen intonational meaning as being either grammatical or emotional, and the discourse functions of intonation as being either textual or social-interactional. She also argues that 'intonational forms have no inherent "meaning"' (1991: 10). Instead, she proposes the analysis of intonation as a set of icons that are interpreted depending on the context and on the shared communicative conventions and norms of the interlocutors. On misinterpretations of intonation, she points out that it is quite typical for hearers to rationalise unfamiliar or inappropriate patterns in emotional or attitudal terms. This is worth remembering as we consider the use and interpretation of uptalk in subsequent chapters.

1.4   Methodological considerations

A full analysis of the methodological issues involved in research into uptalk would be out of place at this point, delaying as it would our entry into discussion of the forms and functions of uptalk. However, and at the risk of replicating information that will be discussed in greater detail in Chapter 10, it is worth commenting briefly on a few considerations that need to be borne in mind when appraising the existing uptalk research.

The first is that different researchers have used quite different bodies of data for their analyses. Some have used small datasets with tasks tailored to the study of intonation in specific speaking contexts or on particular sentence types, while others have relied on large spoken language corpora. While carefully controlled tasks are useful for exploring specific issues (and are particularly important in studies of the perception of uptalk, as we see in Chapter 8), the use of a large body of data is more likely to provide a representative sample for the language or language variety under consideration, and is less likely to be susceptible to experimenter bias.

The second consideration is that uptalk research has used tasks that range from controlled monologues (including sentence reading tasks) to free dialogue. Chapter 3 will show us that some of the predominant functions of uptalk are to check the interlocutor's engagement in the conversation, and Chapter 6 will highlight the fact that uptalk features very strongly in interactional contexts. Since this is the case, studies that rely heavily on non-interactional talk will have more restricted relevance to our understanding of the use of uptalk.

Further considerations concern the type of analysis made of the speech data that have been collected. Impressionistic auditory analysis (possibly but not necessarily linked to transcriptions similar to those introduced in this chapter) is very effective for obtaining broad-picture information relating to questions such as the level of incidence of uptalk in a dataset. For such frequency-of-use studies, it is important to take note of the units over which incidence is being counted. Some studies use intonation groups as the basis for their counting, while others take units delimited by pauses. While in many cases these units will coincide, this is not always the case and the resulting frequencies will not be directly comparable. For more detailed analyses of the forms of intonation, acoustic investigations using speech analysis software can become essential parts of the study (see Chapter 2).

With such considerations in mind, we turn next to descriptions of the forms and functions of uptalk, before looking in later chapters at its distribution in different speech communities and across different speech events.

2   The forms of uptalk

Most descriptions of uptalk – both academic and lay – are based on impressionistic analyses. That is, they describe the general shape or auditory impression of the intonation pattern. Usually this is with reference to the extent of the pitch rise associated with the uptalk, sometimes including an indication of the timing of this rise relative to the text over which it is produced. Both of these aspects are captured in the working definition of uptalk introduced in Chapter 1, which referred to 'a marked rising intonation pattern found at the ends of intonation units'. In addition, some descriptions attempt to define uptalk by comparing or contrasting it with the intonation contours typically associated with other sentence types. In this chapter we will first consider this relationship of uptalk utterances with other sentence types, before then looking in more detail at the forms of uptalk that have been discussed in the literature. This will involve consideration both of descriptions of the phonetic detail of uptalk and of the position that the uptalk pattern holds in the set of intonational tunes constituting the intonational phonology of a language.

It will necessarily be the case that the descriptions we encounter are dependent on the variety of English under scrutiny. Just as the DRESS[1] vowel has a different phonetic quality in British English from that in New Zealand English (where it is closer to the pronunciation of the British KIT vowel) and Canadian English (where it can be more like the British English TRAP vowel), so too the realisation of a single intonational feature can vary from variety to variety (see Warren, 2005a and other articles in the same volume). Although variation of this type exists in the forms of uptalk across varieties, there are commonalities, and this chapter will conclude with a summary of the key features that are shared by uptalk in varieties of English.

To a certain extent, the shapes of uptalk are reflected in the labels used to refer to them. Yet even in discussion by linguists there is some uncertainty or

---

[1]   DRESS (as also KIT and TRAP later in this paragraph) is one of the lexical set labels proposed by Wells (1982). The use of these labels gives researchers a common reference point for the vowels found in English varieties, which can then be described in phonetic detail to elaborate on the commonalities and differences between varieties.

ambiguity in the use of the labels. As we saw in Chapter 1, the label *high-rising terminal* is ambiguous as to whether the contour is a high contour that rises (from a high starting point) or a contour that rises to a high finishing position (from a starting point that could in fact be low).

Australian question(ing) intonation has been remarked on as a particularly unhelpful term – the intonational forms it refers to are not restricted to Australian speakers, and it is not clear that *AQI* is used to ask questions, at least not in the usual sense of that term. The term 'question' itself is ambiguous – does it mean the grammatical form of an utterance, or its function? Finally, unlike *HRT* and terms such as *uptalk* and *upspeak*, *AQI* only indirectly (and inaccurately, as we will see in the next section) refers to the form of the intonation contour, in that there is an implication that it is similar to the forms used in questions.

While *uptalk* and *upspeak* clearly indicate the direction in which the intonation contour is headed, they are in other respects very general and rather vague terms. In addition they are occasionally also used in a different sense, meaning something like raising the interest level or profile of something through how you speak about it, i.e., 'talking it up' (e.g., 'upspeak' is used in this sense by Bramsen et al., 2011). However, the generality of the terms *uptalk* and *upspeak* was given in Section 1.2 as one reason for using *uptalk* as a cover term in this book.

2.1   Comparison with other sentence types

Going up at the end was previously something you did asking questions. Statements went down at the end. The high-rising terminal has messed that up, because it's not a question, it's a statement and there's a certain smugness to it. (Theatre director John Tiffany, quoted by English, 2011)

The working definition of uptalk given in Chapter 1 referred to it as the use of a rising intonation with declarative utterances. Often, however, it has been referred to as the use of question-like intonation with declaratives. From this alternative definition, an obvious starting point for the comparison of uptalk with other sentence types is to consider whether uptalk intonation patterns are indeed like those found for questions in the same variety of English. But as we look at this more closely, we see that there are two further interrelated issues that need to be unravelled. The first is the problem of defining what we mean by 'question', and the second is the relationship between questions and the use of rising intonation.

As pointed out by Bartels (1999: 9), the term 'question' can refer to two overlapping sets of utterances. First, there are utterances that have the clear syntactic form of interrogatives, such as the 'yes–no' question (YNQ, also known as a polar question) in (6) and the 'wh-question' (WHQ, also known as a content question) in (7). Both differ in their syntactic structure from the declarative statement in (5). The YNQ has inversion of the auxiliary (*will*) and subject (*he*), relative to the word order of the statement in (5), and the WHQ additionally employs the question word (wh-word) *when*.

(5)   He'll be at the basketball stadium.
(6)   Will he be at the basketball stadium?
(7)   When will he be at the basketball stadium?
(8)   He'll be at the basketball stadium?

Second, the term 'question' is frequently used to refer to utterances that function as questions (in that they generally expect answers), even though they may not have the syntactic form of an interrogative. For example, questions can also have the form in (8), i.e., they can be syntactically identical to statements like (5). To be heard as a question, the example in (8) would most likely need to have a rising intonation contour. Note that in our discussion here we are separating intonation from syntax, with the latter referring to word order and the morphological marking of grammatical relations. This may of course turn out to be a false separation, because intonation frequently also marks grammatical functions or the grammatical relationships between elements in an utterance.

Questions such as (8) are often used to check what another speaker has just said, perhaps if they haven't spoken clearly or the ambient noise level is high. In English, these are known as echo questions, because they repeat back what one speaker believes the other speaker has said. But the repetition need not be exact, as shown by the example in (9) (from Zwartz and Warren, 2003), where B is checking on information that can be inferred from what A has said.

(9)   A: Jim's just finished a job. That arts show was doing a feature on the architecture of stadiums, and he was getting footage of the basketball one. Can you give him a lift home?
       B: He'll be at the basketball stadium?

Note, importantly, that B's question in (9) suggests that B believes that A is in a position to provide the requested information. As we will see in later chapters, uptalk is clearly functionally distinct from this kind of question, since it is more frequently employed in situations where the speaker of the uptalk is the 'owner' and imparter of information, not the seeker of information, i.e., there is a kind of role reversal compared to what would normally be expected of a situation in which a question is being asked.

A key issue for our working definition of uptalk is whether the intonational forms of questions, including the echo questions in (8) and in B's turn in (9), are different from the form of an uptalk statement. We can refer to the form in (8) and in B's turn in (9) as a syntactically unmarked YNQ. Bartels (1999), who uses the opposition pair *statement* versus *question* to refer to the functions of utterances, and the pair *declarative* versus *interrogative* to refer to the syntactic form of the utterance, calls forms such as (8) and (9) 'declarative questions' (or non-interrogative questions), i.e., utterances that function as questions but have the syntactic form of a declarative rather than that of an interrogative.[2]

This form of asking a question is not that unusual across the world's languages. In a survey of 955 languages from around the world (based on Dryer, 2013), I have found that the use of intonational marking alone for YNQs is far more frequent (19.2 per cent) than the use of word order (1.4 per cent), but not as frequent as the most common form, which is to use a question particle (61.3 per cent). Nevertheless, syntactically unmarked YNQs seem less usual in English, relative to the syntactically marked form in (6). Cross-linguistically, it has been claimed that the difference between questions and non-questions has been the only intonational contrast examined in enough detail in enough languages for anything like a 'universal' pattern to be identified. The generalisation reported by Bolinger (1989) on the basis of a series of studies covering 269 languages is that average pitch levels in questions are higher than those in non-questions. There is variation, however, in how languages realise this higher average pitch. In some languages it is the overall pitch range of a question that is higher, while in others there is a rise in pitch at the end. English employs both possibilities, with a slight preference for final rises, but with the choice seemingly linked to many other factors, such as speaker sex (Séguinot, 1979).

The second major issue that we must address in connection with any discussion of uptalk as the use of 'question-like intonation with declarative utterances' is the assumption that questions have to be marked by rising intonation patterns and statements by falling intonation patterns. I will turn shortly to the use of rises on statements other than uptalk. With regard to questions, there are, of course, many different types, some of which are marked by grammatical features such as word order or the use of special question words, as well potentially by intonation. Some of these question types were illustrated in (6)–(9). It turns out that not all questions in English are marked by rising intonation. For instance, Bolinger (1989), focusing mainly on General American English, lists five types of questions and their typical intonation patterns. For three of these, namely YNQs, complementary questions (*Your name? Your*

---

[2] Geluykens (1987: 483) calls these *queclaratives*: 'Queclaratives are defined here as utterances having the form of a declarative sentence but functioning as requests for information.' This use of the term is perpetuated without critique by Batliner and Oppenrieder (1988) in their response to Geluykens' article, by Geluykens (1989) in his response to Batliner and Oppenrieder, and also for instance by Jones and Roux (2003) and Raithel (2005). However, *queclarative* was first coined by Sadock in the early 1970s (Sadock, 1971, 1974) to refer to an utterance that has the form of an interrogative but the force of a statement, i.e., rhetorical questions in which the speaker effectively negates the proposition used in forming the question, as in 'What use is that?' with the meaning that it is of no use at all (see also Matthews, 2007: 278).

place of birth?) and reprise questions (the second question in *What was that you just said? Am I coming?*), the intonation tends to rise at the end, while in the other two, WHQs and alternative questions (*Is she coming or going?*), it tends to fall. Haan (2002) expresses the relationship between grammatical and intonational marking in terms of a Functional Hypothesis, which predicts that rising or high intonation is most likely when there are no other markers of interrogativity and becomes less likely the more grammatical or morphological markers there are. (For further discussion of Haan's Functional Hypothesis, see Šafářová, 2006: ch. 3. Note that Haan's analysis is largely of Dutch, Šafářová's of American English and of French.) Similarly, across a range of regional and ethnic British English dialects, Grabe (2002) found a negative correlation between the number of grammatical (morphosyntactic) markers of interrogativity and the likelihood of rising intonation on a question. For example, WHQs – i.e., those questions that not only have inversion of subject and verb but also start with a wh-word such as *when, who, what, why* – are more likely to have a falling than a rising intonation pattern. This does not preclude the use of a rising pattern with WHQs in English, but this can in fact be rather marked. This extends also to other languages; one group of researchers found that German WHQs with rising intonation are perceived as challenging (Scherer et al., 1984). The same researchers found that YNQs with falling intonation can also come across as challenging.

In a survey of Canadian English YNQs, Séguinot (1979) reports that rising intonation was used 68 per cent of the time and level intonation 14 per cent, but that there were marked differences between males and females, with the latter using a larger proportion (93 per cent) of rising tunes. However, Bartels (1999) reports corpus evidence from both American and British English that shows falling intonation patterns to be more frequent than rising ones on YNQs. Further, in a study of a small corpus of declarative questions, Geluykens (1987) reports that 63 per cent have falling pitch and only 33 per cent have rising pitch. In other words, the use of rising intonation is not the only way in which an utterance with declarative word order is turned into a question, with contextual factors also playing a role in the interpretation of utterances. Geluykens found that whether an utterance was heard as a statement or as a question did not seem to depend on the intonation contour as much as it did on the pragmatic context (see further discussion in Chapter 8). In summary, questions are not always linked with rising intonation, and some question types may even seem unusual when produced with rising intonation.

A further consideration to note here is that different varieties of English may have different conventional or preferred intonational patterns for the same utterance function. As an example, take the forms of the polite YNQ in British and American English, as discussed by Ladd (2008: 113–114) with the examples *Could I have the bill please?* and *Is your mother there?* In British

English these would be realised with a falling-rising intonation pattern, '*Could I have the 'bill ∨please*, which, however, comes across as condescending to American ears. American English speakers would use a high-rising ('*Could I have the 'bill 'please*) rather than falling-rising tune to realise the same meaning. This example should serve as a reminder that when we come to compare uptalk rises with other intonational forms we need to be mindful of the variety of English that we are considering. Ideally, the formal and functional analysis of uptalk should take account of its position and role within a single system of intonation. Such analyses can then form the background for comparisons of uptalk across the different systems of English varieties.

The discussion above has shown that questions can be found with falling as well as with rising intonation. On the other hand, many declarative statements, which are typically assumed to be associated with falling intonation, are accompanied by intonational rises, and not just in uptalk contexts. For instance, there are varieties of English in which the standard intonation pattern for a declarative statement involves a rise. Thus, the so-called Urban Northern British (UNB) varieties spoken in some cities in the north of England, in Northern Ireland and in Scotland typically have a rise to a high level (the rise-plateau) possibly with a final fall (producing a rise-plateau-slump pattern). We will consider these intonation patterns again in Chapter 4.

More generally across varieties of English, incomplete statements in subordinate or dependent clauses are often realised with rising intonation. So the first clause before the comma in (10) has a generally falling pattern, but potentially finishes with a short continuation rise, for obvious reasons also known as 'comma' intonation. This pattern was shown in Figure 1.2 in Chapter 1.

(10)   Be'fore he can 'go to the ˋbasketball ˌstadium, 'Ben needs to 'tidy his ˋroom.

This falling-rising pattern is frequently used to indicate that the speaker is a) completing one part of the utterance (shown by the fall) and b) connecting this to a following part (shown by the rise). Continuation rises would not usually be included as examples of uptalk, because of their different function.

A further type of rise is found in spoken lists, as in (11), where each of the listed fruits is likely to be spoken with a rising intonation (possibly in a sequence of falling-rising tunes as indicated) apart from the last one, which will have a fall. Figure 1.1 in Chapter 1 showed an instance of this from a New Zealand English retelling of the Cinderella story.

(11)   I 'need ∨apples, ∨oranges, ∨pears and baˋnanas.

So, even if we disregard uptalk, English intonation does not adhere to a simple model whereby statements have falling intonation and questions have rising intonation. Indeed, in a study that attempts to provide quantitative models for intonation patterns, Grabe et al. (2005) report that rather than questions and statements being distinguished by different tunes, they are more consistently distinguished by the fact that questions have a higher overall level of pitch (see the earlier similar comment from Bolinger, 1989, noted above).

Nevertheless, it is the linking of uptalk utterances with the use of rising intonation as a marker of questions that is a recurring feature of both lay criticism of uptalk and expert linguistic analyses of the phenomenon. In one of many articles on the issue of uptalk in the online *Language Log*, Pullum (2006) comments on how a non-linguist journalist misleadingly refers to uptalk as a case of the speaker producing questions. Pullum generously ascribes this error to the journalist's lack of the relevant vocabulary, but at the same time points out that while a journalist writing on a scientific topic would make reference to the appropriate authorities to back up his statements, when the media discuss language issues they rarely see the need to consult with experts. The experts would have been able to point out that the speaker, an Australian in fact, was not asking questions, even though his utterances had frequent rising intonation patterns (Pullum, 2006).

What, then, do the experts say about the relationship between uptalk (in its various guises) and question intonation? Their views range from those who see uptalk and question rises as having effectively identical intonation, through those who see the forms to be similar (although often the extent of the similarity remains unspecified), to those who see clear differences between them.

Among the first type, Ladd, in a discussion of North American and Antipodean high-rising contours, states that

there is to my knowledge no phonetic difference that depends on whether the high-rising contour is used with syntactically marked questions or with statements. It therefore seems reasonable to say that we are dealing with 'the same' tune across varieties of English. The only difference is in the meaning or function of the tune. (Ladd, 1996: 121–122)

Note that Ladd is comparing high-rises on statements with those on syntactically marked questions in these varieties of English, so is comparing high-rising contours on statements with those on syntactic forms such as (6) above. The lack of a phonetic difference here might not be crucial to the distinction of two otherwise highly similar utterances, since the differences in their word order should ensure the correct interpretation. In a later edition of this work, Ladd (2008: 126) no longer makes the above claim about the lack of a phonetic difference, but does state that 'the differences are subtle, and arguably gradient', and that it may be plausible to 'analyse HRT statements as having the same phonological representations as high-rising question contours'.

Ladd is not alone among linguists in claiming an overlap in form between uptalk and question intonation. In an earlier observation, Lakoff

(1973: 55) describes the statement rise as a 'rising inflection typical of a yes–no question', although here it is not specified whether the question type she has in mind also has the syntactic marking of a question. In some of their early work, Guy et al. (1986: 47) stated that there was not much evidence that uptalk 'ever had a phonetic form different from the normal English tone 2', where the latter is a reference to Halliday's (1967) system of tones for British English. They concede that while it is possible that there are phonetic differences between statements and questions, 'we treat the HRT in declarative clauses in AE as the same tone unit – tone 2 – as the HRT in interrogatives' (Guy et al., 1986: 25)

In a further discussion of rises on yes–no questions and statements in Australian English, McGregor (2005: 17ff) notes that while they are not identical they can appear to be similar in form although they clearly differ in meaning. She maintains that despite their formal similarity they will not usually be confused by speakers of the same variety, because contextual clues will make it clear what the speaker intends. Guy and Vonwiller (1989: 21) allow for some phonetic differences, claiming only that uptalk rises are 'similar in form to the intonation of *yes/no* questions'.

What is of greatest interest perhaps is whether the same similarity of question and statement tunes is found when the questions are not syntactically marked but are identical word strings to the statements (as in a comparison of (5) and (8) above). Bartels (1999) notes that in American English, both low-rises and high-rises can appear either on syntactically marked YNQs (the low-rise being more usual) or on 'non-interrogative questions'. Several of her examples of the latter are taken from the literature, and are borrowed from others' discussion of uptalk, and it is not clear whether these are really questions rather than high-rise statements. Bartels remarks, however, that it is the high-rise rather than the low-rise version of non-interrogative questions that had recently become widespread, presumably as uptalk. This implies that uptalk favours high-rises and questions favour low-rises, and that there is at least a distributional difference in the rising tunes associated with statements and questions (although note that the opposite pattern – with lower onsets for statement rises – has been claimed in recent analyses of Australian English, see Section 2.2).

Other studies have noted further similarities of uptalk with the intonation of other utterance types. For example, in an early study of Australian English rises, Bryant (1980: Appendix, A-4) found that a subset of AQI rises that were realised over a narrow pitch range were difficult to distinguish phonetically from other narrow-range rises such as those used in lists, as might be found in the example in (11).[3] Tomlinson and Fox Tree (2011: 60) extend this link of uptalk with list intonation, reporting that 'uptalk in rising declaratives

---

[3] This seems at odds with statements elsewhere in her thesis that AQI 'shares the acoustic features of the pitch rise of yes/no questions but not of lower rises such as list tone' (Bryant, 1980: 3).

has been described as similar to list intonation'. On the other hand, Britain (1992: 78) notes that the intonation of HRTs in New Zealand English is 'similar in many respects to the contour often used in English polar questions' (these are what were referred to above as YNQs, as in (6)), and also to the intonation used to turn statements into questions (as in (8)).

In addition to these observations of identity or similarity of intonation patterns in uptalk and other utterance types, there are comments that highlight differences. For example, in his language blog, linguist Robert Beard states of uptalk that '[t]he intonation is not that of a question, however, because it does not simply rise at the end of the sentence but before the end and is sustained. It sounds very much like the intonation of "you know what I'm sayin?" superimposed on a statement' (Beard, 2006). The opposite pattern was reported by Bryant (1980), who found in her study of Australian uptalk (AQI) that statement rises were later and more dramatic than question rises, an observation echoed for New Zealand English in Warren (2005b). Fletcher (2005) found that most terminal high-rises in a corpus of Australian English map task dialogues were the final part of complex or compound tonal movements – for example, the rise part of a falling-rising pattern – and were therefore different from the rises typically found on YNQs.

The discussion above suggests that there may be varietal differences in uptalk forms. Indeed, in one of his *Language Log* contributions, Liberman (2008b) conjectures that there are differences both in function and form between Antipodean uptalk and American uptalk. As far as the form is concerned, he suggests that while the Antipodean variant may have a rise that continues to the end of the utterance, the American one is more likely to have a rise then a level (and indeed is similar in shape to the UNB rise-plateau, which is a default statement intonation pattern in some northern British cities). This rise-and-level he claims to be a more typical form of uptalk than the late rise used by poet Taylor Mali in his rendition of his poem *Totally Like Whatever* (Mali, 2005). Liberman suggests that this late rise (which incidentally looks much like the New Zealand English statement rises reported by Warren, 2005b) may be a performance of uptalk by someone who is not a native uptalker, and who believes that uptalk is indeed a type of yes–no question. In other words, and in the context of the American patterns, Mali has interpreted uptalk as indicating a questioning nature, and is reproducing this with an intonation pattern he associates with questions.

Certainly a comparison of two instances of 'uptalk' from the above-cited performance of the poem by Mali in Figure 2.1 with an instance of a YNQ from his performance of another (but not 'uptalked') poem *What Teachers Make* (Mali, 2000) in Figure 2.2 shows a strong similarity in the onset of the rise, which is part way through the accented syllable (the first syllable in *talking about* and the only syllable in *tone* and in *make* for the three utterances). There

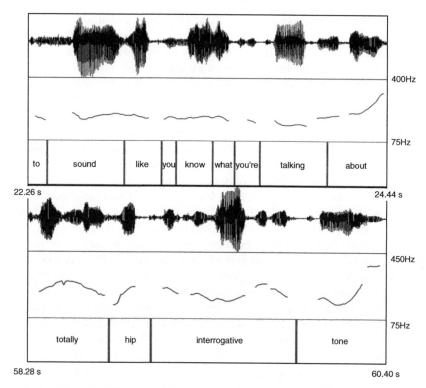

Figure 2.1 Two instances of performed uptalk from Taylor Mali.

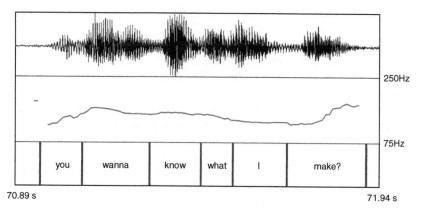

Figure 2.2 Instance of yes–no question from Taylor Mali.

is a marked difference though in the extent of the rise, which is considerably higher in the examples of uptalk. It should be noted, however, that these utterances are performances and the question may be no more a genuine question for this speaker than the uptalk examples are genuine statements.

Some of the distinguishing features of uptalk mentioned in the paragraphs above will be discussed in more detail in the following sections. What we have seen in this section is that the assumption that uptalk is 'question-like intonation on a declarative utterance' is problematic on many counts. The notion of 'question' is ambiguous between function and form; the belief that there is any single type of 'question intonation' is misplaced, as is the assumption that questions necessarily have rising intonation; and even if we accept that 'question-like intonation' is shorthand for the type of rising intonation often found on YNQs, then there is lack of agreement concerning whether that type of rising intonation is identical or even similar to uptalk.

Some of the confusion may result from the fact that different varieties of English have different styles and uses of uptalk (see further discussion in later chapters, including discussion of cross-linguistic patterns of statement and question intonation). A contributory factor here may be that different varieties have reached different stages in the development, spread and use of uptalk, with some varieties starting to make novel distinctions between the forms of uptalk rises and the forms of other rises. House (2006) makes a suggestion along these lines when discussing Fletcher and Harrington's (2001) evidence that Australian English speakers were distinguishing statement and question rises, with higher pitch accents on the questions than on the statements. Making a new phonological distinction by means of different intonation patterns is, House claims, a natural resolution of a prior and potentially confusing situation where multiple functions were associated with one pattern. She notes that there was no evidence of a new intonational distinction between statement and question rises in her study of British English (Shobbrook and House, 2003), which may reflect the later uptake of uptalk in that variety. She does not rule out a future phonological split in British English between question and statement rises.

Note, however, that other factors may make such a split unlikely to happen precipitously. As Guy et al. (1986) pointed out in their discussion of Australian English, even if there is no phonetic difference between uptalk rises and question rises, ambiguity is unlikely, as contexts will clarify the intended meaning. That is, true questions usually include some anaphoric reference to a previous utterance, and will usually be at the end of a turn. By contrast, uptalk tends to provide new information, and the speaker of uptalk typically continues to hold the floor. 'If these clear contextual and textual differences were not sufficient to disambiguate between the two meanings, we might expect structural change to occur: for example, phonetic differentiation of the contours or disuse of the contour for one of the meanings' (Guy et al., 1986: 27). It may be that recent phonetic differences between uptalk and question intonation patterns noted for Australian and New Zealand English indicate that a level of potential confusion has been reached that requires such differentiation. Thus Adams, in an early study of intonation in Australian English, observed that 'evidence points to the fact that certain sequences regularly occur with particular structures, and when an intoneme other than the usual one is used it is recognised that the substitution has been made, intentionally or unintentionally, to signal some special meaning' (Adams, 1969: 104). At a later stage, however, the phonetic detail of the shape of a rise may come to carry additional social significance. Podesva (2011) makes a similar distinction between a categorical choice of contour to convey pragmatic meaning, and the selection of a particular phonetic contour that carries social meaning.

Finally, in this section comparing uptalk with other sentence intonation patterns, spare a thought for the computer scientists trying to programme computers to interact with humans using speech. In an article in the *New Yorker*, Seabrook (2008) wrote the following: 'language isn't static; the rules change. Researchers taught machines that when the pitch of a voice rises at the end of a sentence it usually means a question, only to have their work spoiled by the emergence of what linguists call "uptalk".'

2.2   Uptalk shapes

Before looking at some of the individual features of uptalk, such as where the rise starts and how extensive it is, let us consider some observations on its overall shape or shapes. There is little general agreement concerning the shape of uptalk. This no doubt reflects the fact that it may vary from one variety of English to another (Fletcher et al., 2005; Wilhelm, 2015), as well as potentially varying within one variety and indeed within the speech of one talker. Such variation will be a contributing factor to the lack of expert agreement. As Liberman (2008c) points out in connection with nine examples he presents on his language blog, whether you treat these utterances as instances of one intonation pattern, or as nine different contours, or something in between, you will almost certainly find researchers with more or less the same analysis as yours (as well, presumably, as many who have different analyses). There may be some commonality to be found in the notion that an uptalk rise is dramatic or dynamic, but the way in which that is realised need not be the same across varieties. In some varieties, the distinction between uptalk and question intonation may be in terms of the size or range of a pitch rise, while in others it may be in terms of either the pitch level or the temporal alignment of the starting point of the rise (Fletcher et al., 2005; Warren, 2005b). The following paragraphs summarise some of the observed patterns of uptalk rises in different English varieties.

A general statement of uptalk or HRT rises in New Zealand English was given by Warren and Britain as 'salient rises in pitch at the end of *non*-interrogative intonational phrases' (Warren and Britain, 2000: 153, emphasis in original). Although the salience of such rises makes them easily identifiable, the details show considerable variation in rise shape. Warren and Britain refer to Britain and Newman's (1992: 4) observation that there can be 'an impressive variety in the shape of the F0, a variety which one would hardly expect simply on the basis of the label (High Rising Terminal) for the phenomenon'. Britain and Newman found that the rise could be less than 50Hz or more than 100Hz, depending on the speaker's pitch characteristics and that the rise could be on the final syllable of the intonational phrase, or across more than one syllable of the last word, or across more than one word, or could consist of a general rise across several words with a significant additional rise on the final syllable. Ainsworth (1994) mentions an additional 'weak HRT' for New Zealand English that does not rise as much as the full uptalk rise in that variety.

Fletcher and Loakes (2006: 42), summarising Fletcher and colleagues' extensive study of uptalk in recent Australian English (e.g., Fletcher and Harrington, 2001; Fletcher et al., 2002a; Fletcher, 2005), point out that the phenomenon covers a wide array of intonational shapes, including 'simple high rises, expanded range fall-rises or rise-fall-rises, and compound or split fall-rises'. Earlier, Bryant (1980) noted that AQI rises in her data were late (on the final syllable) and sharp, but that there was some variation in the extent of the rise. Bryant groups the rises into McGregor's (1979) categories of narrowed, normal and widened, using a range/duration ratio, i.e., a Hertz per second measure of the steepness of the rise. Normal variants have a rise factor of 700Hz/sec or above, and widened variants range from 1,100 to 2,000Hz/sec.[4] Allan (1984: 28) describes the Australian rise as 'a step up from mid to high key', which can happen either before the final stressed syllable, or immediately after it, i.e., in the tail. The tonic itself is rising, and can be the second part of a compound fall-rise, as is also evident from Fletcher's work mentioned above. In their instrumental studies, Guy et al. (1986: 25) found that rises typically showed an increase in F0 of at least 40 per cent, and that they began on the last tonic syllable of the intonational phrase, rising sharply through to the end of the phrase.

In her analysis of a small sample of British English uptalk rises, Bradford (1996: 22) describes the shape of these as 'a steep rise in pitch on the last word and a concomitant lengthening', and that phonologically the pattern is 'a

---

[4] Bryant (1980: A-3) in fact reports these factors as 7,000 and 11,000–20,000, but it would seem that her calculations are out by a factor of ten.

fall-rise tone which begins on the tonic syllable and continues to fall over the rest of the unit, or levels out after the original fall, until the accented syllable of the last word where a dramatic change in direction to a steep rise is made. The rise is highlighted and achieves extra height via a lengthening of the vowel(s).' It is not clear whether the 'accented' syllable in the last word refers to the second part of a fall+rise sequence or whether by accented Bradford means stressed (rather than pitch accented). This notwithstanding, Bradford notes that the extent of the fall before the rise depends on the amount of phonetic material between the tonic syllable and the end of the phrase. If these are close together, then there is only a slight dip before the final rise (see also Bradford, 1997).

In their study of Southern Californian (SoCal) English, Barry and Arvaniti (2006) find that uptalk typically takes the shape of a low-rise (77 per cent L* H-H%), with some high-rises (18 per cent H* H-H%) and a few fall-rise patterns. In a later study, however, Ritchart and Arvaniti (2014: 7) propose that 'the melody typically used with questions in SoCal English is L* H-H% and that used with statements is L* L-H%', which might be characterised following Ladd (2008) as a low-rise and a narrow range low-rise respectively (see Figure 1.6). Fought (2003) notes that while uptalk generally starts at a mid-point in the speaker's range, in Chicano (i.e., Mexican American) English it starts higher.

For Canadian English, James et al. (1989) note that uptalk contours have a significant rise at the end of the utterance, but that the extent of the rise in their data ranges from 37Hz to 226Hz. Talla Sando (2009) adds that in his data he typically finds that the rise begins on any accented syllable and finishes on the final syllable, but is frequently preceded by a falling movement. Lacey et al. (1997) provide phonetic details for one male and one female speaker from their data, and find that the female, for instance, has a mean pitch rise of 102.5Hz, representing a 54 per cent rise from the beginning of the nuclear accent, or 38 per cent from the beginning of the rise. From her data from adolescents, Halford (2007) reports a similar average rise of around 100Hz, often followed by a slight fall of around 20Hz.

Even within English varieties, then, we find considerable variation of the overall shape of uptalk rises. Some of the variation involves the pitch levels involved and some is due to different temporal alignment of rising patterns. The following sections explore each of these in more detail.

2.3   Pitch levels

2.3.1   Starting pitch level

From the descriptions of uptalk shapes above, it is clear that there is variation in the starting pitch level of the rise. As noted earlier, one of the criticisms sometimes made of the use of the 'high-rising terminal' label is that it implies that the starting point is already high in the speaker's pitch range. For example, Tench (1997) cites examples of HRT from Britain, Australia, New Zealand and Canada, each of which has a starting point in a high key. In other work, Tench (2003: 217) states that the difference between the rises found on declarative questions and on uptalk is based on the higher starting point for the latter. He calls this tune 'raised rising' to avoid the ambiguity of the high-rising terminal label, and presents examples from Watt (1994) for Canadian English, and from Britain and Newman (1992) for New Zealand English. He also gives an example from Bradford (1997) for British English, though it should be noted that Bradford herself describes this example as a fall-rise pattern, albeit with only a slight dip before the rise because the tonic syllable is late in the intonational phrase.

Fletcher and Harrington (2001: 223–224) found some support for an observation by Ladd (1996: 121) that statement high-rises in Australian English may be associated with onsets that correspond to low-pitch accents (L* H-H%) as well as those that correspond to high pitch accents. However, 84 per cent of the declarative high-rises in their sample had low onsets, while 91 per cent of YNQ rises had high onsets. McGregor (2005) similarly looks at the onset pitch level of uptalk and question rises in Australian English. She distinguishes high (H*) and low (L*) pitch accents as the initial pitch feature of the rises. If the rise is associated with an H* accent, then it begins from a mid or high point in the speaker's range, whereas a rise associated with an L* starts in a valley or trough that is low in the speaker's range before rising steeply to a final high point. McGregor reports (2005: 94–95) that her female informants were more likely to distinguish questions and statements on the basis of the pitch level at which the rise starts, with high starting points for questions and low for statements, and with a greater rate of F0 change in statements. Her male speakers, on the other hand, preferred high starts for both, although when they used low-pitch accents these tended to be accompanied by an earlier rise start for questions than for statements. Overall, however, her speakers 'did not appear to have made systematic choices in relation to tune onset on the basis of the grammatical function of the HRTs' (McGregor, 2005: 269).

In a study of American English at Cornell University in New York State, McConnell-Ginet (1983) distinguishes high-rises from low-rises (the latter including fall-rises). These were used by the same speakers, predominantly women, and the main difference between them was that the high-rise communicated a higher level of incompleteness or questioning. This suggestion that low-rises are less likely to indicate 'questioning' is compatible with the findings from Australia that statement rises are more likely than question rises to have a rise that starts low in the speaker's register. As noted in the preceding section, Bradford (1996, 1997) also found that uptalk contours in British English were shaped by a fall followed by a sharp rise.

Although Watt's (1994) examples cited by Tench (2003) suggest that uptalk rises in Canadian English have a high onset, Talla Sando (2009) reports a Canadian English shape that is more like the Australian and American contours, with a fall across the accented syllable into the following syllable followed by a dramatic rise to the end of the phrase.

This brief summary suggests either that there is no consistent difference between the starting pitch level of uptalk rises and that of question rises, or that if there is a difference then it depends on the variety of English (see Fletcher et al., 2005), with high-onset rises for uptalk in Canadian (possibly) and in New Zealand English, and low-onset rises or fall-rises in Australian, American and British English.

2.3.2   Extent of pitch rise

It has frequently been claimed that one of the most noticeable features of uptalk is the size of the final pitch rise. For Australian English, Guy et al. (1986) noted that pitch rose to a value that was typically at least 40 per cent above that at the starting point of the rise. In their acoustic analysis of New Zealand English, Britain and Newman (1992) remarked on considerable variety in the shape of HRT rises. Most notable was the variation in the overall size of the increase in F0 values. The 40 per cent value quoted above suggests a sizeable rise for uptalk contours, but Fletcher and Harrington (2001) found that four of the five females in their Australian sample had higher endpoints for questions, although none of their males did. Overall, they conclude that the starting value (L* vs. H*) is a more salient indicator of statement versus question rise than the pitch value at the end of the rise. It is probably the lower L* starting value that contributes to the size of the rise, rather than any difference in the height of the endpoint.

Di Gioacchino and Crook Jessop (2010: 2) suggest that the 'pitch excursion of the phrase boundary [is] the defining feature of uptalk, which distinguishes it from falling declarative phrases'. While this amounts to little more than a statement that uptalk has rising rather than falling contours, they also hypothesise that the important aspect of the extent of the rise may not be the absolute size of the movement but its height relative to the speaker's overall pitch range. This is not controversial, since most analyses of intonation recognise that pitch values (highs and lows) and pitch movements are judged relative to a speaker's usual range. Di Gioacchino and Crook Jessop claim on the basis of a small set of Canadian English contours that the uptalk rise is 'steeper than those of other declarative statements, but not as steep as those produced in question intonation'. It is clear from their data that there is also much more variation in the rise size for uptalk than for questions.

Ritchart and Arvaniti (2014) observed for Southern Californian English a rise for non-floor-holding statements that was roughly half the range of that used in questions, in confirmation requests and in floor-holding statements.

2.4   Temporal aspects

A number of studies have considered temporal aspects of uptalk tunes. These include the point at which the rise takes place (i.e., the alignment of the rise) and the duration of the rise.

2.4.1   Alignment

Media statements about when the rise of the uptalk contour actually happens are understandably vague, but tend to emphasise that it is late in the utterance: 'Other teens engage in "uptalk" which involves phrasing a declarative sentence so that it ends like a question. The speaker, usually a female, will raise her voice toward the end of the sentence as if she's asking for your opinion on what she has just said' (Fergus, 1994).

Bryant (1980, Appendix A) carried out a small-scale acoustic study in which she compared uptalk and question rises over the same material. She took 13 examples of uptalk (AQI tokens) from the connected discourse of one speaker, and asked the same speaker to reread the utterances as questions, but keeping the same word order, i.e., to read them as 'statement-as-question' utterances. Bryant found that the question rise started earlier and covered the final 72 per cent of the final syllable, compared with the final 50 per cent for the uptalk rises. In addition, the question rises had a greater range of F0 across the utterance preceding the rise, whereas the uptalk rise had a narrow range of pitch (85Hz) across this region. As pointed out by Steele (1996), these features make the uptalk contour in Australian English more dramatic than the question rise. We must be cautious, however, in our interpretation of Bryant's results, since her study involves a comparison of spontaneously produced uptalk with read examples of questions, and the intonational forms produced in reading reflect different pragmatic constraints from those resulting from spontaneous speech (Speer et al., 2011). See Chapter 10 for a discussion of the effect of task demands.

In a more recent analysis of adolescent Australian English, McGregor (2005) found considerable variability in the alignment of the starting point of rises, but her overall findings show that females started their rise contours later than males, that rises with low (L*) onsets started later than those with high

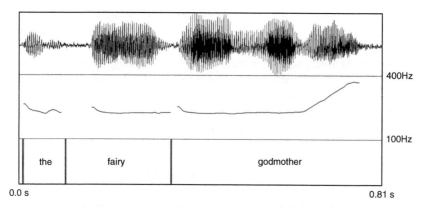

400Hz

100Hz

| the | fairy | godmother |

0.0 s   0.81 s

Figure 2.3 Speech wave, pitch track and orthographic transcription of a New Zealand English uptalk rise, female speaker (Warren, 2005b).

(H*) onsets and, importantly for our discussion here, that statement rises had later onsets than question rises. If the accented syllable is followed by further syllables within the intonational phrase, then rises that started later than the accented syllable were typically aligned with a metrically stressed syllable in the tail, rather than with an unstressed one.

In their study of New Zealand English, Britain and Newman (1992) also noted considerable variation in the alignment of the uptalk rise, with the actual location depending in large part on the make-up of the intonational phrase. Britain and Newman also report that there were no examples of late rises on a final unstressed syllable unless that syllable was itself a word. Warren (2005b), however, found that late rises were aligned either with a metrically stressed post-nuclear syllable or – in the absence of such a syllable in the inton-ational phrase – with a final unstressed syllable. An example is reproduced in Figure 2.3, taken from a retelling of the Cinderella story. In this figure, the rise is associated with the accented first syllable of *godmother*, but is realised on the final unstressed syllable.

Warren (2005b) builds on research reported in Warren and Daly (2005), who looked at the alignment of rise starting points in questions and state-ments from six male and six female young speakers (16–19 years of age) of New Zealand English taking part in an interactive task (i.e., the map task, see Chapter 10). They found that both groups of speakers, and particularly the male speakers, had an earlier onset in question rises than in statement rises. This finding contrasts with Ladd's (1996) statement quoted earlier that there is no phonetic difference between question and statement rises. Warren and Daly conjecture that the result from the map task data may be an early sign of a functional distinction emerging between rise types, a suggestion that was followed up in an analysis of a more extensive dataset that included also mid-age (30–45 years) speakers (Warren, 2005b). This analysis confirmed that the alignment difference was more marked for the younger speakers, i.e., the younger speakers were starting their rises even earlier for questions. In terms of an Autosegmental-Metrical analysis, and building on work by Grice et al. (2000), Warren (2005b: 225) suggests that the difference between the early (question) and late (statement) rises can be described in terms of whether there are two anchor points for the H phrase accent or one. When there are two anchor points, then the first is on the nuclear syllable and the second is either on a metrically strong post-nuclear syllable (MSPNS) in the tail of the intonational phrase or on the final unstressed 'peripheral' syllable. When there is only a single anchor point, then this is one of these two later points (i.e., on a MSPNS or on the final unstressed syllable as in Figure 2.3). These anchor point differences result in an early rise with a convex rising pattern for the questions and a late rise with a concave rising pattern for the statements, for the younger group of New Zealand English speakers.

The data from Australian English cited above (Bryant, 1980; McGregor, 2005) give some indication of a similar difference in alignment for statement and question rises, but generally it has been found that statement and question rises in Australian English are more likely to be distinguished by the type of pitch accent (L* vs. H*) than by rise alignment (Fletcher and Harrington, 2001; Fletcher and Loakes, 2010). One recent study of alignment in Australian English (Webb, 2008), specifically looked for a parallel to Warren's findings in statement and question rises, using narratives and interactive tasks from four young Australian speakers (22–30 years of age), and concludes that there is no evidence that Australians are using the alignment of the phrase accent, and therefore of the starting point of the rise, as a phonological device to distinguish statements from questions.

Elsewhere, however, an alignment difference between statement and question rises has been noted for South African English (Dorrington, 2010a, 2010b). Dorrington categorised a set of rises from six females in the 20–22 age range according to whether the rise onset is on the nuclear accented syllable, on a MSPNS or on a weak syllable in the tail. Statement rises in her data were much more likely to start after the nuclear accent, and in particular on a weak post-nuclear syllable. Ritchart and Arvaniti (2014) report data from Southern California that show a similar pattern of rise alignment differences to those reported for South African English by Dorrington and for New Zealand English by Warren (2005b), with rises on questions typically including the last stressed vowel (which Ritchart and Arvaniti assume to be the accented vowel), but those on statements starting after this vowel.

2.4.2   Duration

Tomlinson and Fox Tree (2011: 60) suggest that time might be the 'missing ingredient' in studies of how the different meanings of rises might be indicated. Specifically, they investigate experimentally whether the duration of the segmental material associated with an uptalk rise might distinguish between a backward-looking function to signal uncertainty and a forward-looking function to indicate that further information is upcoming. Their experiments show that listeners are more likely to interpret uptalk as forward-looking (as reflected in significantly shorter word-monitoring times for a word in the following sentence) if the rise is combined with lengthening of the final syllable in the intonational phrase, than if there is no such lengthening. There is no such effect of duration when the intonation contour is falling. Tomlinson and Fox Tree also show that this effect of uptalk duration is not found if the listeners believe the speaker is an expert with regard to the content of their utterance. It would thus appear that the effect is primarily associated with uncertainty (in that it is not found when the speaker is presented as an expert), and might therefore indicate that the backward-looking, uncertainty interpretation is cued by rises over shorter speech material.

It is important to note that the length of the final syllable was a between-item variable in this study, i.e., it was not deliberately manipulated over otherwise identical stimuli. Therefore it is unclear whether the length variable interacted with other features of the intonational contour. For example, the F0 values given in the Appendix to Tomlinson and Fox Tree (2011) indicate a greater pitch movement (169Hz versus 134Hz) on rises that were produced on utterances that had a shorter final syllable when compared with those with the longer final syllable. It is therefore possible that the duration effect is actually an effect of either the size or slope of the rise, with the latter being more dramatic for the shorter syllables. The alignments of the contours in this study are also not clear, except that one of the defining features of prolonged versus non-prolonged stimuli is that the rise reaches its high point near the end of the shorter final syllable, whereas the prolonged contours reach their peak nearer the middle of the syllable and remain high from there. There is no comment, however, on the starting point of the rise.

In a study of final –er, the pronunciation of which is a marker of ethnic identity in Australian English, Kiesling (2005) finds that Greek Australians in particular use a cluster of three apparently linked features. These are the use of a backed vowel in –er (e.g., *better* realised as [bɛra]), lengthening of –er, and the presence of uptalk on the –er word. While this might appear to indicate a link between uptalk and duration, it is more likely that the lengthening is a consequence of the full-vowel realisation of the –er, which in turn results from the rhythmic type of Greek Australian English (being more syllable-timed, i.e., with less reduction of weak syllables than Anglo-Australian). Indeed, an earlier study of Australian English (Bryant, 1980) reported no consistent durational difference between syllables carrying uptalk and the same syllables without uptalk.

2.5   Phonological analyses

The question of how to analyse uptalk in terms of the intonational phonology of a language or variety is a vexing one. In his description of cross-linguistic and cross-varietal differences in intonation, Ladd (1996, 2008) outlines four possible types of distinction, based on earlier analyses of segmental differences between varieties (Wells, 1982). These types are semantic, systemic, realisational and phonotactic, which we can consider here in terms of possible varietal differences in uptalk.

Semantic differences are those where the same tunes occur in the varieties of a language, but they are used to convey different meanings. An example would be where two varieties have the same rising tunes in their inventories, but while one variety uses them to express questions, the other uses them both for this and to convey the meanings associated with uptalk. Confusions between uptalk and question intonation, which form the basis of much popular criticism of uptalk (see Chapter 7), rather straightforwardly imply semantic differences between the variety being criticised (where one form can convey either a question meaning or an uptalk meaning) and that of the critic (whose system allows only the question meaning).

Systemic differences are where the varieties have different inventories. For uptalk, this would require the forms of uptalk rises and question rises to be different and to be regularly associable with the different meanings of uptalk and questions.

Realisational distinctions involve differences in phonetic detail that do not result in differences in the inventory of phonological contrasts. If, as suggested in the preceding section, there are phonetic differences between uptalk forms and other rising intonation, then a crucial issue is whether such distinctions are systemic or realisational. If the differences do not (yet) systematically distinguish uptalk and other meanings, then we might treat them as realisational differences, without perhaps being able to determine the contexts that determine the choice of realisations. For instance, the reported differences might happen to be chance encounters with otherwise unmotivated variation in realisation. Such realisational variation may, however, be latent systemic variation waiting to become established as a means of contrasting uptalk and other meanings more systematically.

Phonotactic differences include differences in tune-text association and in the permitted tune structures. Ladd's (2008: 116–119) example of phonotactic differences relates to how the calling contour is realised on names in a set of European languages. He points out, for example, that both English and French use a sequence of a high tone followed by a downstepped high tone (H ...!H). In English the first H tone is associated with the stressed syllable of the name and any preceding syllable has low pitch. In French, however, each tone is associated with one syllable. On two syllable names such as *Annie* (which has stress on the first syllable in English) and *Louise* (with second-syllable stress), this will result in differences in how the calling contour is realised, with the second syllable of *Louise* 'split' in English and realised as two syllables in order to accommodate both H tones, and with the addition of a preceding low pitch on the unstressed syllable, as in (12):

(12) French
      H* !H   H* !H
      L o u i s e   A n n i e

      English
      L H* !H   H* !H
      L o u i – i s e   A n n i e

A parallel from uptalk research might be the differences that have been noted for some varieties of English in the alignment of the rise onset, or differences in the pitch height of the accent before the rise.

The summaries in the preceding section of a range of phonetic features that have been linked to uptalk indicate that there is no single phonetic shape that distinguishes uptalk rises from other types of rise. To an extent, this may be a consequence of including a range of varieties of English in our scope, since the phonetic realisation of a particular rise type need not be uniform across varieties, any more than we would expect the realisation of the KIT, DRESS or TRAP vowels to be the same in different varieties. These varietal differences in rise shapes may account for some instances of what have been described as 'multiple and conflicting definitions of uptalk' (Di Gioacchino and Crook Jessop, 2010: 2), and for transcriptions that 'are often inconsistent' (Di Gioacchino and Crook Jessop, 2010: 6). Yet even within a single variety there is rarely a clear indication of a distinctive uptalk pattern.

However, the summaries do point to some differences between uptalk and question rises. A number of these relate to features of the starting points of the rises concerned. In particular, some researchers have found that uptalk rises start at a lower point in the speaker's range than question rises, while others have found the uptalk rise starts later than the question rise. Since there is little consistent indication of any difference in the endpoint of the rises, it seems that both patterns lead to a more dramatic intonational rise for uptalk than for questions, as well as to a higher average pitch for questions than for uptalk. A conclusion along these lines was drawn in a perceptual study of question versus statement rises in New Zealand English (Zwartz and Warren, 2003; Warren, 2005b).

How, then, might these differences be captured in a phonological account? Some researchers do not seek to do this at all, assuming instead that the forms of uptalk are realisational variants of existing shapes and are not phonologically distinctive. Thus Di Gioacchino and Crook Jessop (2010: 1–2) state of the ToBI transcription system (see Section 1.3.1) that 'its shortcomings become evident when trying to provide a representation and analysis of uptalk. The ToBI system is designed to characterise phonologic intonation patterns and is not necessarily equipped to deal with the apparent phonetic variation that exists between particular intonation contours.' The implication from Di Gioacchino and Crook Jessop is that uptalk is phonetic variation.

The question of phonological distinctiveness is, of course, linked to meaning as well as to form. This is seemingly trivial at the segmental level; we can use minimal pair contrasts to determine that since 'pit' and 'pet' have different lexical meanings, we can establish two phonemes /ɪ/ and /e/. However, as we saw in Section 1.3.2, and as we will see specifically for uptalk in Chapter 3, intonational meaning is multilayered. Phonological distinctiveness may apply only to some of these layers of meaning, and other aspects might better be described as paralinguistic or extralinguistic expressions of meaning. Grammatical oppositions such as that between question and statement seem to be an obvious candidate for phonological contrasts in intonation, especially if these can be conveyed by intonation alone (e.g., by different contours on the same word string). This is less clear for contrasts between rising patterns such as uptalk and continuation rises, particularly if there is some commonality in meaning that might correspond to possible similarities in shape. A more modest goal than establishing a phonological description that distinguishes uptalk from other contour types might initially be to see how well the description of uptalk fits within the existing phonological framework provided for intonational analysis. If it turns out that the best description involves a departure from that system, then we might infer that uptalk has indeed become phonologically distinct from other intonation patterns. It is possible, of course, that there is no such phonological distinction, for some if not for all varieties. For example, there may be neutralisation of a contrast between questions and statements, for some speaker groups in some contexts.

We should not assume that a phonological description of intonation proposed for one variety of English will apply equally to another variety, for uptalk just as for any other intonational pattern. As parallels on the segmental level, the fact that 'cot/caught' merger exists in some varieties of American English but not in others results in a difference between varieties in their phonological inventories, and the ongoing merger of NEAR and SQUARE in New Zealand English might ultimately result in a difference in inventories between New Zealand English and other varieties. Similarly, phonological distinctions in intonation patterns in one variety may not exist in other varieties. It is indeed problematic to assume that an existing phonological system for one variety can readily be used for another variety, or that a new intonational phenomenon can be accommodated without modification of a transcription system. In his approach to rising tunes in Tyneside English, Local (1986: 182) emphasises that the analyst has to do the phonology, to identify what count as the same or different tunes: 'That is, there are not any ready-made, simply identifiable "tones", they are the result (not the starting point) of phonological analysis.' So when we consider the phonetic variation noted by Di Gioacchino and Crook Jessop, we need to determine whether such variation is sufficiently systematic to warrant a modification of the phonological description in order to capture what is a relatively new contrast, one for which existing ToBI transcription systems were perhaps not intended. That is, the problem perceived by Di Gioacchino and Crook Jessop is only a problem if it is assumed that the phonological system of variety X also applies to variety Y, which may be separated from it either geographically or historically. (See also Warren, 2005a, especially pp. 349–350.)

A number of ToBI-style transcriptions have been offered for the description of uptalk, and understandably – given the phonetic descriptions presented earlier in this chapter – these vary from region to region. For Canada, Shokeir (2008) considers rises and falls on declarative sentences in a study of recordings of speakers from southern Ontario. The 'contours' that Shokeir (2008: 19) includes in her analysis are L* H-H% (which she calls the 'traditional uncertainty contour'), L-H% (the 'continuation contour') and L-L% (the 'standard falling contour'). The last two labels are combinations of phrase accents and boundary tones rather than complete contours, but it is clear from an earlier conference abstract (Shokeir, 2007) that Shokeir assumes these follow a H* pitch accent, i.e., the entire set of three contours being surveyed is L* H-H% (uncertainty), H* L-H% (continuation) and H* L-L% (standard falling). The first two contours appear to be considered uptalk rises by Shokeir, with the 'uncertainty contour' often interpreted by listeners in her perceptual study to also show continuation. Di Gioacchino and Crook Jessop, also investigating Canadian English (for speakers from Ontario and British Columbia), similarly include the continuation rise as an example of uptalk: 'Traditionally in the ToBI system, uptalk, also known as a continuation rise, occurs at an IP boundary and is characterized by an L phrase accent followed by an H boundary tone' (Di Gioacchino and Crook Jessop, 2010: 6). So to Shokeir's transcriptions we can also add Di Gioacchino and Crook Jessop's continuation rise with a low pitch accent, transcribed as L* L-H% (see their Figure 1). These authors also refer to work that assigns uptalk the same boundary patterns (H-H%) as YNQs. In particular they refer to discussion of high-rises by Hirschberg and Ward (1995), who focus on the H*H-H% pattern, which they call the 'high-rise question contour'. However, Di Gioacchino and Crook Jessop (2010: 9) found no instances of this tune in their data. In summary, uptalk transcriptions for Canadian English include L* H-H%, L* L-H% and H* L-H%, all of which are also suggested as transcriptions for contours with other meanings (albeit meanings frequently also associated with uptalk).

Hirschberg and Ward (1995: 407–408) contrast H* H-H% with the L* H-H% pattern, which they say conveys a request for a simple yes or no response (whether it is on an interrogative or a declarative form). They claim that this interpretation is not appropriate for H* H-H%. Hirschberg and Ward's illustrations of the uses of H* H-H% show that this is an uptalk rise. Although they do not explicitly state the variety they are describing, the content of their examples suggests that it is American English. In another analysis of American English, McLemore (1991: 42) states that the types of final rise that typically occur in her data from Texan sorority speech have L* pitch accents followed by H- (at intermediate phrase boundaries), H-H% or L-H% (both of these at intonational phrase boundaries, with the latter indicating a delayed rise). This seems to be at odds with Hirschberg and Ward's description of uptalk as H* H-H%. Levis (1996), however, indicates that in Midwestern American English H* H-H% (high-rise) and L* H-H% (which he calls a 'low-long-rise') are not functionally distinct, although he says that it is possible that they may have different sociolinguistic distributions. From their analysis of uptalk in Southern California, Ritchart and Arvaniti (2014) conclude that question rises typically have the pattern L* H-H%, while statement rises (uptalk in the sense used here) have the pattern L* L-H%, leading to a phonetic distinction between early and late rises as well as between higher and lower rises. So for American English (which admittedly is a broad category) we have transcriptions for uptalk of L* L-H%, L* H-H% and H* H-H%, with the first two more likely in Texas, the first in Southern Calfornia (where the second tune is more likely on questions) and the third in the Midwest.

Fletcher and Harrington (2001) found that declarative (i.e., uptalk) rises in Australian English were more likely to have an L* accent, while question rises had H*. Since both were found with a H-H% boundary combination, this means that the opposite pattern is reported for Australian English to that reported by Hirschberg and Ward (1995) for American English, who claimed that L* H-H% was used for YNQs and H* H-H% for uptalk. The pattern noted by Fletcher and Harrington is also reported for a subset of Australian English in Fletcher et al. (2005), and the suggestion is made that although both shapes are found on statements and questions there may be some system-internal distinction arising to separate statement rises (L*H-H%) from question rises (H* H-H%). However,

McGregor and Palethorpe (2008) claim that both H* H-H% and L* H-H% patterns are found on Australian statements (i.e., as uptalk forms), but with different meanings. In particular, uptalk with H* conveys new information, to be added to the listener's belief set (or, alternatively, information that the speaker wishes to present as if it were new), while L* uptalk presents information that is not new and therefore serves as a reminder. They similarly contrast question rises following H* and L* pitch accents, with the former carrying an expectation of a positive ('yes') response to the question, and the latter having an expectation that the listener will provide some information in their response. In a further twist, Fletcher (2005) reports that a closer look at terminal high-rises in a corpus of Australian English (from map task dialogues) reveals that most of the rising movements are in fact the final part of a split fall-rise movement (e.g., in a H* L* H-H% sequence) and therefore different in that respect from YNQ rises. Uptalk in Australian English therefore appears to include the forms L* H-H% and H* H-H%, along with H* L* H-H%

In her analysis of British uptalk, Bradford (1997: 30–33), like Fletcher and her colleagues for Australian English, also argues for a fall-rise pattern (i.e., H* L-H%), with a fall beginning on the tonic syllable and either falling to a low level or involving a gradual fall until the final accented syllable in the intonation group, at which point a dramatic rise takes place. In some cases this rise is realised as a high step up rather than a glide, and the rise can be given extra height by lengthening of the segmental material over which it is realised. Non-uptalkers would, by contrast, have a falling movement through to the end of the intonation group. Note also that Bradford comments that the extent of the falling part of the fall-rise depends on the amount of material between the tonic and the final rise. Sometimes this can be so brief that the fall is barely noticeable. The most marked aspect of this fall-rise is clearly the rise. A possible transcription for this has been suggested by Ladd (see Section 1.3.1), i.e., the high range fall-rise H*+L H-H%.

What should be clear from this summary of transcriptions offered for uptalk is that there is some commonality but also much difference across varieties. A sequence of a high phrase accent and high boundary tone (H-H%) is found in most descriptions, but variably preceded by a low or a high pitch accent. In addition, low-rises (L* L-H%) are reported in North America, and various types of fall-rise are also mentioned in most regions. The position of the transcribed tunes in the intonational system of the varieties also differs, with some analyses offering labels that distinguish between question rises and uptalk, but with most descriptions remaining unclear about the tune's status. Additionally, of course, the phonological descriptions, while indicative of the phonetic form of the rises and often accompanied by a description of their shape, may not indicate the same phonetic tune in different varieties, even when the transcriptions coincide, i.e., there may be realisational and/or phonotactic differences.

2.6   Summary

In this chapter we have seen that the description of uptalk as the use of question intonation on declarative statements is too narrow. Questions do not always require rising intonation, and indeed for many questions – especially those with morphological or syntactic marking of their questionhood – the preferred pattern is a fall. If question intonation is interpreted as a shorthand for rising intonation, then the description is still not accurate, since there are rises on declaratives that are not uptalk. Even if we put aside the particular intonation patterns of the Urban Northern British dialects, we still find rises in list intonation or being used to mark continuation or the linking of one part of a statement to the next in a way that is quite different from uptalk.

We have also seen that there is considerable variation in the phonetics and phonology of uptalk across the varieties of English in which it has been studied. Because of the description of uptalk as the use of question intonation on declarative statements, our starting point has been to consider whether there are any ways in which the forms of uptalk differ from those of questions. We have seen claims that the average pitch levels of uptalk are lower than those of questions, that uptalk rises start later in the intonation group than question rises and that they start from a lower pitch level than question rises. These last two observations (later rise, rise from a lower level) would of course result in the first (lower overall pitch), but they also result in a more dramatic rising pattern for uptalk, either more sudden or more extended. These different claims concerning the phonetic shape of uptalk rises are to an extent dependent on the variety being described, but even within single varieties there are different descriptions.

We should perhaps not be surprised that the phonological analyses of uptalk, as reflected in the suggested ToBI transcriptions, show differences between English varieties. These varieties differ in other aspects of their intonational systems, which is in turn reflected in the development of different ToBI transcription sets, for example, for General American and for Australian English. When we couple this with differences in the phonetic forms of uptalk, it is unlikely that we will achieve a consensus. The single common feature in the transcriptions listed above is the high boundary tone (H%). Many, but not all, also have a high phrase accent (H-).

Phonological considerations of course also include the consideration of meaning, and it is to the meanings of uptalk that we turn in the next chapter.

3   The meanings and functions of uptalk

It seems that there are almost as many functions and meanings ascribed to uptalk as there are magazine articles and letters-to-the-editor dealing with the phenomenon. The range of functions is also extensive in academic texts. For example, on the basis of previous research, Shokeir (2008: 17) lists uncertainty, continuation, deference, verification, facilitation, checking, grounding, negotiation, implication and lack of confidence. These functions need not of course be mutually exclusive, but the range of meanings is clearly extensive.

Guy and Vonwiller (1989: 21), writing mainly about Australian uptalk, state that of the various questions about this type of intonation, the most contentious is perhaps what it means. At around the same time, in their study of uptalk in Canadian English, James et al. (1989: 15) note that the tune has many shades of meaning, including meanings that convey emotion and attitude. It is therefore not surprising, they point out, that the tune occurs in diverse contexts and that it is consequently difficult to establish a definitive set of semantic features to characterise the contour. In a more recent review of declarative rises and models of intonational meaning, Šafářová (2006: ch. 5) concludes that some rising declaratives commit neither the speaker nor the addressee to the truth of the proposition they contain, some commit the speaker to its truth, and some are only used if the addressee is already committed to its truth. She also notes that rising declaratives can seek an evaluative response, that they can be considered to be more polite and friendly than falling declaratives, and that the paralinguistic interpretation of high rising intonation is uncertainty.

In an early investigation, Guy and Vonwiller (1984: 2) start with an initial hypothesis that since uptalk employs a tune frequently associated with questions, then its use is to question something, 'even though it is not questioning the yes/no polarity of the clause'. They point out that it is not practical to ask people what uptalk means, not least because the intonation has acquired a stereotype. They then explore what this stereotype is, in terms of meanings and associations, i.e., as a sort of exercise in post-hoc justification of uptalk's possible meanings. Since it is typically associated with the speech of young females, they say, we might therefore assume that it expresses uncertainty or lack of confidence (associated with being young) and deference, self-effacement or social powerlessness (stereotypically associated with females). The first of these meanings (uncertainty) is closer to the questioning meaning often associated with rising intonation patterns. Guy and Vonwiller go on to point out that this characterisation is inadequate, since uptalk is also widely used by men, and is not used exclusively by young people. They see that the main significance of uptalk is interactional, seeking verification of the listener's comprehension. At the same time it can convey different shades of meaning such as 'are you with me emotionally?' (affective feedback) or 'is it all right to go on?' (a turn-taking regulator). They look at the text types with which uptalk is likely to be used, and find that it occurs more with narratives and descriptions than with opinion texts; this suggests that the referential meaning of uptalk may be quite different from its social and emotional meanings. That is, if it conveys uncertainty then we would not expect it on narratives and descriptions, and if it shows deference then we would expect to find it more in the context of opinion texts (see also Warren and Britain, 2000).

More generally, the lack of a clear or regular mapping from intonational forms to meanings is noted by Hirschberg (2002: 67–68), who comments that although intonation researchers frequently look for such regularities, they typically encounter too many exceptions even for generalities such as a link between an increase in the prominence of a pitch accent and a heightened focus on the item made prominent. She points out that detailed interpretation of intonational features depends heavily on the context of use. Cruttenden (1981) had earlier acknowledged the difficulty in finding universal meanings for falls and rises, and settled instead on rather more abstract commonalities, namely 'closed' for falls and 'open' for rises (see Section 1.3.2). The individual characteristics or meanings associated with 'open' include limiting (doubt), question, continuity, open-listing, non-conducive (i.e., disagreement is possible), statement with reservations and conciliatory (amiable) (see also Horvath, 1985), many of which we find associated with uptalk.

Half a century ago, Bolinger (1964: 842) also considered the difficulties faced by any attempt to find universals of intonation:

The toughest objection is how it will be possible to find criteria of meaning that will transcend individual languages. Take a foreign speaker who misuses an intonation and is misunderstood. The naïve cultural relativist looks at this and takes it for proof of an accidental similarity in form only. But this is giving up too easily. It fails to make a distinction between meanings and values. For example, a low-pitched fall in two languages may mean finality in both, but finality may be frowned upon sometimes in one community but approved in the other.

In other words, there is layering of meaning in intonation that can result in apparently similar forms having equivalence on one layer, but not on another.

In one attempt to identify these layers of meaning, specifically with reference to uptalk (high rising tones), House (2006: 1554) considers the different orientations of intonation, which can be towards the speaker, towards the linguistic content or towards the discourse context. If an instance of uptalk is seen as speaker-oriented, then this highlights affective meanings associated with the Frequency Code (Ohala, 1983), such as 'politeness, deference, timidity, vulnerability, or friendliness'. If the focus is on the linguistic message, then a possible interpretation is that the speaker is expressing uncertainty. House cites here Gussenhoven (1984), who ascribes a 'testing' function to rises, whereby the speaker chooses not to make their own commitment to the relevance of adding the linguistic content of their utterance to the discourse, but is inviting the hearer to make an assessment. Finally, if the orientation is towards the discourse context or towards interaction with the listener, then the high tone of an uptalk contour could signal 'open-endedness, continuity, non-finality, or a need to check with participants in the interaction that they are successfully negotiating common ground'.

Bolinger's (1964) focus in the passage cited above was on the comparison of intonational meaning across languages, but the 'objection' he raises applies equally to the comparison of varieties of a single language. For example, Cameron (2001: 114) has pointed out that uptalk need not have the same meaning in different dialects. I would argue that in addition it need not have the same meaning at different points in time, and that it may not be interpreted in the same way by different speaker groups within a dialect region. So, typically, we see that at the early stages of the uptake of uptalk, older and more conservative listeners interpret this tune – understandably given their own intonational inventories – as questioning and/or as expressing insecurity, whereas the intentions of the speakers in producing the uptalk may be quite different; for example, to show openness and inclusivity. In terms of the types of orientation discussed by House (2006), the 'out-group' (the older generation listening to younger speakers) is oriented more towards the linguistic content, whereas the 'in-group' (the younger generation) find themselves oriented towards the speaker or towards the goals of the interactional context.

Similar differences in interpretation were highlighted by McConnell-Ginet (1975) in her review of Lakoff's *Language and Women's Place* (Lakoff, 1975). Lakoff had given what is one of the earliest published examples of uptalk, as in the following interaction, originally used by her in a journal article (Lakoff, 1973: 56):

(A) When will dinner be ready?
(B) Oh ... around six o'clock ...?

Lakoff (1975: 54) suggests that the questioning nature of the intonation in turns such as B's above creates an impression 'that the speaker lacks authority or doesn't know what he's talking about', although in this particular example it potentially also serves as a check that the suggested time is good for A. Lakoff's view is that a greater tendency for women to use uptalk is not a direct expression of gender identity but rather a reflection of their greater likelihood to take stances that indicate uncertainty or their unwillingness to assert an opinion. McConnell-Ginet, however, emphasises that although uptalk may indicate uncertainty, it is also being used to keep the interaction going. Interestingly, she maintains that this rising tune can imply an 'unexpressed question', and that the meaning of this question will depend on the context in which the uptalk occurs. Thus, if a speaker uses an uptalk contour to identify themselves after they have been asked their name, then this uptalk (*I'm Paul ⟋Warren*) might indicate 'Who are you and why do you want to know my name?', but it does so without being openly confrontational, in that the implicit question can be ignored. In another context, someone using uptalk on the introduction *I lecture in lin⟋guistics, at Victoria University of ⟋Wellington* is not indicating uncertainty about what they teach or who they represent, but is probably using the rising intonation as an opening gambit to get the listener to reply and to engage in a continuing interaction.

It is clear also that the nature of the interactional context and the status of the speakers in that context need to be added to the orientations discussed by House (2006). In her study of uptalk amongst sorority members in Texas, McLemore (1991) notes that junior members with minimal speaking rights in business meetings use uptalk with an effect of insecurity (they were also hesitant speakers and used many hedges), while senior members use it in the same contexts but from their position of authority in order to elicit involvement. In different speaking contexts – for example, at social events – junior members can appropriately use uptalk to introduce new topics. The nature of the discourse contexts and the status and orientation of individuals within those contexts are crucial to the interpretation of the uptalk intonational contour.

For organisational purposes, I have arranged further discussion of the various meanings and functions of uptalk into three main groupings below. The first two correspond largely to negative and positive orientations towards uptalk. These groupings are largely for convenience. It might seem odd to start with the negative meanings attributed to uptalk, but doing so allows us to subsequently indicate that many of these negative features actually correspond to some of the positive functions for uptalk that are further explored in the subsequent section. The third group covers some of the interactional functions of uptalk in maintaining conversation, and this too is somewhat artificially demarcated from the other meanings and functions, since, for instance, the use of uptalk to show deference or to avoid confrontation will also serve interactional functions.

3.1   The downside of uptalk

One of the most frequently cited meanings of uptalk, particularly in media commentary, is that it indicates that speakers are uncertain about what they are saying or that they are generally insecure and lacking in confidence, or – in the words of playwright Alan Bennett – that they are using 'that lilting interrogation with which young people can cast doubt on any certainty' (cited in a review of his appearance on *The South Bank Show* by Wollaston, 2005). For example, when tapes were released of phone conversations between former White House intern Monica Lewinsky and her friend Linda Tripp, speech expert Sam Chwat was cited in the *New York Post* (Morris, 1998) as characterising Lewinsky's speech as having 'classic late teen-ager upspeak patterns' with 'a lot of insecurity'. This interpretation of uptalk is reflected also in advice given in the *Chicago Tribune* to potential interviewees (Kapos, 2004): 'no giggling at the end of sentences – a habit many women succumb to when they're nervous – no cell-phone use, no verbal upspeak or sing-song language'. According to Barbara Pachter, a communications expert cited in the article, this 'all shows you are uncomfortable and it takes away from your credibility'. In his early study of uptalk in Australian English, McGregor (1980: 1) pointed out that the 'apparent need of the speaker for regular encouragement' had led some commentators to suggest 'perhaps somewhat jocularly, that the form is a reflection of a deep seated insecurity which pervades the Australian psyche'.

In addition to this rather anecdotal evidence, experimental data produced by Smith and Clark (1993) shows that when participants are unsure of their answers to a question (as revealed by a test of their 'feeling of knowing'), then they are more likely to use rising intonation as well as hedges such as 'I guess'. It is unclear, however, whether the rising intonation patterns observed in that study are instances of uptalk.

In her discussion of high pitch as an illocutionary device, Holmes (1984: 356) refers to Brown and Levinson's (1978) argument that there is a universal association of high pitch with tentativeness. It has frequently been claimed that high pitch is a fundamental signal of incompleteness or non-finality, and that a high-rise conveys tentativeness, hesitancy and uncertainty. There are, of course, circumstances where such expression of uncertainty is strategically important, as noted by Shepherd (2011), who studied classroom interactions, in particular students' responses to questions from their teachers. Shepherd found that rising intonation on these responses did appear to function as an indicator of uncertainty. The effect seemed to be that the student was presenting an uncertain answer to the teacher for evaluation and feedback. Interestingly, such use of rising intonation did not pattern according to the demographic variables of sex and ethnicity associated with the use of 'uptalk'. A further positive perspective on uptalk as marking uncertainty is found in a study of New Zealand children (Ainsworth, 1994) in which it was again concluded that uptalk is used by children to seek verification and can therefore function as a positive politeness device.

Gunlogson (2002: 130) makes a generalisation concerning declaratives with rising intonation that they 'fail to commit the Speaker to their propositional content'. However, the same author elsewhere (Gunlogson, 2001: 27) allows that some rising declaratives can commit the speaker to the truth, as in *My name is Carl? I'll be your waiter tonight?* She notes, however, that such instances are not the focus of her research, which is on declarative questions. For our purposes, note that the frequent negative interpretation of uptalk as showing uncertainty fits well with the fact that declarative rises are frequently associated with questions and therefore with the absence of commitment from the speaker to the propositional content. What is also interesting is that Gunlogson (2002: 130) points out that a consequence of the failure of rising declaratives to commit the speaker to the truth of their content is that these rising declaratives allow for a range of speaker attitudes. We should not therefore be surprised to find that uptalk is similarly associated – by listeners at least – with a range of speaker attitudes.

In her study of courtroom interactions in New Zealand, Innes (2007) reports that the less powerful participants tend to have a higher rate of uptalk usage. Although uptalk is therefore associated with relative powerlessness, Innes points out that this is not the only explanation for its distribution in her data. Rather, discourse functions and the interlocutors' goals are also significant factors, with uptalk being used to seek verification from the listener or to show politeness.

Uptalk can also have a defensive flavour, such as in the following interaction, where a waitress has just been asked back to the table by the customer because the latter felt a rather hostile attitude from the restaurant staff (Jacobs, 2004):

'I'm sorry, there's no hostility!' the waitress said, slipping into self-righteous uptalk. 'We're just all … super-super-busy?'

Fletcher and Harrington (2001: 227) note that Australian uptalk 'has been associated variously with lack of confidence, low social status, extreme youth, and a high degree of friendliness'. But closer scrutiny of when and where uptalk is used has challenged the widespread claim that it indicates insecurity. For instance, analyses of the text types in which uptalk occurs show that it is frequently found in just those cases where it would be detrimental for the speaker to show uncertainty or insecurity. This includes expressions of fact or opinion, where the speaker would be highly motivated to convey the accuracy or acceptability of what they are saying (Guy and Vonwiller, 1984, 1989; Warren and Britain, 2000; Horvath, 2004). In his *Language Log*, Liberman (2010) gives examples of uptalk from the spoken commentary of a python wrestler and from the actor William Hurt as illustrations that uptalk is not exclusively used as an indicator of 'feminine insecurity and need for reassurance'. McConnell-Ginet (1978: 554–555) similarly argued that rising intonation is not the marker of female tentativeness that it is often claimed to be, since it is also used by men, including when they respond to questions to which they have the answer. In their study of Australian English, Fletcher et al. (2002a) show that the low-onset rises typically associated with uptalk (see Chapter 2) have a forward-looking function such as indicating continuation, rather than a backward-looking function expressing questioning or tentativeness.

House (2006) links a speaker-oriented interpretation of uptalk with the notions of deference and vulnerability, and cites in this context the Frequency Code (Ohala, 1983). As explained in Chapter 1, the Frequency Code links differences in pitch in mammalian and aviary vocalisations to differences in size – higher pitch suggests that the organ producing the vocalisation is smaller. In humans, this reflects the differences in larynx sizes between women and men – post-puberty, the male larynx is in its front-to-back dimension approximately twice the size of the female larynx. More generally, the association of the Frequency Code with physical size differences has been linked to a dimension of dominance versus submissiveness, with high pitch indicating subordination.

Deference also features in an early analysis of uptalk forms, where Lakoff (1973: 56) comments that they share features with tag questions and hedges, in showing 'unwillingness to assert an opinion'. This has also been presented as a popular view among 'standard-speaking middle classes' in New Zealand, who see uptalk as showing 'deference to the hearer or alternatively hesitation about the validity of what [the speaker is] saying' (Britain, 1992: 92). On the basis of the distribution of uptalk rises by speaker sex and social class in Guy et al.'s (1986) Australian data, Eckert (1989: 253) assumes that this intonation 'can be associated with subordination regardless of sex'. In his analysis of uptalk in Australian English, Allan (1986: 54) argues that deference is a natural aspect of high pitch, but claims that this is a general effect of a higher register, and not a specific attribute of uptalk.

As we have seen above, the view that uptalk is used to show deference and is therefore to be negatively evaluated contrasts with McConnell-Ginet's (1975) interpretation of Lakoff's early examples. McConnell-Ginet focuses on the positive effect of uptalk in the maintenance of conversation. Showing deference, or being backward in coming forward, will be more likely to maintain an interaction than would result from taking a confrontational stance. A subordination account for deference is anyhow unlikely given the greater likelihood of uptalk in conversations between equal status friends (Guy and Vonwiller, 1984: 11–12). More recently, Lowry (2011: 215) has pointed out that it is unlikely that uptalk indicates 'the relative subjugation of females' suggested by Lakoff, since it has become associated with 'stereotypically socially ambitious, appearance-obsessed young women'. In a *Rolling Stone* article on teenage girls in Connecticut, Dunn (1999) writes of how these girls have an 'abject fear of offending. This extends to their speech, which has a noncommittal, nonconfrontational, questioning intonation.' But she goes on to point out that 'these girls … are confident consumers, secure in their opinions'.

A positive slant on deference is also taken in an early study of uptalk in American English (Ching, 1982). Ching lists examples from his data of rising intonation with a range of uses and then points out that '[i]n all of the categories … deference is shown to the listener by the speaker' (Ching, 1982: 105). The speaker might do this, for instance, by begging the listener's indulgence, by indicating the tentativeness of the information being conveyed or a desire for correction, or by requesting confirmation that the listener understands what is being said. In each of these examples, deference is not showing subordination but is part of a collaborative approach to the management of interaction.

Ogden and Routarinne (2005) point out that the deference interpretation of uptalk focuses on a consideration of the social relationships between conversational participants, and they argue that further insights can be gained from a focus also on the function of intonation in contributing to the management of interaction. In addition to frequent use of uptalk in narrative contexts, Ogden and Routarinne report a number of instances in 'suggestions' in their data from adolescent Finnish females. They argue that making a suggestion usually implies that the speaker has some authority, and that the function of uptalk in such contexts is to mitigate such an implication.

Finally, uptalk is often associated with casual speech. It is not entirely clear whether casualness is a negative or positive attribute, but Cruttenden (1986: 134–135) describes uptalk as a feature that is 'typical of a number of teenage groups in Australia and America, for whom casualness is the "in thing"'. One blog states: 'There is nothing wrong with uptalk and it tends to sound friendly and casual.' However, the blogger continues, 'if you want to sound professional, it can work against you. The constant upward intonation makes it sound like you are seeking approval and that you are not quite sure if what you are saying is okay' (VoicetowordBlog, 2011).

3.2   The upside of uptalk

As the comment on casualness indicates, not all interpretations of uptalk are negative. For instance, the profile of a director of Nickelodeon preschool television makes a link between uptalk and enthusiasm: 'Although clearly immersed in commerce, Johnson makes the impression of an enthusiastic student of everything around her. She has a penchant for uptalk, her phrases often rising into an implied question' (Hayes, 2008: 37–38).

In a further positive take, uptalk has been linked with authority. While Ladd (1980: 111) characterises low-rises as, among other things, 'self-assured', and Brazil (1997: 98) interprets rises more generally to show dominance, McLemore (1991) gives examples from her sorority study of high-rises being used to show authority. Further, Cheng and Warren (2005) show that rise tones are used much more frequently by the authority figure in business meetings and in graduate supervision meetings. In their study, Cheng and Warren considered the relative use of rise tones by the 'designated dominant speaker' and by other participants in the interactions in a corpus of Hong Kong English. They found that the relative proportion of rises used by dominant and non-dominant speakers changed from an equal share of around 50:50 in conversations, to 67:33 in placement interviews, 75:25 in business meetings and 85:15 in academic supervisions. Elsewhere, Liberman (2005b, 2010) similarly notes that authority figures such as President Bush use uptalk.

Of course, it could be that it is because they are in a position of authority that dominant speakers find they can use uptalk with relative impunity. Another explanation, however, is offered by McLemore (1991: 3), in terms of the fact that there are two physical parameters that determine voice pitch, namely larynx size and the rate of vibration of the vocal folds. As we have seen, the Frequency Code links high pitch with the smaller larynx size of smaller and less dominant individuals. At the same time, however, increased vocal fold vibration is linked with increased arousal and tension. So high pitch can indicate a higher level of involvement, which might be associated with taking an authoritative position. In addition, McLemore's finding of uptalk use by sorority members in a leadership context underscores McConnell-Ginet's (1983) view that uptalk need not indicate powerlessness.

Perhaps the most widely discussed use of uptalk as a positive feature is in the context of reducing social distance (Meyerhoff, 1991; Bradford, 1997). Bradford (1997: 34–35) discusses this in the context of highlighting both affective and referential functions for uptalk. The affective dimension acts 'as a bonding technique to promote a sense of solidarity and empathy between speakers and hearers'. That is, the rising intonation pattern reduces social distance by exploiting a conventional interpretation of rises as indicating openness and shared experience, and has the 'psycho-social effect of making the speaker sound less assertive or authoritative'. At the same time, uptalk has a referential function of signalling important chunks of information, and this function simultaneously maintains the hearer's involvement. What the speaker is doing, Bradford argues, is presenting 'new' information as though it were in fact part of the common information shared by speaker and hearer. By doing this, the speaker is showing that this information is assumed to be of mutual interest.

As outlined also by Britain (1992), uptalk is inclusive of the other conversational participant, building common ground between speaker and hearer, and conveying a meaning along the lines of 'can I assume that you (have enough information to) understand what I am saying?' (Warren, 2005a). Britain points to extensive distributional analyses of uptalk in New Zealand and Australia, and to the fact that Lakoff's (1975) claim that uptalk shows lack of commitment and confidence cannot explain how uptalk is distributed. He urges a move from thinking of uptalk as a negative politeness marker, i.e., hedging and showing deference (in Lakoff's (1973:56) terms 'leaving a decision open, not imposing your mind, or views, or claims, on anyone else'), to a positive one, inviting the addressee to participate in the production of talk and emphasising the in-group membership of speaker and hearer (see also Warren and Britain, 2000; Fletcher et al., 2005). Podesva (2011: 245) further argues that uptalk use can be subsumed under a general politeness strategy 'enabling the speaker to express concern for the hearer'.

3.3   Interactional functions

The positive aspects of uptalk discussed in the preceding section are linked to the interactional functions of this tune, since building common ground and being inclusive of the hearer clearly contribute to the maintenance of interaction. As has been stated, '[t]he meaning of the HRT is at the centre of debate, but there is a consensus that it has to do with the speakerhearer relationship' (Leitner, 2004: 117). Guy et al. (1986) characterised the broader communicative function of uptalk in their analysis of Australian English as being an interactional one, by which speaker and listener jointly construct a text. Similarly, McGregor and Palethorpe (2008: 174) summarise uptalk rises as 'collaborative structures, used by speakers in task-oriented discourse, such as a narrative, where the intention is to achieve a common goal'. More broadly speaking, the use of intonational rises for interactional functions is not really surprising given that increases in pitch range are frequently used to manage conversations (Ayers, 1994).

A range of interactional functions have been claimed for uptalk. These include checking, seeking a response, sharing, qualifying, connecting, floor holding, showing surprise, signalling information structure and committing the interlocutors to the truth value of the content. As pointed out by McLemore (1991: 81), these interactional meanings are not direct but need to be inferred from the discourse context.

3.3.1 Checking

The checking functions of uptalk include both interactional and informational checks (Watt, 1994: 99–101). These relate to uses on the two parallel 'tracks' of conversation highlighted by Clark (1996). One of these tracks is used for discourse management, while the other carries the subject matter or content of the discourse. Interactional checks serve discourse management and are used to 'obtain feedback about the listener's reaction to an utterance, negotiate a longer turn, secure listener empathy' (Britain, 1992: 79). The speaker uses them to track the listener's continuing involvement in the conversation (Horvath, 1985; Innes, 2007). Informational checks relate to the content track but have similar functions. One is that they are used to 'ensure that the hearer has grasped the meaning of the utterance in question' (Britain, 1992: 79). Watt (1994) calls these 'ideational' checks (see also Allan, 1984; Guy and Vonwiller, 1984). A further function of informational checks is to test the listener's general opinion of the relevance of the contribution (Watt's 'appropriateness' check). This includes checking whether the information conveyed is shared by the listener (Gussenhoven, 1984). Lakoff's (1973) example noted earlier and repeated below might be seen as an appropriateness check. Lakoff states that the effect of the uptalk in B's response is 'as though one were seeking confirmation, though at the same time the speaker may be the only one who has the requisite information'.

(A) When will dinner be ready?
(B) Oh ... around six o'clock ...?

The use of uptalk to check for comprehension is supported by Guy and Vonwiller's finding that uptalk incidence is related to the degree of semantic complexity of the speaker's turn (Guy and Vonwiller, 1989: 25). Uptalk is frequent, for example, in narrative text, where the development of the plot depends on what has gone before, and the speaker needs to repeatedly check that the listener is following. It turns out that uptalk is used in this way more often in narrative texts than in statements of fact or of opinion, which tend to have a much simpler structure. In their study of the management of information structure in interviews involving British adolescents, Cheshire and Williams (2002: 229) found that while the boys in their sample primarily want to impart factual information, the girls are more interested in the interviews as a conversational opportunity, and so were more likely to use uptalk to check the interviewer's understanding: 'They gave as much attention to how [the interviewer] might perceive their answers as to whether they were providing an adequate response to the question.' Also working with children, Brazil et al. (1980: 78) note that school students frequently use uptalk in answers to teachers' questions. Their interpretation is that the student is 'requesting an evaluative, high key follow-up by ending their answer with high termination'.

A more specific check of understanding is described in connection with the 'try marker' intonation rise noted by Sacks and Schegloff (1979: 19). This is used to check the listener's understanding of a reference, as in their example *well I was the only one other than than the uhm tch <u>Fords</u>?, Uh Mrs. Holmes Ford? You know uh the the cellist?* Each of the question marks indicates a rising tone and is followed by a brief pause for the listener to provide some sort of confirmation. When that is not forthcoming, the next 'try marker' is produced. This new try marker conveys additional information but still has a rising intonation as the speaker continues to seek confirmation. A similar use is noted by Clark (Clark and Wilkes-Gibbs, 1986; Clark, 1992).

Jeannette McGregor (2005: 174–175) discusses uptalk in terms of Clark's (1996) model of interaction and the contributions that participants make to a conversation. She suggests that uptalk aligns with two types of contribution that serve to establish grounding. One is 'trial constituents' where the speaker makes a contribution that they are not sure is correct or for which they may not be sure that there is mutual understanding. The listener can respond by asking a question, suggesting an alternative or just confirming what the speaker has said, and so the speaker then continues. The other type of contribution, which she refers to as 'instalments', are when speakers are telling a story or giving instructions – at each step the speaker makes sure that the listener understands. Robert McGregor earlier made similar claims for Australian English uptalk. He observed that the rising tone suggests a question that in its least insistent form means something like 'Are you following me?' (McGregor, 1980: 1). In its more insistent form, however, it can convey a meaning such as 'Aren't you impressed by what I'm saying?' McGregor highlights a 'social reinforcement' function for uptalk. Note, however, that in another early analysis of Australian English, Bryant (1980: 13) suggested that it might not make sense to think of uptalk in narrative texts as having a checking function, because this type of text typically has a clear and often chronological sequencing of the events that are being recounted. This sort of sequenced narrative should be less likely to require checking than, for instance, procedural or expository discourse.

Increasingly, however, the 'are you following me?' meaning has been suggested for uptalk in a range of English varieties. For instance, MacNeil and Cran (2005: 177) claim in a survey of American English that such a meaning is more likely than an indication of uncertainty. A similar meaning has been suggested for British English by House (2007) who takes a Relevance Theory approach to prosody in interactions. She interprets rising tones in a map task as a device used by the speaker to check that the listener is updating their cognitive environment using the content that the speaker is expressing. Uptalk is an overt signal of feedback elicitation. House argues that when prosody used in this way it is encoding procedural meanings, in a manner that is comparable to discourse particles, rather than conceptual meanings. Danesi (1997: 458) characterises uptalk in the speech of North American adolescents as an 'Emotive Language Programming' trait that 'probably indicates the need of teenagers to ensure the full participation of their interlocutors'.

In a study that involved both spontaneous interactional speech and the original speakers' re-reading of that speech from transcripts, Ayers (1994: 28) found that her two participants used high-rising tones to check the listener's comprehension in their spontaneous interactions. In the example *I was an interdisciplinary ↗major | you have any idea what that ↗is*, the rise on the first phrase seems to foreshadow that on the second. While the second phrase does not have syntactic marking of an interrogative, such as inversion, it clearly functions as a question. The first phrase has an identical tonal pattern, and takes on the same questioning meaning, despite its declarative structure. This suggests that the meaning of the rise in the first phrase parallels the explicit meaning conveyed by the text and rise together in the second phrase, i.e., it serves to check the listener's comprehension. Interestingly, when the participant reread this interaction, under instruction to do so as if it were spontaneous, they realised the first intonational phrase with a falling declarative intonation, with the high-rising intonation only on the actual question in the second phrase. The 'do you follow what I am saying?' meaning is conveyed by Ayers' other participant through the rise on *I kind of invent characters to help me with my ↗teaching*. Again, the reread version of this utterance did not have the high-rising tone, supporting the notion that the tone has a predominantly interactional function that is difficult or deemed unnecessary to recreate from transcripts.

In an experimental manipulation, Tomlinson and Richardson (2007) found that uptalk with the function of what they call a 'confirmation contour' (i.e., seeking affirmation in a proposition) was more likely in contexts where the speaker believed that the listener could see photographs of a 'talking head', a discussant whose opinions both speaker and listener had just been listening to. That is, checking for common understanding was more likely in the context where there was already some common ground (in this case, the visual information about the discussants). In such contexts, the uptalk contours were also more likely to be followed by simple back-channel devices, i.e., expressions used for feedback by the listener, such as 'uh-huh' or 'OK'.

Bolinger (1989: 140) also pointed out some checking functions for high-rising contours. On the one hand, they can be used to elicit repetition of a prior utterance that has not been fully understood. On the other, they can serve 'as a ploy to create the impression that the speaker has the knowledge he is supposed to have (and might be embarrassed at not having) and only needs to be reminded of it'. Earlier, the same author commented that

[m]any speakers of American English in giving a running account of something will use exactly this kind of terminal rise at the end of practically every sentence – clearly a channel-clearing device that says, in effect, 'Are you listening?,' for unless one gives a clear sign of attention, the monolog comes to a halt. (Bolinger, 1978: 510)

3.3.2   Seeking a response

The checking functions outlined above often seek a response from the listener in terms of some non-verbal feedback or possibly a minimal verbal response, indicating that the listener is still following. As pointed out by McGregor (2005), feedback from the listener has an important function to play in turnholding. Guy et al. (1986) noted that minimal and often non-verbal responses from the listener (back-channels) are enough to secure grounding and to maintain the interaction. Indeed, Bryant's (1980) study included videotapes of the interlocutors and showed that non-verbal feedback often provided sufficient acknowledgement after an instance of uptalk for the speaker to know that they could continue. Allan (1990) found that about a third of uptalk instances were followed by a minimal response. Since his analysis is based on utterance transcriptions without visual information, there may well have been non-verbal minimal responses after other instances too. In their discussion of uptalk as a checking device, Guy et al. (1986) considered the uptalk to be the first part of an adjacency pair. Clearly the examples discussed above show that the second part of such a pair can be a minimal verbal or non-verbal response. Not only is the speaker of the uptalk not seeking an elaborated response from the hearer, but also the uptalk does not invite a change in speaker. Thus, uptalk frequently occurs turn-medially, indicating that it is not expressing a genuine question to which a more extensive answer is required. In a study of overlapping talk in collaborative interactions, Salazar (2009: 52) finds support for the idea that uptalk invites minimal feedback, and that it is by providing such feedback that the participants in a conversation demonstrate their understanding of the norms of interaction, thereby establishing common ground and displaying group membership. Likewise, Wichmann and Caspers (2001) found that while listeners expected high-rises on questions to result in a change of speaker, they felt that high-rises on statements would be followed by back-channelling, a finding that is consistent with the view that high-rises on statements are used to elicit hearer acknowledgement.

In their analysis of narrative uses, Ogden and Routarinne (2005: 167) identify two functions for uptalk: allowing the listener to mark herself as recipient of the information being imparted by the speaker, and indicating that the speaker intends to continue their turn. The first use is reflected in a high proportion of minimal responses from the listener, with a smooth transition back to the original speaker.

In a cross-linguistic study, Beeching (2007) considers a number of pragmatic particles that she claims have the common feature that they serve some qualificatory role in face-management. These include terms expressing smallness (*a little bit*, *un petit peu* in French, *–chen* in German) and approximation (*well, sort of*), as well as interrogation forms including rising intonation, tag questions and uptalk. Beeching's interest is to track the changes in meaning of such forms from their source meaning to their new qualificatory meaning, which she claims is at the same time both 'semantically bleached' and 'pragmatically enriched'. In the case of interrogation forms, the source meanings of lack of knowledge or uncertainty are extended metaphorically onto a declarative statement to carry the conventional meaning 'do you agree?' and/ or 'I allow you to demur about this'. They can also create common ground, by allowing back-channelling, but are clearly not intended as genuine questions as shown by the fact that responses other than back-channelling are not required.

In their analysis of interactions concerning experiences of breast surgery, Stirling and Manderson (2011:1593) observe that the use of a high rising tone by a post-operative patient on *I was too frightened to look down?* is to seek acknowledgement from the listener, who provides this with *mm*. Uptalk-type intonation patterns have also been observed with attempts to get more than a minimal response. Ching, for example, reports a piano salesperson producing strings of rising contours as he offers choices to a customer, as in *We have Mediterranean in pecan? This piano in walnut? Light oak?* The salesperson described his use of rising intonation as seeking to make the listener respond to whether the wood type was a good choice (Ching, 1982:103).

Šafářová (2006: 73–74) found that rising contours (L* H-H%, H* H-H% and L* L-H%) were strong predictors of whether declarative utterances would be interpreted as 'seeking an evaluative response from the listener', which was defined to the judges in her experiment as being where 'the speaker stops talking and expects that the addressee will confirm or negate what has just been said' (2006: 73). Note, however, that speakers will not always stop speaking when they seek an evaluative response, as minimal verbal or non-verbal feedback is often a sufficient response. Šafářová conjectured that such rises 'serve as expressions of epistemic uncertainty'.

Fletcher et al. (2002a: 247) discuss uptalk produced by speakers in the instruction-giver role in a map task corpus. These rises were associated with 'forward-looking' communicative functions, i.e., were used on utterances that influenced the subsequent interaction, as contrasted with 'backward-looking' functions such as responses and acknowledgements that reflect the previous discourse. Gernsbacher and Jescheniak (1995) also suggest that uptalk may be a cataphoric device, signalling a forward-looking connection in discourse, as in their example linking *professor* to the following elaboration: 'So, y'know what? I have a pro↗fessor, 'n' he …' Fletcher et al.'s study distinguished between low-onset high-rises, labelled L* H-H%, and high-onset high-rises, labelled H* H-H%. They found that low-onset high-rises were typical on explanations, opinions and instructions, and they found high-onset high-rises mainly on requests for information (see also Fletcher and Harrington, 2001). The two types would clearly expect different kinds of response. They are also linked to differences in informational structure (see Section 3.3.3).

Head nods from the speaker have also been found to co-occur with high-rising contours in turn-final position, often in conjunction with yes–no questions, as found by Aoki (2011) in a study of uptalk and head nods in Japanese interactions. In non-turn-final position, an uptalk contour from the speaker will frequently be accompanied by a head nod from the listener as a back-channel acknowledgement.

Finally in this section, a further interpretation of the response-seeking nature of uptalk is reflected in a newspaper article that attributes to expert opinion the view that uptalk originated in Australia and that it is 'based on a colonial desire to please – as in, "please agree with me?"' (Kenny, 2007).

3.3.3   Signalling informational structure

It has been suggested that uptalk plays a role in identifying the informational structure of discourse, i.e., whether information is either new or already shared by the interlocutors. For instance, a study of British English (Bradford, 1997) indicated that 'upspeak' is used to introduce new information to the discourse, but importantly it does so as if it were part of the 'common ground' (see Section 3.3.4), i.e., information that can be assumed to be shared by both speaker and listener or to be of value to them both. This serves to indicate to the listener that the content is assumed to be of mutual interest.

In her study of adolescents in the south of England, Cheshire (2005) considers the ways in which her informants mark items as being new to the discourse. One category of mechanisms by which they do this is by using a linguistic form that creates interspeaker involvement. These include lexical means such as tags like *and stuff* and particles such as *like* and *you know*. To these she adds high-rising tones. Cheshire sees the imprecision in many of these forms to be part of their function as positive politeness markers, since they signal an assumption on the speaker's part that speaker and hearer share enough common ground for the hearer to understand the speaker's meaning.

Richardson et al. (2009) measured the incidence of rising intonation in their study of the effects on speech patterns of the speaker's beliefs about whether an addressee shares the same visual information. The visual information involved in this study was related to a short opinion-based video that speaker and hearer

had just seen. At the time of speaking either the speaker could see a still pho-
tograph of the actor from the video and believed that the listener could not
(or vice versa), or the speaker believed that they both had the same visual
information. Richardson et al. included rises in their study because they can
'serve as an implicit request to the listener to confirm the truth status of the
speaker's current utterance' (2009: 1476). More rises were found when the
speaker believed that the hearer did not share the same visual information than
when they believed they did. The role of these rises is thus considered to be
to coordinate the attention of the speaker and hearer, but as a function of what
the speaker believes is in the common ground (see also Tomlinson and Fox
Tree, 2011).

McLemore (1991) found that final rises in weekly sorority business meetings at a Texas university indicated that a meeting contribution is new in some
way. For instance, while falling intonation typically accompanied reminders
of events or other issues that had already been discussed, rises were used on
announcements of new plans.

In a second language learning context, Chaudron (1982) surveyed vocabulary instruction in Canada, and noted that instructors of English as a second
language used high-rising tones to signal to learners that a linguistic element
such as a word was new or being elaborated upon. The example in (13) is given
in connection with explaining the lexical item *abandon*:

(13)   You just leave them ... you couldn't ⟋drive them, you couldn't ⟋move them, you
       you couldn't do ⟋anything

Chaudron sees this prosody as part of an instructional style, although we can
see parallels here to its use in other contexts, i.e., not only is new information
being introduced, but it could also be claimed that the instructor is checking
for comprehension.

McGregor (2005) discusses the forms of uptalk in terms of a compositional
approach to meaning within the framework of Autosegmental-Metrical phonology (Pierrehumbert and Hirschberg, 1990). In particular she compares rises
with high- and low-pitch accent onsets, concluding that rises with H* accents
occur when there is new information to be added to the listener's belief system,
and rises with L* are found when there is salient information but that is not
necessarily to be added. A parallel in yes–no questions is that H* is used when
it can be expected that the listener will provide a confirmation ('yes') and L*
when the listener is expected to provide information or if the speaker is not
sure what sort of response the listener will make. While Pierrehumbert and
Hirschberg (1990) claim that a high rising statement with a L* pitch accent is
infelicitous, McGregor (2005: 179) suggests an amendment to allow for the
incidence of this form in Australian English, 'used for the sake of completeness,
or as a reminder'. A further suggested amendment (after Hobbs 1990: 314) is

that H* signals 'new' and L* 'not new'. McGregor (2005: 206) proposes the following explanation of how both H* and L* rises are used with statements in her map task data:

high (H*) pitch accent onset statement HRTs are used by speakers to check for listener understanding of the ('new') proposition; low (L*) pitch accent onset statement HRTs (associated with 'not new' information) are used to check that the listener is following the talk so far.

As noted earlier, McGregor sees a distinction here between what Clark (1996) calls trial constituents and instalments, respectively.

Also working within the Autosegmental-Metrical framework, Hirschberg and Ward (1995: 409) point out that descriptions of the meanings of high-rises in terms of confirmation-seeking, tentativeness, or uncertainty 'fail to capture a crucial distinction between high-rise contours and general rising question contours – namely, that this contour functions to assert information while also inviting a response'. They note that the characterisation offered by Pierrehumbert and Hirschberg (1990) for this contour is that it invites the hearer to add information to the set of shared beliefs held by speaker and hearer, while also indicating that there is some questioning of the relevance of that information for the hearer. Hirschberg and Ward (1995) modify this analysis, stressing the significance of the speaker's stance regarding the private (i.e., non-mutual) belief space of the hearer. That is, by using the uptalk contour, speakers are asking their interlocutors to make a link between the information being conveyed and their private beliefs; for example, speakers are questioning whether the information is already familiar to the hearer or they are inviting the hearer to link the information to what they already believe.

3.3.4   Sharing and connecting

A consequence of checking, response-seeking and signalling the transmission of new information should or could be the establishment of common ground (Guy and Vonwiller, 1984), and a sense of sharing in the developing interaction. Leitner (2004: 237) characterises uptalk in mainstream Australian English as a reflection of modern norms of interaction as involving 'sharing'. He observes that for younger speakers this contrasts with falling tunes that are 'telling' and have a sense of finality, as if the speaker is talking *at* rather than *with* their interlocutors. He sees the movement from telling to sharing as indicative of a 'shift in underlying norms of communication' (2004: 238).

It is interesting in this context that in their review of previous work on uptalk, predominantly in New Zealand English, Warren and Britain (2000: 165ff.) highlight its use as a positive politeness marker, overcoming barriers to communication (see 'checking' features discussed above) and ultimately helping to establish solidarity between speaker and listener (see also Britain, 1992). This approach enables them to explain the greater incidence of uptalk among women, and among Māori compared with New Zealanders of European descent (for further discussion see Innes, 2007). Women and non-Western societies such as the New Zealand Māori community are independently argued to place emphasis on using talk to establish and maintain relationships (Edwards and Sienkewicz, 1990; Holmes, 2002).

Rising tunes are of course commonly associated with non-finality or continuation (cf. list intonation and continuation rises or comma intonation, e.g., at the end of initial adverbial clauses). That is, they are used to indicate the connection of one portion of speech with the next. Such connections can be made between adjacent segments of one speaker's turn or between different speaker turns. By metaphorical extension, rises also indicate connection between the interlocutors themselves, and not just between their turns. In her study of Texas sorority speech, McLemore (1991: 75) states that 'the signalling value attributable to [phrase-final rises] across occurrences is "connection"; how members of this culture use the form as a strategy to accomplish more specific communicative ends is related to their shared goals and values'. Interestingly, members reported that they would use uptalk when addressing members of another sorority but not when addressing members of a fraternity, as it would make them appear weak. Status within the community is also an important consideration in the interpretation of uptalk, and McLemore also cites an example of a junior sorority member using uptalk to address a meeting and being perceived as seeking approval.

A specific aspect of continuation that is occasionally mentioned in connection with uptalk or uptalk-like rises is floor-holding. Fletcher and Loakes (2006) found in their study of Australian adolescents that speakers used a range of tunes as floor-holders, including mid-level plateaus, fall-rises and high-rises, whereas there was a stronger tendency for final falls at turn-yielding positions. Guy and Vonwiller (1984: 4) also suggest that uptalk might serve to negotiate a longer turn. At the same time, however, they suggest that these rises provide an opportunity for the listener to intervene if they have a good reason to do so, such as no longer being able to comprehend.

3.3.5   But ...

It is interesting that although many linguistic analyses of uptalk indicate that it has positive interactional functions, a scientific article on suicide prevention includes in a section called 'Establish rapport' advice that 'it is important to speak slowly and calmly, in short declarative sentences. Downspeak, where the pitch of the voice drops at the end of sentences, results in declarative statements. This contrasts with upspeak, which implies a question through a raised tone at the end of sentences, connoting uncertainty and tentativeness' (Granello, 2010: 223).

3.4   Multiple functions

The preceding section has highlighted quite clearly the range of meanings and interactional functions that have been associated with uptalk. As we saw in Chapter 1, it is widely acknowledged that intonational meaning has multiple layers (e.g., linguistic or lexical meaning; discourse, interactional or social meaning; paralinguistic or attitudinal meaning) and that a single intonational contour can convey meanings simultaneously at more than one of these layers. It should not be surprising, therefore, to find descriptions of uptalk that attribute multiple meanings or functions to this intonational form. Guy and Vonwiller's (1984) study of interview data concludes that two different kinds of meaning are linked to uptalk forms – the referential or experiential meaning of an utterance, and the social evaluation of that utterance. Just as the choices of phonetic or lexical variants to express the same message will provide indicators of the speaker's social background, so too will intonational choices. So in their study, the primary meaning intended by the speaker was to verify that the listener was understanding the speaker's utterances. The social meaning is most likely not even something that the speaker is consciously aware of, and might include deference, insecurity or youthfulness, depending among other things on the listener's interpretation of the intonation.

There are also descriptions of uptalk that reveal multiple functions or interpretations within one layer of meaning. In an early perceptual study, Uldall (1964) found for example that listeners associated high-ending rises with both 'submissiveness' and 'pleasantness'. Nilsenová (2002) points out some shortcomings of emotional and discourse/epistemic approaches to intonational meaning, and suggests a game-theoretic solution to the analysis of the meanings of rising declaratives. She bases her approach on a typology of speech acts developed by Merin (1994). The account Nilsenová gives for this type of intonation contour involves the settings of some parameters that are associated with the 'game' being played, this game being to establish the proposition as part of the common ground of speaker and hearer. One parameter determines who starts the game; in the case in point this is the speaker. A second determines whether the proposition will be adopted, and this is controlled by the addressee. This effectively indicates that the speaker expects the addressee to show some commitment to the truth of the proposition (see also Gunlogson, 2001). A third parameter indicates who has dominance in the game, and this is also set to the addressee. The notion of dominance is interpretable in several ways, and can signal for example who has the bargaining power or who dominates socially. Because the addressee is assumed to have dominance, they are in the position to force commitment to the proposition. This situation can arise either when the speaker does not have enough information themselves to commit to the truth of the proposition or when the speaker hands dominance over to the addressee as a signal of politeness or submissiveness. By invoking this notion that dominance can be assigned, Nilsevoná neatly aligns two of the meanings frequently associated with uptalk, i.e., speaker uncertainty and submissiveness.

In earlier work, Ching (1982: 98–99) also used speech act theory. In his corpus of uptalk he identified six functions of declarative rises: the topicalisation either of the whole unit of discourse or of a component of the discourse; the emphasis of particular words or phrases; the combination of an assertion with a question to determine the listener's understanding of or agreement with the assertion; an indication that the speaker is uncertain or is asking for correction; the demonstration of deference by the speaker by dramatising what they are saying to make it more interesting, or by begging the listener's indulgence, or by ingratiating themselves with the audience; the enactment of mitigation or politeness by downplaying the strength of an assertion. As Ching points out through examples, many instances of uptalk would appear to carry more than one of these functions. For instance, a topicalisation function also has the illocutionary force of a directive, getting the listener to pay attention to the topicalised information, and can be seen as a requestive, 'begging indulgence of the listener' and showing mitigation and politeness. But he also points out that in all of the usage categories deference is simultaneously being shown by the speaker to the listener. The speaker 'seems to have the welfare of the audience in mind when using this speech pattern' (Ching, 1982: 105).

Finally, a television review in the *Guardian* newspaper (Freedland, 2002) describes the character David Brent portrayed by the actor Ricky Gervais in *The Office* as '[ending] his sentences with an upspeak "yeah" or "all right"'. Freedland is here commenting on the modern dynamics of offices and other workplaces, in which bosses convey two meanings. They attempt to be 'matey' while also having to be bosses. Tench (1997: 17) expressed this duality of uptalk in the following way: 'HRT is a clever and efficient way of doing two things at the same time: giving information and checking on comprehension. It also seems to act as an indicator of in-group solidarity.'

3.5   Summary

Perhaps the most controversial aspect of the analysis of uptalk is what it means. We have seen that intonation has many layers of meaning, including linguistic, discoursal and attitudinal meanings. There are meanings that tell us something about the speaker, meanings that tell us about the content of what the speaker wishes to say, and meanings that help manage conversations. It is not surprising then that uptalk is also interpreted on many levels, reflecting these different intonational meanings. As a consequence, both positive and negative interpretations have been given for uptalk, the difference between these reflecting the stance of the commentator, such as whether they are a member of the in-group of people who use uptalk in a certain way, or belong to the out-group. To paraphrase Bolinger's comment on low-pitched falls cited earlier in this chapter, a high-pitched rise in two varieties may mean openness in both, but openness may be frowned upon sometimes in one community but approved in the other. As a result, there are tensions in the interpretation of uptalk: it can indicate insecurity but is also used in the expression of fact; it is a feminine trait but is also used by macho men; it shows deference but is common among equal status friends; it signals subjugation but is used by the socially ambitious.

Finally, it is clear that the interactional functions of uptalk are central – it is used for checking and for seeking feedback, which is often given through verbal or non-verbal responses. It is used to mark new information and to invite the listener to make links between information being conveyed and their existing beliefs. It asks 'are you following me?' It shares rather than tells.

4   Uptalk in English varieties

Cruttenden (1995) notes two main geographic areas where wider use of rises has been reported than for either British Received Pronunciation or General American. These are on the one hand Urban Northern British (UNB), covering a group of northern British cities (Belfast, Derry, Glasgow, Newcastle, Liverpool, Birmingham), and on the other hand the Pacific Rim (Australia, New Zealand, California, Canada). The two areas have different characteristic rises, with the rise-plateau and rise-plateau slump patterns of UNB different in shape, distribution and function from the high-rise terminals or uptalk of the Pacific Rim (Cruttenden, 1995: 168–171). It is clear, however, that uptalk has a wider geographic range than just the Pacific Rim. In a summary of phonological features of English varieties around the world, Schneider (2004: 1126) comments that uptalk (HRT) occurs 'fairly generally in British, American, Caribbean, Australian and New Zealand dialects and occasionally in Africa and Asia; in general, the phenomenon is assumed to be spreading globally among the young'. In this chapter, I review studies of uptalk across a range of English varieties worldwide. In terms of Kachru's (1992) classification, the discussion in this chapter will be mainly of uptalk in inner-circle varieties such as British, American, Canadian, Australian and New Zealand English. But I will also include varieties such as Indian and Hong Kong English sometimes labelled as outer-circle or extended-circle varieties and New Englishes.

It is important to remember again that discussions of uptalk, HRT, upspeak, AQI and so on may not be discussions of precisely the same phenomenon. That is, an Australian's questioning intonation may not have the same form nor the same function as an American's upspeak or a New Zealander's high-rising terminal. This difficulty is compounded by the fact that researchers based in different countries or even in different university departments in the same country may not be using a common set of terms, nor a common method of intonational analysis. What might work as a set of intonational descriptors for one variety may not work for another. While Rahilly's (1997: 110) comment that 'the lack of an appropriate model for analysing prosody tends to beleaguer all varieties of English except RP [Received Pronunciation]' may sound extreme (after all, the ToBI model has for instance been successfully applied to both General American and Australian Englishes), the point remains that cross-varietal comparisons can be problematic (Warren, 2005a). So the discussion in this chapter is of a fairly broad set of phenomena that have been characterised as uptalk (under its various names); it should not be assumed that we are always dealing with precisely the same intonation in the different varieties under consideration.

4.1   Australian English

I start this survey with Australian English (AusE) partly because some of the earliest mentions of uptalk-like tunes are for this variety, but also because this variety is placed in focus by the most widely used terms for uptalk that include any geographic reference, Antipodean Rise and Australian Questioning Intonation. In an early description, Mitchell and Delbridge (1965: 56) comment on an 'interview tune' that they find in a survey of Australian adolescents, based on recordings made between 1959 and 1961. While they suggest that this tune may be peculiar to the interview situation in which their speech data were gathered, the characterisation is very much that of 'uptalk', with their participants tending to 'end with a rising terminal a sentence which would normally fall away to a low terminal'. The tune has an interactive function meaning 'I've finished with that. What are you going to ask me next?' Mitchell and Delbridge also observe that this tune is frequently heard in radio and television interviews, 'especially with naïve subjects'. This comment suggests that this form of intonation was in widespread use in Australia by the mid-1960s, at least among non-professional speakers and in dialogic discourse contexts such as interviews. In her 'Survey of Australian English intonation', Adams (1969: 106–107) found that nearly half of the statements produced in response to questions had a rising intonation, but only a few of these had the 'interview tune' reported by Mitchell and Delbridge. Interestingly, in a footnote to her overview statements about her participants, Adams suggests that Mitchell and Delbridge's 'interview tune' is a tune that might 'upset the normal intonation patterns' (Adams, 1969: 84).

Surprisingly, Delbridge (1970) makes no mention of a distinctive rising intonation pattern, despite his earlier finding of uptalk-like tunes in broadcast interviews (Mitchell and Delbridge, 1965), and despite referencing Adams (1969) (who as we have seen mentions an unusual incidence of rises) as the only substantial study of intonation in AusE at that time. By the mid-1970s, however, there is growing evidence of uptalk in AusE. Burgess (1973) is able to confirm Adams' earlier observation of a high incidence of rises on statements. Burgess performed an acoustic analysis of a set of read sentences (based on Gimson, 1962) produced in 1972 by a mix of males and females across a spread of ages.

While there is no clear discussion of a feature that could be clearly isolated as uptalk, Burgess does tentatively note some 'tendencies worth further investigation' (1973: 325) that include a finding that statements ending in words of more than one syllable frequently have rising intonation over that word.

An intonational form much more recognisable as uptalk emerges by 1974. Writing in the *Sydney Morning Herald*, Bernard (1974) comments on 'the rising intonation which is unfortunately becoming more and more common in declarative statements (not only among broad speakers)'. By 1979, uptalk (high-rising terminal intonation) is noticeable enough in AusE to become the topic of a Master's thesis (McGregor, 1979), using recordings made in 1977. In a subsequent report based on that thesis, McGregor (1980: 1) comments on how the high-rising terminal is widespread in Sydney, and that it has been reported elsewhere in Australia. He suggests that 'it may be that this intonation contour will in time be recognised as a characteristic marker of Australian English'. In his 1977 data, it was still largely limited to younger speakers (up to around 25 years of age).

In her BA(Honours) thesis, Bryant (1980) noted that rising intonation at the end of declaratives was 'apparently solely Australian' and gives 'an impression of questioning to utterances without converting them to questions proper', leading her to coin the term 'Australian Questioning Intonation'. Bryant comments that of a range of rising tunes, Mitchell and Delbridge's 'interview tune' is closest to this form, 'but is not readily mistaken for AQI, which rises to a high level from a low preceding syllable' (Bryant, 1980: 2). Bryant's survey, conducted in Canberra, found that uptalk was used by speakers up to about 50 years of age, although more by younger than by older speakers in this group, and predominantly by females. It was also more likely to be found in the speech of female speakers in lower-status occupations than in any other group. This pattern of social distribution reflected in McGregor's and Bryant's work – younger working-class females showing higher incidence than other groups – is fairly typical of innovative language use (Kroch, 1978; Labov, 1982), and seems to indicate that the late 1970s was still an early period of uptake of uptalk in AusE.

By 1984, sufficient attention was being paid to high-rising terminals that questions were being asked about their meaning. Guy and Vonwiller (1984) used a 'subjective reaction test' containing two 30-second passages from each of three speakers. For each speaker, one passage contained a high-rising terminal pattern and the other did not. The goal was to determine what meanings were associated by naïve listeners with texts containing uptalk. The overall results from 97 listeners suggested that uptalkers were less suitable for higher-status employment and were considered less forceful, as well as generally less confident, but more attentive to the listener's needs, friendlier and younger, as well as more expressive. Guy and Vonwiller set these results against popular views of the meaning of uptalk in AusE, namely that it expresses uncertainty, deference (or powerlessness) and/or that is has an interactional function of checking the listener's comprehension (see Section 3.3). They also consider the content being expressed by uptalkers, and conclude that the most likely single meaning or function being conveyed by uptalk in AusE is the checking function relating to ongoing listener comprehension. However, because of the newness of the use of this intonational form with declaratives and its association with younger speakers in particular, they claim that there is some uncertainty about its meaning (see also Allan, 1984, who comments further on Guy and Vonwiller's analysis).

In 1985, Horvath reported an extensive study of interview data collected in Sydney between 1978 and 1982 (Horvath, 1985). Her book devotes an entire chapter to the high-rising tone, at the beginning of which she comments that '[n]o study of variation in Sydney English which was started in the late 1970s … could fail to investigate a particular intonation pattern, namely, a rising contour on declarative clauses' (Horvath, 1985: 118). As McGregor and Bryant before her, she notes that this contour was most likely to be found in the speech of younger females, particularly from the lower or working classes. In addition, it was associated with either Greeks or Anglos, but not with Italians (Horvath, 1985: 122). For her quantitative analysis, Horvath included 107,685 tone groups from a core group of 130 speakers. 1,724 high-rising terminals were coded, amounting to 1.6 per cent of the declarative clauses in the dataset. She comments that given the low incidence of this particular form of intonation, it is surprising that it receives so much attention.

Guy et al. (1986) further analyse data from Horvath's corpus (see also Guy and Vonwiller, 1989). They argue that the AusE rise that they analyse is different from the American examples given by Lakoff (1975) and Ladd (1980) because the latter have meanings such as deference, hesitation or tentativeness, which the AusE rise does not. They also point to phonetic differences. For instance, the American rise can start lower, rise more slowly and finish at lower levels than the AusE one. They acknowledge, however, that the rise under investigation is not unique to AusE and that some of the rises in Canada, California and the southern United States could be examples of the same phenomenon.

Guy et al.'s analysis shows that uptalk usage is higher among younger speakers. They point out that such an 'apparent time' stratification is only indirect evidence of an ongoing change, and so they supplement their analysis with a comparison between their data from the late 1970s and early 1980s and that of Mitchell and Delbridge (1965), also collected in Sydney, but 20 years earlier. Comparing teenagers in the two samples, Guy et al. (1986: 41–42) find about 3 per cent use of uptalk in their sample, compared with 0.3 per cent in the earlier sample. What is more, the 20–39-year-old group in their sample, which would include the age cohort of Mitchell and Delbridge's teenage sample 20 years earlier, showed 0.5 per cent uptalk usage, suggesting that linguistic behaviour remains relatively fixed after adulthood.

While the literature reviewed in the preceding paragraphs indicates that uptalk has been present in AusE since the 1960s, it is still occasionally commented on as a novel intonational form, even into the twenty-first century. In a review of features of AusE for *English Today*, Courtney (1996: 27) mentions rising tone, as an 'interesting recent phenomenon', but only in a parenthetical remark in his section on the Australian accent. He comments that it is 'used quite widely by young people, and seemingly to express a deference or uncertainty of response'. Kiesling (2006: 77) comments that it is a recent innovation in AusE and New Zealand English, and that the innovation is being led by Māori in New Zealand and by Greeks and Italians in Australia.

However, other recent writers comment on how uptalk has become established in AusE, with incidence levels reportedly as high as 16 per cent (McGregor, 2005) and 19 per cent (Fletcher and Loakes, 2006), much higher than Guy et al.'s 3 per cent in 1986.[1] Forman (2009: 17.3), in his review of a study of intonation and English grammar by Halliday and Greaves (2008), points out that 'it is correctly noted that the high rising terminal ... is becoming the unmarked option for a statement among some speakers in Australia and New Zealand'. Cox and Palethorpe (2007: 346), however, stress that 'it is important to recognise that HRT users also employ standard falling and fall-rise tunes'. Moore (2008: xix) comments that the high rising tone is 'very noticeable' as a distinguishing phonological feature of AusE, and Leitner (2004: 116) notes that uptalk is so prominent in AusE that any foreigner will notice it quickly. He also illustrates with examples that it is used on 'utterances that are grammatically in the declarative mood and, by the speakers' intent, declarative speech acts or statements'. Uptalk has become such a strong feature of AusE that voice coach Bruce Shapiro feels the need to point out that Australian actors have to learn not to uptalk when speaking with American accents (Iowa Center for the Arts, 2008). Uptalk in AusE continues to be the subject matter of extensive thesis research (e.g., McGregor, 2005; Webb, 2008).

Recent phonetic work on AusE intonation, especially by Fletcher and her colleagues, has explored in more detail the forms of uptalk and the differences between uptalk and other utterance types. For instance, and as noted in Chapter 2, Fletcher and Harrington (2001) test the claim (Ladd, 1996) that there is no phonetic difference between statement high-rises and question high-rises.

---

[1] Note, however, that these three samples use different speech tasks: Guy et al. used sociolinguistic interviews, i.e., conversations with a researcher; McGregor used an interactive map task; Fletcher and Loakes used data from peer-to-peer conversations. Task differences will be discussed further in Chapter 10.

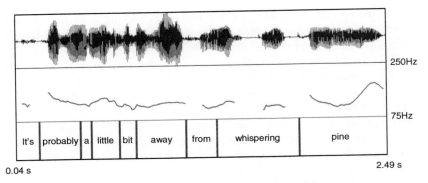

Figure 4.1 Fall-rise uptalk pattern in Australian English.

While the height of the rise appears not to differ, they report a greater tendency for low (L*) onsets for statements (84 per cent) but for high (H*) onsets for questions (91 per cent). Statements were also likely to have high-range fall-rises. It has since been suggested that a number of what were previously analysed as low onsets (L*) in L* H-H% statements could in fact be the second part of bitonal accents in fall-rise patterns. These seem to be particularly prevalent in utterances that convey forward-looking functions, i.e., those that influence the forthcoming discourse (Fletcher, 2005). Figure 4.1 shows an example of such a fall-rise pattern (on *pine*) from AusE map task data (my thanks to Janet Fletcher for permission to present this example, which formed part of the dataset analysed by Fletcher et al., 2002a).

4.2   New Zealand English

Referring to fieldwork carried out in the period 1963–1965, Benton (1966: 71) talks of a 'distinctive rising intonation' among ethnically Māori speakers of New Zealand English (NZE), 'especially marked in the speech of 5 to 8 year old children, but present in a modified form in the speech of older children too'. The areas in which Benton noticed this form were predominantly regions where knowledge of the Māori language was 'negligible', suggesting that this intonation form was not a direct influence of the Māori language on English. He also reported that Pākehā[2] children in these areas seemed to show the same pattern. Bauer (1994: 396) remarks that by 1980 uptalk (the high-rising terminal) had become so widely used in New Zealand that it was no longer considered a particularly Māori feature, although subsequent

---

[2] Pākehā is common New Zealand parlance for referring to New Zealanders of European descent.

studies have shown that uptalk is still strongly associated with Māori English (Warren and Bauer, 2004; Holmes, 2005), and also with Pasifika English (Stanton, 2006).

There is some suggestion that uptalk dates back even further in NZE than Benton's initial observations. For instance, Gordon (1998; Gordon and Trudgill, 1999) reports an analysis of 21 randomly selected speakers from New Zealand's South Island who were recorded in the 1940s by the Mobile Disc Recording Unit of the New Zealand Broadcasting Service. One speaker, born in 1874, had 'significant usage', another (born 1868) used a few uptalk rises at the beginning of her interview, and three further speakers showed rises that had a marked increase in pitch and that did not seem to be continuation rises.

After Benton's comments in the mid-1960s, there is little discussion of uptalk in NZE until the 1990s, although Gordon (2010) reports that in 1977 Denis McEldowney, then editor at Auckland University Press, wrote to her stating:

there is one tonal habit that I have become very conscious of among the Auckland young. This is the habit in ordinary narrative, of raising the pitch at the end of nearly every sentence, as if the sentences were questions, though they are not intended as questions. 'I was walking down Queen St? And I saw a group of Hare Krishnas? And they were chanting and ringing their bells?'

By the 1990s the intonation pattern was clearly punching above its weight, in that it was widely commented on despite relatively low incidence levels. For a review of some of this early work on uptalk in NZE, see Warren and Britain (2000).

In 1990, Allan opens a chapter on rises in NZE intonation with the following words: 'The question most often asked by New Zealand students when the topic of intonation is introduced is "Why do we raise the pitch of our voices at the end of everything we say?"' (Allan, 1990: 115). Allan presents a small-scale study that provides an initial comparison of uptalk in NZE with that reported by Horvath and others for AusE (see Section 4.1). He reports an uptalk incidence level of 3 per cent (i.e., three out of every 100 intonation groups) in his recordings from nine female 25–35-year-olds from the town of Levin (in the southern part of the North Island of NZ), higher than the 1.6 per cent reported by Horvath, but not as high as the 4.35 per cent in Auckland reported a few years earlier by Kaiser et al. (1987). Kaiser et al.'s sample apparently included younger speakers and also some particularly nervous informants. Allan also reports a higher incidence of uptalk from speakers of Māori ethnicity than from Pākehā speakers.

A more comprehensive study of NZE uptalk was conducted by Britain (1992, 1998a, 1998b). This involved interviews with 75 residents of Porirua, just north of Wellington. The sample represented three age groups (20–29, 40–49, 70–79), two sexes, two ethnicities (Māori and Pākehā) and two socioeconomic

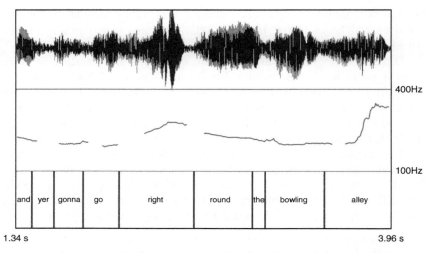

| and | yer | gonna | go | right | round | the | bowling | alley |

1.34 s   3.96 s

Figure 4.2 Uptalk rise from a young New Zealand female taking part in a map task.

groups (working class and middle class). Overall uptalk use was at 4.12 per cent. There was higher uptalk usage among young Māori speakers of NZE and amongst young Pākehā women than among the other groups. Class differences were not significant. Britain interpreted the uptalk usage as a positive politeness marker (see Section 3.2), as did Meyerhoff (1991). Bell (Bell and Johnson, 1997; Bell, 2000) also found that women, particularly Pākehā women, were more likely to use uptalk than men, and also that uptalk was more likely when the conversational partner is a woman.

Britain and Newman (1992) present further analysis of Britain's uptalk data, including phonetic descriptions. The rises vary both in the extent and the location of the pitch movement. Some rises are less than 50Hz and some more than 100Hz, and the rises can be over the final syllable of the intonation group, or over more than one syllable of the final word, or even over more than one word. As with Australian English (see Section 4.1), some of the more recent work on uptalk in NZE has considered the possible phonetic differences between question and statement rises (see also Chapter 2). One set of studies suggests that a major difference is in the alignment of the starting point of the rise, with later rises for statements than for questions (Zwartz and Warren, 2003; Warren, 2005b). An example of an uptalk rise from NZE is given in Figure 4.2, taken from a female New Zealand English speaker taking part in a map task (Warren and Daly, 2000), where she is describing to her conversational partner the configuration of a map so that the partner can draw the details on her own map.

The final accent of this phrase is on the first syllable of *bowling*, but the rise does not start until the final unstressed syllable of *alley*.

In an analysis of uptalk usage by much younger speakers, Ainsworth (1994) found a rate of around 9 per cent among NZE children, with more from the nine-year-olds in her sample than from the four-year-olds (14 per cent versus 2 per cent). The lower uptalk rate for the younger children is in part attributable to the difficulty in extracting narrative talk from these children, narratives being one of the text-types in which uptalk is most frequently found in the speech of the older children, as well as in that of adults. In a student project, Brown (2000) also found an uptalk rate of around 9 per cent, in this case in an Auckland NZE sample of informants in the 19–23 age range. She also found higher rates among students than workers. As in previous studies, females were stronger uptalk users, and there was more uptalk in narratives than in other text types.

Innes (2007) analysed interactions in the courtroom, an interesting context because of the power dynamics that exist there. She found that while there was some association of uptalk with power, the factors that might predict uptalk use are actually quite complex, and involve discourse functions, speaker roles and the interlocutors' goals in the interaction (see Chapter 3).

Finally, it is interesting to note that one visitor to New Zealand, from Toronto in Canada (see Section 4.4), comments on the demise of a standard in NZE, as exhibited by a coach tour operator, noting that the latter's 'commentary was in "uptalk," with a rising intonation in most sentences' (Fitzgibbon, 2007).

4.3   Pacific English Varieties

In a study of the English used by Niueans resident in New Zealand (who outnumber Niueans still living in Niue by a factor of around 15:1), Starks et al. (2007: 143) found that young, female, New Zealand-born speakers were more likely to use uptalk than older, male speakers. Indeed, one younger female speaker had around 11 per cent uptalk use on declarative utterances, while a middle-aged Niue-born male had none. It seems most likely that uptalk is a feature of Niuean English that has entered this variety via New Zealand English. No evidence is supplied concerning whether English spoken in Niue also has uptalk.

In Fiji, according to Tent and Mugler (2008: 259), the intonation patterns found in Indo-Fijian English include a final rise similar to that used in English yes–no questions. This is a form that is typically associated with expressions of surprise in Hindi, and is carried over with that meaning into Indo-Fijian

English. Since this meaning is different from those identified earlier for uptalk, it would seem that the rise in question is not an uptalk rise.

4.4   Canadian English

One of the earliest mentions of uptalk-like features in Canadian English is found in a survey of the English used in Carbonear, Newfoundland, based on recordings made in 1965 (Paddock, 1981). Paddock noted that visitors 'from other dialect areas of North America have informed me that they often respond incorrectly to a statement as if it were a "yes–no" question with a rising [terminal contour]' (Paddock, 1981: 34). He offers two possible explanations. One is that speakers are in fact producing a rise where the visitors would produce a fall, and the other is that they are not producing a rise, but a sharp change in key.

While it is unclear whether what Paddock was describing for Newfoundland really was uptalk, a more explicit investigation of an 'apparently new' intonational feature in Toronto English was carried out by James et al. (1989). These authors monitored an amateur (student) radio station in Toronto and noted instances of uptalk, which were predominantly from young females. Their analysis included asking both naïve and linguistically informed participants to note any unusual aspects in a set of recordings from their database. While some participants commented on the uptalk intonation, many did not, and when it was drawn to their attention they would comment along the lines of 'That's unusual?' or 'Everyone does that' (James et al., 1989: 16). The authors take this to suggest that uptalk was already well established by 1989, although Talla Sando (2009) claimed 20 years later that uptalk was only a recent phenomenon in Canadian English, and in a book review, Whittaker (1999) suggested that for a novel set in Toronto in the early 1970s, the uptalk of one character is 'wildly anachronistic'.

Analysing a small corpus of speakers from a region close to Toronto, namely from south and south-west Ontario, Lacey et al. (1997) noted that while uptalk was more prevalent among females, it was not restricted to young speakers – one 51-year-old male used it a lot, but acknowledged that this was probably due to the influence of his teenage daughter. The speakers in the survey were middle-class, but on the basis of other observations the authors argue that the usage does not seem to be greater among the working class than the middle class, and is thus different from patterns recorded in Australia and New Zealand. The shape and size of the rise in Lacey et al.'s examples is comparable to that found in other analyses. Similar rises are found in some of the Canadian speakers in the IDEA database (International Dialects of English Archive, 2013). The example in Figure 4.3 is from a narrative by a 25-year-old

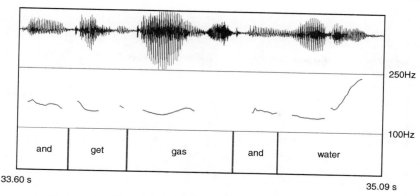

Figure 4.3 Female Canadian uptalk rise.

woman from British Columbia describing her family holidays. The rise on the final syllable of *water* follows a low pitch accent on that word. The height of the rise is clearly greater than the continuation rise on *gas* at the end of the preceding phrase.

Liberman (2008b), however, suggests that the Canadian uptalk rise may have a different shape, with a rise followed by a sustained high pitch. An example is given in Figure 4.4, using a sound file from the Linguistic Data Consortium's online collection of telephone conversations (Cieri et al., 2004), from a female Canadian, describing men's behaviour when affected by colds.

In further research on English in southern Ontario, Shokeir (2007) noted a greater incidence of uptalk among women than men, and found that men are more likely to interpret uptalk as an indicator of uncertainty. She did not find any evidence that uptalk use was on the increase.

In addition to the southern areas of Ontario, uptalk has been noted in the speech of speakers from most regions across Canada. These include Alberta, New Brunswick, Newfoundland, Nova Scotia, Ontario more generally, Quebec, Prince Edward Island and Saskatchewan (Talla Sando, 2009), as well as 'Central Canadian' (Watson, 2000). In her recordings from 2004, Halford (2007) finds that uptalk is also strongly present in British Columbia (specifically, Vancouver Island). In fact, more than 30 per cent of the contours produced by the teenagers in her corpus have final high-rises, with just 10 per cent of those being on questions. She also notes that uptalk sequences are common, in a kind of coordination that is reminiscent of the narrative structures indicated for other English varieties. Halford notes that the large proportion of rises is in contrast to her earlier 1996 corpus, where falls were more common.

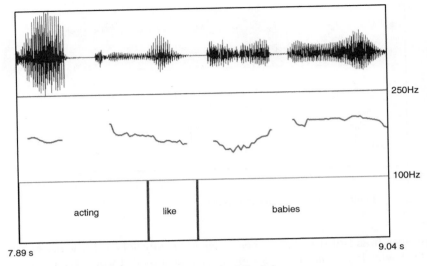

Figure 4.4 Female Canadian sustained final rise.

4.5   United States English

There is evidence of uptalk or uptalk-like intonation patterns in various communities in the United States as early as the 1970s. For instance, Tarone (1973)
conducted a survey of the intonation of informal black American English in the
Seattle region, comparing the patterns with white American English and formal
black American English. She reports a greater use of rising (as well as level)
intonation on statements in the informal black American English, usually in a
context where a response was expected, as part of what she refers to as the 'call
and response' nature of black American interactions (Tarone, 1973: 33). Since
this type of interaction is quite different from the uptalk-plus-minimal response
pattern noted in Chapter 3, it is likely that this is a different type of rise from
the uptalk rise. Indeed, in a later study, Pratt-Johnson (2005, 2006) noted that
uptalk was largely absent from the English of black Americans except when
talking with whites.

Edelsky (1979) carried out street interviews of more than 300 informants
in Miami, and compared the use of level, falling, rising and rise-fall-rise patterns in the responses given to the interviewers' questions. She also used a
matched-guise task to assess listeners' impressions of the different patterns.
Her production data showed only rare use of a simple rise on the participants'
responses, but a greater use by women than men of a rise-fall-rise pattern,
especially when interacting with a female interviewer. The overwhelmingly
predominant contour from all participants was, however, a falling contour.

Interestingly, her listeners attributed stereotypically feminine characteristics (more submissive, warmer, less aggressive) to the simple rise, but also rated women with falls and rise-fall-rise patterns as warmer, less aggressive and more easily influenced than men using the same patterns.

As noted earlier in Section 3.3.1, Bolinger (1978: 510) commented that American English speakers use terminal rises in narrative contexts as 'a channel-clearing device that says, in effect, "Are you listening?"'. He goes on to state: 'It would not be hard to imagine such a habit becoming a contagion, after which, with interlocutors weary of giving the countersign, the language could be said to have a rising intonation as a mark of clause terminals in general.'

In an early study focusing explicitly on 'question intonation on assertions', Ching (1982) refers to Lakoff's earlier mention of this as a strategy used typically by women to avoid a strong commitment or to prevent conflict (Lakoff, 1973, 1975). Ching also quotes from a 1963 item in *Esquire* that seems to contain uptalk (Southern, 1963), and from a 1976 novel by John Updike. Southern (1963) provides a description of a visit to Oxford, Mississippi, where the author encounters a 17-year-old from Macon, Georgia, who speaks 'in that oddly rising inflection peculiar to girls of the South, making parts of a reply sound like a question' (Southern, [1963] 1990: 155). Updike (1976) describes uptalk-like intonation from a character, Sally, who has been married ten years so is not an adolescent, although the portrayal of Sally and Jerry's love affair is very much that of two impassioned teenagers. (So much so that it is a surprise to learn on p. 10 that they are both married with children.) As Ching notes, the *Esquire* piece places the uptalk in the southern United States, while the Updike novel locates it in Connecticut. Ching himself focuses on speakers from the south (Tennessee), and concludes that the 'question intonation' on assertions is used to express deference and can serve as a means of mitigation when presenting information that may be unpleasant to the listener.

Despite some of the early references mentioned above, later writers associate uptalk with American English in the 1990s. Thus, Kyff (1995) refers to uptalk as the 'worst linguistic trend' of 1994, and later talks of it as 'the annoying uptalk that infested young women's speech during the late 1990s' (Kyff, 2004). In 2001, uptalk was so strongly associated with teen speech that one television reviewer highlighted the fact that a teen series did *not* have uptalk (McDonough, 2001).

In addition to Ching, other researchers have identified uptalk features in the southern states. Weldon (2008), for instance, reports that declarative sentences in Gullah, a creole spoken on the South Carolina and Georgia coasts, frequently end in high, mid or rising tones, where a fall would typically be found in standard American English speech. In her study of sorority speech in Texas, McLemore (1991) identifies uptalk as a strong feature of the speech of young women in the southern states in the early 1990s. Johnstone (2003: 80), however, notes that even if early academic discussions such as those by Ching and McLemore associated uptalk as 'southern' it appeared to spread rapidly across the United States.

Indeed, uptalk rapidly became associated not with southern US English, but with the West Coast, especially California. As a result, rather than it being seen as a southern feature of Tennessee and/or Texas, MacNeil and Cran's study of American English notes that rising intonation is one of many Californian features that are spreading across the United States (2005: 176). In 2006, Wolfram and Schilling-Estes describe how 'the use of so-called uptalk ... is now becoming a prominent trait of West Coast dialects ranging from Los Angeles to Portland' (2006: 124), and is spreading from females to 'young people of both sexes in many parts of the US'. Indeed they highlight the fact that uptalk is unlike other changes within US English because it has spread from the west to the east. Although Wolfram and Schilling-Estes point out that uptalk is a general West Coast phenomenon, its stereotyped linkage with Valley Girl-speak[3] means that it is sometimes argued to be a Southern California trait (Smith, 2011:22). One detailed study focuses on Southern Californian (SoCal), and presents a comparison with the intonation patterns found in London English (Barry and Arvaniti, 2006). For SoCal they note that most uptalk takes the shape of a low-rise (77 per cent L*H-H%), with some high-rises (18 per cent H*H-H%) and a few fall-rise patterns (5 per cent H+L*L-H%).

Still on the West Coast, Conn (2006: 154) comments on 'up-speak' in Portland, Oregon. He notes that it is not restricted to female speakers, nor to younger speakers. In an earlier MA thesis on high-rises in Portland, Wolff (2000) studied 16 speakers grouped by age (11–14, 15–19, 20–39, 40+), sex and class (middle and working). Her examples show considerable rises, some from quite low starting points. She reports an overall uptalk rate of 4.4 per cent, slightly higher among females than males, and stronger among the younger speakers, especially the younger females. Wolff presents clear examples of uptalk sequences in narrative texts.

Finally, Liberman's *Language Log* includes a series of pieces on uptalk in American English (Liberman, 2005a, 2005b, 2006a, 2006b, 2008a, 2008b, 2008c, 2008d, 2008e, 2008f, 2010). In these, Liberman looks at the forms and functions of uptalk as well as its distribution, and provides some useful commentary on issues such as the terminological differences between 'uptalk' and 'HRT' and on the differences between uptalk in different varieties. He also

[3] 'Valley Girl' is a term used to refer to middle- and upper-middle-class young women living in the Los Angeles commuter towns of the San Fernando Valley in the early 1980s. Valley Girl-speak or just *Valleyspeak* or even *Valspeak* is used to refer to the Californian English dialect typically associated with such speakers.

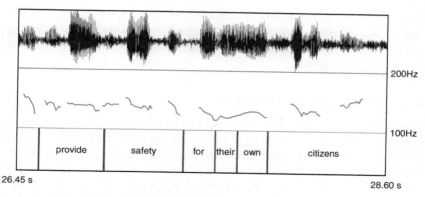

Figure 4.5 Uptalk from George W. Bush.

notes with illustrative examples the increased use of uptalk in the speeches of former president George W. Bush. One example is given in Figure 4.5, using audio files of a speech made in 2005, which was published on Liberman's blog site. This pattern is typical of the examples Liberman presents. The uptalk rise is not large, but it is a noticeable characteristic of some of Bush's speeches.

4.5.1   Mexican American English

Also referred to as Chicano English, Mexican American English is spoken by Mexican immigrant families. Fought (2006) notes that some Californian Chicano English speakers have incorporated into their speech some of the features of the local Anglo dialect, i.e., the 'Valley Girl' dialect. Though she does not mention it explicitly, this could well include uptalk.

Elsewhere, Fought (2003: 72–73) refers to an earlier description by Metcalf (1974: 55) of a pattern of intonation in Chicano English which to speakers of other varieties sounds 'wishy-washy and a little crazy … as if [the speaker] is asking a question when he should be making a statement, expressing doubt when he should be certain'. Fought relates this to a rise-and-sustain pattern in Mexican Spanish that had been reported much earlier (Matluck, 1952). She notes, however, that the Chicano English rise differs from most descriptions of uptalk in that it starts high in the speaker's range, whereas uptalk is typically from a mid-range point.

Santa Ana and Bayley (2008: 231) point out that a rising glide can occur anywhere in a Chicano English utterance to show emphasis or contrast. The pitch level usually falls after the glide but if it is on the final stressed syllable, the pitch level can remain high. Thomas and Ericson (2007) report a similar rising glide and note that it is more frequent in Mexican American English than in Anglo English. Earlier, Penfield (1984) had argued that in Chicano English this pattern does not necessarily express doubt, surprise or questioning as it does in American English. It is not clear, therefore, whether what is being described here is uptalk.

4.6   Caribbean English Varieties

A number of researchers have commented on uptalk-like intonation patterns in Caribbean varieties of English. In an early commentary, Allsopp (1972: 4) notes that the oral tradition of Caribbean cultures and their West African ancestral cultures results in a consultative and casual speech style, which includes signals to encourage the involvement of the addressee. These signals include specially patterned intonation styles often described as 'sing-song'. Cassidy (1961: 29) had earlier commented on the fact that Jamaican conversations often feature an upturn on declarative sentences, which is never as great as the rise on questions, but which 'when heard by an outsider, [gives] a peculiarly tentative or inconclusive effect, as if the speakers were perpetually in doubt about something'. He gives an example from recordings made in 1952, in which a narrative has noticeable uptalk-type rises at the end of most intonation groups. Cassidy describes some of the theorising around where this intonation pattern originated. He finds little support in terms of settlement patterns for the often cited hypothesis that a Welsh influence is responsible, and conjectures instead that the intonation derives from the ancestral tone languages of West Africa. In Twi, for instance, stress on nouns falls either on the first high-toned syllable or on the syllable immediately before it. Applied to English, this second type of relationship between stress and tone might result in patterns such as opPOⁿenⁿ, or PAⁿper (Cassidy, 1961: 32), where ___ and ‾‾‾ indicate low and high pitch. Morales-Muñoz et al. (2009) similarly suggest that the incidence of declarative final rises and final high-rises in Caribbean creoles is a result of influence from West African languages, as has also been suggested for Dominican Spanish by Megenney (1982).

Childs and Wolfram (2008: 252–253) point out that Bahamian English is characterised by final high-rises on affirmative sentences. They note the similarity with Australian and New Zealand English and with the speech of younger American English speakers from some regions. But they also comment that this intonation pattern has been a characteristic of Bahamian and other Caribbean English for some time. Wolfram et al. (2006: 185) mention that Bahamian statements sound like questions to most North Americans.

Youssef and James (2008: 334) note a 'peculiar intonational characteristic' in Trinidadian and Tobagonian, namely 'a rising intonation at the end of an utterance as if the speaker is in doubt or questioning'. They suggest that the speaker is seeking a response from the hearer much as they do with the local tag form *Right?* Aceto (2008) refers to work by Sutcliffe (2003) on intonational features in Eastern Caribbean, including the presence of high-rise intonation. Wells (1982: 580) refers to work by Warner (1967) claiming that final rising contours are more frequent in Trinidadian than in Received Pronunciation.

Although the relevant volume of the Mouton Varieties of English project carries very little mention of prosodic features, in his synopsis of phonological variation in the Americas and the Caribbean, Schneider (2008: 397) says that uptalk is found 'variably in all American and Caribbean varieties under consideration, with the sole exceptions of [Cajun English] and [Tobago Creole]'.

4.7   British English

It would seem that uptalk had made its presence known in Britain by the mid-1990s. For example, Cruttenden (1997: 130) notes that uptalk had spread to the United Kingdom by 1995, with most reports of its use being from London. Bradford (1997: 33), who uses the label 'upspeak', claims that Britain was seeing a form of rise that was different from existing statement rises in some varieties of English (e.g., UNB, Bristol, Wales, Norfolk, Indian, Caribbean) in that it is not systematic. Wichmann and Caspers (2001), presenting an analysis of map-task dialogues from the IViE corpus recorded in the period from 1997 (Grabe et al., 2007) report very few cases of the high-rise, which they say is an interesting finding in itself. They note that high-rises on statements are a recent innovation in British English. As late as a 2007 thesis, Barry (2007, 2008) concludes that uptalk remains still a marked feature of London English, compared with its more unmarked use in Californian English. A journalist noted around the same time that uptalk was 'still a burgeoning trend' (Marsh, 2006), while the BBC's Radio 4 series Word4Word in 2005 (summary of programme 6) refers to 'intonation patterns such as *Upspeak* (attrib [sic] to *Neighbours*) which may just be waning' (Word4Word, 2005). In 2011, however, it was reported that uptalk was now 'ubiquitous in the UK', although still more typical of young females (Wichmann, 2011: 187). By 2011 it was also well-enough established that it was a suggested topic for secondary school study of language change in the United Kingdom (Gregory, 2011: 206).

Given that there are many and often quite distinct varieties of English in Britain, the remainder of this section considers several of these separately. A further good reason for doing this is that, as stated by Upton (2008: 281) in his summary of phonological variation across the British Isles, 'the extent to which the feature of terminal intonational raising is related across different regions is currently unclear'. That is, there is some uncertainty whether the forms of rise attested in Bristol, Wales, Norfolk and elsewhere are forms of uptalk, or different features altogether, and it is also not clear whether they are

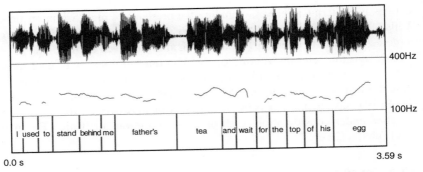

400Hz

100Hz

| I | used | to | stand | behind | me | father's | tea | and | wait | for | the | top | of | his | egg |

0.0 s

3.59 s

Figure 4.6 'I used to stand behind me father's tea and wait for the top of his egg'. Sing-song pattern, featuring uptalk-like rises on 'tea' and 'egg', from an elderly Bristol woman (see text).

interrelated. Note in addition that Irish English, including that used in Northern Ireland, is treated in a separate section.

4.7.1   Bristol, Wales and the West Midlands

Elmes (2005: 38–39), in his discussion of the English spoken in Bristol in the south-west of England, writes of 'that rising questioning inflexion that used to be more or less limited to Bristol and Belfast but that has, with the popularity of American and Australian soap operas, become an international phenomenon known as "Upspeak"'. He goes on to declare that this Bristolian intonation has 'a much longer pedigree' than the more recent forms of uptalk. It is also, he maintains, quite different from other intonation patterns in the south-west of England, so much so that it could be considered a feature that marks Bristol speakers off from the rest of the region. Elsewhere in the same text (2005: vii) he points out that 'the constantly uplifted ends to sentences' are now found across the country, but that these newer forms stem 'from Bondi [referring to a beach district in Sydney, Australia] not Bedminster [a district of Bristol]'. This seems to be an acknowledgement that uptalk is not Bristolian in origin, although it is not clear whether the historical forms of 'Bristol Upspeak' and 'uptalk' in other parts of Britain are different. Elsewhere (Warren, 2014b), I have suggested that the Bristol rises are part of a general sing-song pattern found in that region. Figure 4.6 shows a sample from a woman from Bristol, taken from the 1979 BBC cassette tape *English with a Dialect*. The rises on *tea* and *egg*, in a narrative description of the speaker's childhood, are certainly similar to uptalk rises, but are less dramatic than the rises illustrated above for Australian and American English. The more general 'sing-song' intonation pattern contrasts with the pattern found in samples from other varieties, where a gently falling pattern culminates in a marked rise, as Figure 4.2 for New Zealand English.

Welsh English is particularly well known for the 'sing-song' quality of its intonation, which has been ascribed by Tench (1990: 140) to a large amount of pitch movement on pre- and post-tonic unaccented syllables. Thomas (1994: 122) cites Pilch (1983/1984) who commented on an unusual frequency of rising pitch patterns in what he calls 'Cambrian English', and suggested that this had led to the impression of the Welsh speaking English on a very high pitch, as well as in a sing-song manner. Walters (2003a, 2003b) notes in particular a tendency for pitch to rise from stressed syllables in the English of the Welsh 'Valleys', which he links to intonation patterns in the Welsh language. Since this is a feature of stressed syllables generally, and not just the terminal, the pattern over the utterance as a whole is typically a sequence of rising tones, and is therefore quite different to the typical uptalk pattern of a steadily falling contour finishing in a dramatic rise.

Nevertheless, Tench (1996) reports hearing an uptalk intonation in Cardiff as early as the 1970s, and Mees and Collins (1999: 195) similarly attest it in recordings dating from 1976, primarily in narrative texts, as found also in Australia, New Zealand and elsewhere. Collins and Mees (1990: 101) point out that with respect to intonation, Cardiff English is generally closer to dialects from England than to other Welsh English dialects such as those of neighbouring Glamorgan and Ghent. Their description of the Cardiff English uptalk tune is of 'a high-pitch terminal rise ... [reaching] a far higher pitch than in RP [Received Pronunciation]'. They note that it is strikingly similar to the pattern heard in the Bristol accent. Mees and Collins (1999) also recall that English visitors to Cardiff in the 1950s commented along the lines of 'Why do Cardiff people always seem to be asking questions when they're actually trying to tell you something?' Coupland (1988: 32–33) provides discussion of this rising pattern in Cardiff English.

Some of the cities of the West Midlands, such as Birmingham, belong to the group of urban centres that have been claimed (Wells, 1982: 91) to have rising tones where other accents have falling tones. Biddulph (1986: 3) suggests that the Black Country accent in the West Midlands has a 'peculiar' intonation pattern with final rises in statements. On the other hand, Cruttenden (1995: 162) argues that while the Birmingham accent does have an above-average number of rises in final position, along with instances of occasional rise-plateau tunes on declaratives, this pattern is not the unmarked tune that is found, for instance, in Belfast.

4.7.2 South-east and East Anglia

Ellingsæter (2014) surveyed two age groups (young: 17–23 and old: 66–87), born and raised in Surrey in the south-east of England. She found that her younger informants used final rises on 8.8 per cent of their statement utterances, while the older speakers produced only 0.4 per cent, all of which were attributable to a single speaker. She also found more uptalk rises from the young men she interviewed than from the young women, but again a single speaker was responsible for this overall difference.

Elmes (2005: 150) comments that the East Anglian region has an intonational pattern 'that swings the speaker along on a series of rollercoaster upward inflexions, rather like the so-called "upspeak" that's become a national standard among young people, perhaps in imitation of Neighbours, but especially in Norfolk repeated throughout the sentence'. Trudgill (2008: 192), however, mentions only a characteristic rise on yes–no questions, with an initial low level becoming a high level on the stressed and all following syllables.

4.7.3   North of England and Scotland

The Urban Northern British (UNB) statement rises are often (typically, I suspect, by researchers outside the United Kingdom) grouped together with uptalk. However, and as noted at the beginning of this chapter, Cruttenden (1995) is quite clear that there is a distinction in form and distribution between UNB rises and those found in the Pacific Rim. In addition, Ladd (1996: 125–126) explains that there is a 'systemic' difference between UNB and other varieties, since the UNB statement form is 'a tonal sequence that does not occur in RP or American English'.

Beal (2008) underlines the differences between the UNB rise and the high-rising intonation found in Australia and New Zealand. Other authors similarly point to the differences between UNB and uptalk rises. For instance, Local (1986: 182–184) highlights both formal and functional distinctions between rises in Tyneside speech and rises in other English varieties, as well as a clear phonetic difference (see Knowles, 1981, for similar comments on Liverpool English). Phonetically, the Tyneside rise starts on the tonic syllable and is followed by sustained but level high pitch over the post-tonic syllables (see also Pellowe and Jones, 1978). Functionally, the rise typically signals completeness, unlike uptalk (see Chapter 3). In this, Local's comments match those by Strang (1964), who also claimed that Tynesiders regularly use a final rise 'for positive affirmative statements, for non-yes-or-no questions, in short, for finality', and are reflected by Foulkes and Docherty (2007: 71), for whom the UNB rising pattern has a 'Closed' category meaning. On the other hand, Local claims that one of the attested functions of uptalk, i.e., 'understanding checks', involves falls from high to low in this variety.

Stuart-Smith (2008) comments that the majority of English accents in Scotland have a typical sequence of falling tones in statements. Glaswegian English, however, shows a tendency towards final high-rises (Stuart-Smith, 1999) similar to those found in Northern Irish English (an accent that may have influenced the

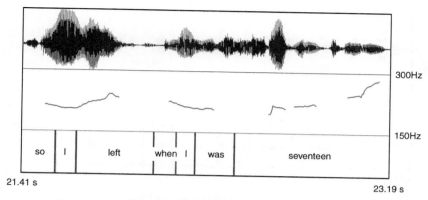

Figure 4.7 Uptalk rise in Glaswegian English.

English of Glasgow), but unlikely to be linked to uptalk (Cruttenden, 1997: 129). In fact, Cruttenden (2007) points out that Glasgow is the only area of Scotland reported to have the intonational features of UNB. However, he reports data on a single speaker of Glaswegian English who he claims is intonationally diglossic. In free conversation, this speaker shows a pattern of tone types that is typical of UNB (with high proportions of rises and rise-slumps), while in a reading task she shows tonal usage closer to that of RP (with a high proportion of falls and sentence medial low-rises). One of the features of the conversational but not the reading passage is the presence of 'full rises', functioning as a checking device, even within narrative sequences where it frequently occurs in clusters. Cruttenden concludes that this full rise 'indicates further spreading of the High Rise Terminal' (Cruttenden, 2007: 270). Sullivan (2011: 152–153) presents examples that she conjectures are uptalk rises in Glaswegian English. She notes the appearance of rises without a final low tone in both non-questions and questions, with the function of 'are you following me?' Sullivan presents an example of a non-question that shows a rise starting early in the accented word and continuing to the end of the phrase. A similar example is shown in Figure 4.7, taken from the IDEA corpus (International Dialects of English Archive, 2000), and is part of a sequence of rises from a young female speaker describing her life story. The rise here is visually as well as auditorily different from the rise-plateau shape shown in a further example from the same speaker in Figure 4.8. But the uptalk rise in Figure 4.7 is clearly less dramatic than the rises seen above for Australian, New Zealand and Canadian English.

Earlier, MacAfee (1983: 37) noted that Glasgow and Edinburgh, as well as Belfast, have low-rises as a dominant form of intonation on statements, but also that all three cities 'share the prevailing use in English of a high rising terminal as a marked intonation, expressing "open" meanings [and] it would not be

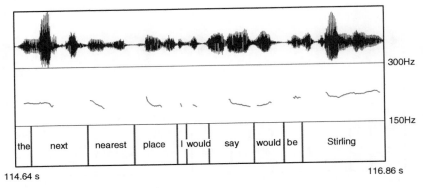

| the | next | nearest | place | I would | say | would | be | Stirling |

114.64 s   116.86 s

Figure 4.8 Rise-plateau from same speaker as Figure 4.7.

surprising if the frequency of rising terminals in Glasgow speech was heard by some groups as expressing hesitancy and lack of confidence'.

Despite examples such as that shown in Figure 4.7, it would seem that the north of England and Scotland are – on the whole – not uptalking regions, perhaps because of the presence there already of the UNB rise. However, there is suggestion that some speakers may be using uptalk.

4.8   Irish English

A 2001 profile of singer Sharon Murphy (McCarthy, 2001) recognises uptalk as a prominent speech feature in Ireland: 'The so-called high-rise terminal, the mark of today's youth-speak in Ireland, was actually the strongest indication that Murphy had survived [a childhood exposed to brutality].' It seems to have been a fairly recent innovation, however, judging from a retrospective newspaper article suggesting that it had not caught on in Irish English in 1997 but had by 2007 (Kenny, 2007).

A question that has often been asked is whether rise patterns in various varieties of English are due to an influence from Irish (presumably via Irish English, see also Chapter 5). Dalton and Ní Chasaide (2005) note the similarities between Belfast English rises and rises in Gaoth Dobhair (Ulster Irish) and remark that these are hardly coincidental, i.e., that there may be a contact influence from Irish on Belfast English. They also note that Cruttenden (1997) and Knowles (1975) have both commented on the possible influence of Irish intonation patterns on the rising contours found in some of the UNB dialects, generally for UNB in the case of the former and more specifically for Liverpool English in the case of the latter. Rahilly (1997: 113) argues, however, that there is little substance to such a claim, simply because analyses of Irish have not

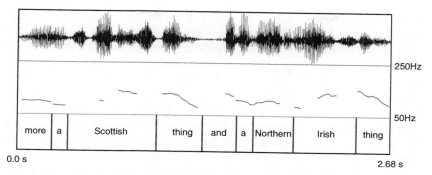

Figure 4.9 Rise-plateau-slump patterns for a male Northern Irish speaker.

shown support for the notion that Irish is characterised by a high incidence of rising tones. She acknowledges that further research is needed in this area.

There is little research on variation in intonation in Irish English. Barry (1982: 110) notes a striking intonation in south County Cork, which is different from other Irish English intonation and similar to Anglo-Welsh intonation (see above). Most research on intonation in English in Ireland has focused on Northern Ireland, and in particular on Belfast, which is typically included in the group of Urban Northern British cities that have an unmarked intonation pattern of rises where falls would be found in other varieties of English. Hickey (2008) mentions that there are distinct patterns of intonation in northern Irish English and refers to Rahilly (1997) who notes that there are rises in Belfast English where falls would be found in southern British. Lowry (2002) suggests that falls are used in Belfast English as accommodation to southern British English, and that as a consequence falls are associated with higher degrees of formality. Jarman and Cruttenden (1976) had earlier pointed out that rising intonation is the normal pattern for statements in Belfast, with their data showing that 70 per cent of contours are rises (McElholm, 1986, reports a higher figure for Derry English). Rahilly (1997) also notes that high pitch serves as a prominence marker in Belfast.

As noted above, the UNB rises differ from uptalk rises. First, they are an unmarked form and so indicate completeness, rather than having functions such as checking that have been identified for uptalk. Wells and Peppé (1996), analysing speech data collected in the mid-1970s in a study of the prosodic marking of turns in Ulster English, note a conversational structure where turns ending with UNB rise patterns are both intended and interpreted as complete. Second, UNB rises have distinct phonetic shapes, typically taking the form of a rise followed by a plateau and a final optional 'slump'. Figure 4.9 (from Warren, 2014b) shows this pattern for a Northern Irish speaker (recording courtesy of *BBC News Magazine*, 2014) across the sequences *Scottish thing* and *Irish thing*.

Sullivan (2010) argues that rises in Belfast do not always show the final slump, but finish rather on a high tone and can be distinguished therefore from the rise-plateau-slump pattern found for instance in Glasgow English. Grabe and Post (2002) give largely overlapping intonational transcriptions for the Belfast questions and statements in their database, but note that while both utterance types have rise-plateaux, only the statements in their recordings have the rise-plateau-slump pattern. While Sullivan entertains the idea that Belfast rises may have resulted from a rightwards shift in the alignment point of the high pitch accent in what was previously a rise-fall, she is unable to find convincing empirical support for this idea (Sullivan, 2009). Indeed, she suggests that Belfast rises 'may not in fact be distinct from the phenomenon of High Rising Terminals (HRTs)/"Uptalk" in other English varieties' (Sullivan, 2010), although we have seen that other researchers (Cruttenden, 1995; Ladd, 2008) see these as quite distinct, both formally and functionally.

Cruttenden (1981) suggests that the open versus closed meanings that are found on rises versus falls in other varieties are realised in Belfast English in terms of a contrast in either pitch height or pitch range, with the UNB rise-plateau and rise-plateau-slump shapes being truncated falls. Sullivan (2010) indeed reports an experiment showing that in Glasgow and Belfast questions and statements both have rises but are distinguished by the pitch ranges involved. See Section 2.3 for further discussion of pitch level and range differences between statement and question rises.

4.9   Falkland Islands English

Sudbury (2001) reports that uptalk is widespread among Falkland Island English speakers, and conveys her impression that it is more typical of younger speakers than of older speakers and of females than of males. However, no systematic social study or acoustic analysis has been carried out. Along with other features, the high incidence of uptalk in Falkland Islands English leads Sudbury to suggest its categorisation as a southern hemisphere variety.

4.10   South African English

The status of uptalk in South African English (SAE) is somewhat unclear. In a review of international varieties of English, Bauer (2002: 90) commented that uptalk did not yet seem to have been adopted in SAE, yet in an early study of the pronunciation of SAE, Lanham (1967) comments on an intonational form found in 'extreme SAE', particularly among schoolchildren in the Eastern Province. The utterance type in question starts on a mid-pitch then rises to a

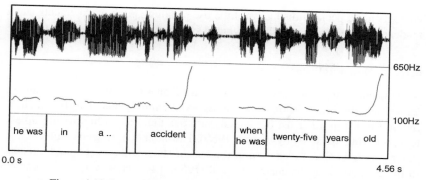

Figure 4.10 Sequence of uptalk patterns from a South African woman.

high pitch, which is then sustained until the end of the utterance, where there is a brief 'down turn'. From this description this pattern sounds similar to the UNB rises, yet apart from the final down turn this is highly similar to many descriptions of uptalk. As has also been noted for other varieties, Lanham observes that speakers of a more conservative SAE comment that this form sounds like the speaker is asking a question. Lanham goes on to note that 'if there is a peculiarly South African trend in intonation patterns then it takes the form of a consistent tendency to end "statement" intonations at a higher level' (Lanham, 1967: 101). More recently, Dorrington (2010a, 2010b) carried out a study of uptalk in young female SAE speakers. She notes that, as previously found in research on New Zealand English (Warren, 2005b; Warren and Daly, 2005), 'rises in declarative clauses [in SAE] have a later onset than those in question contexts'. The example in Figure 4.10 is from a South African woman who is presenting a narrative about her son who had been in a coma following an accident (*Today*, 2006). The example clearly shows the late and dramatic rises that we have seen for other southern hemisphere varieties, with the first rise starting well into the final unstressed syllable of '*accident*, and rising from around 180Hz to about 620Hz. The speaker is urging listeners to not give up on people in a coma, as her son recovered following treatment with a particular drug. In this context, it is unlikely that the speaker would want to appear insecure or uncertain about what she is saying.

Finn (2008: 215), in his analysis of the phonology of English spoken in working-class neighbourhoods in inner-city Cape Town, points to research that indicates a large proportion of rising intonation patterns, with these being especially noticeable in the case of statements. Earlier work by Malan (1996) similarly notes rising intonation as a feature of Cape Flats English, and reports an earlier study of children's language where a rising terminal was the unmarked style for narratives. Of 'Coloured English', Lanham (1982: 343) states: 'Intonation contours are especially distinctive: little use of falling pitch in statements and a tendency for pitch to rise in final accented syllables'.

4.11   New Englishes

A small number of studies have commented on rising tones in varieties of 'New Englishes' (i.e., outer-circle Englishes). Pennington et al. (2011) include Indian English in their list of English varieties that have a high-rising uptalk tone, referring to a study by Bansal (1969). The latter does indeed comment that 'the rising tone sometimes used at the end of statements must sound unusual to the R.P.-speaking listeners' (Bansal, 1969: 144). However, the examples given by Bansal include *I 'found that I was ꞵrong* (for which it is claimed the corresponding RP pattern would be a fall on *wrong*) and *'Don't take any 'notice of ꞏthem* (RP would have falling nucleus on *notice* or a falling-rising tone on *them*). Without more information on the contexts in which such forms are found, it is difficult to determine whether they are uptalk. Note that contrary to Pennington et al.'s claim that Bansal shows high-rise tones in Indian English, the transcription given by Bansal (according to the key on p. iv of his text) is of a *low* rising pitch.

Cheng and Warren (2005) consider the use of both rise and rise-fall tones in a corpus of Hong Kong English. Their corpus covers a range of discourse types: conversations, service encounters, informal office chat, placement interviews, business meetings and academic supervision meetings. Across their data, Cheng and Warren found that rises were more likely to be used by the dominant conversational partner. While they were evenly distributed between partners in conversations, they were used more by business managers and lecturers in business meetings and academic supervisions respectively (see also Section 3.2).

In a summary chapter on the pronunciation of Brunei English, Deterding and Sharbawi (2013: 45–46) observe a number of rises that are difficult to explain, and some which are very dramatic in form. They conjecture that these forms might in fact be uptalk.

It thus seems that uptalk-like intonation is being uncovered in these new varieties, but that the forms and meanings of the attested patterns are not yet sufficiently well understood for us to be certain that we are dealing with uptalk rather than with some other pattern that might be the result of contact with the substrate languages in the relevant regions.

4.12   Non-native speaker English

Given the extent to which uptalk is found in native speaker contexts, as shown in some of the previous sections of this chapter, it is not surprising that educators have started to consider whether more attention should be paid to this form of intonation in non-native English. Learners are certainly aware of the phenomenon, as indicated in a reflective study of the experiences of advanced learners in community placements. One student commented on the 'Kiwi [i.e., New Zealand] style' of one set of interactions and observed: 'They usually raised their tone in every last word of sentence casually no matter asking or answering' (Andrew, 2011: 231).

Park (2011) talks of the decisions that teachers have to make in the context of language changes or shifts, and cites uptalk as an example of such a shift. Should teachers encourage learners of English to use innovative forms such as uptalk? Wells (2006: 38) advises learners of English that if they were born before about 1980 they should avoid uptalk altogether, and if they were born after 1980 then they can imitate how native speakers use it, but they should not overdo it, they should remember that it is never essential and they should be mindful that it may annoy older listeners. Park's own advice to students when he noticed them using uptalk (2011: 12) is that while they might hear young people speaking that way, falling intonation on statements is a more standard pattern. Jenkins (2004) recommends the adoption of a discourse-based approach to the teaching of intonation, which would include explanation of the functions of uptalk to signal solidarity and participation.

A negative view of uptalk is taken by Park in his study of non-native intonation. Park asked native speakers to annotate recordings of non-native speakers (NNS) for accuracy of intonation, and instructed the native speakers to mark uptalk as non-native like. He subsequently argues that one learner's lack of apparent improvement in intonation may have been due to his use of uptalk on statements. Park also highlights the difficulties that the raters had due to the presence of uptalk, and due to the uncertainty about whether the participant was using uptalk or signalling continuation.

Hincks (2005) notes that Swedish learners of English sound more lively in student presentation contexts if they have greater variation in their intonation, but that some of these students, mainly females, have greater variation because of the use of final high-rises, which she claims can lead to the perception of uncertainty. Hoff (2014: 58) attributes uptalk in the speech of the learners she analysed to task effects, saying that it resulted from nervousness about being recorded and consequently made it difficult to obtain accurate ratings of their intonation.

On the other hand, uptalk is valued in other NNS research. Kang et al. (2010) carried out a multiple regression analysis to assess the possible contribution of a number of acoustically measured suprasegmental characteristics to raters' scoring of NNS utterances on scales of proficiency and comprehensibility. They found a positive relationship between both of these scales and the choice of high-rising tunes. That is, the more high-rises the NNS used, the more proficient and comprehensible their samples were rated. One factor that they think may play a role here is that learners who show low levels of rising tones may be more focused on the language itself and not on their listeners, i.e., they are not showing the native speaker pattern of using rising intonation as a communicative device, and so come across as less proficient and/or less comprehensible (Kang et al., 2010: 562).

Many learners assimilate quite readily the intonational patterns of the native speakers they interact with. A review of training activities for international teaching assistants at a Canadian university (Du Steinberg, 2007) notes that some of the participants on the training programme adapt their speech behaviours towards those of the North Americans in the classes they teach, including adopting uptalk. Grieve (2010: 204) comments on how when German native speakers living in Australia took part in role-play telephone conversations with Australians they hedged their responses using a number of politeness strategies, including uptalk. In a study of the use of general extenders ('and things like that', 'and stuff') by native New Zealand English speakers and by German native speakers in New Zealand, Terraschke and Holmes (2007) report a number of instances where the German speakers used uptalk in their English language interactions with New Zealanders. Some – but not all – of these were on the general extender expression. The authors argue that the intonation, like the general extenders, is being used to appeal to the interlocutor's understanding and solidarity.

4.13   Summary

Uptalk has a wide geographic spread, and appears to be spreading globally among the young, and particularly among young female speakers. The focal regions for the analysis and discussion of uptalk are Australia and New Zealand, where it dates from the late 1950s and early 1960s, along with the United States and Canada, where similar dates are given for the earliest instances. As we will see in more detail in the next chapter, the precise origin and pattern of spread of uptalk in the English-speaking world is difficult to determine. Uptalk is also present, but less markedly so, in the British Isles and in South Africa as well as in a few other regions. In Britain in particular the rise of uptalk appears to be later than and therefore possibly influenced by the other main areas mentioned above, and although there are possible pockets of earlier uptalk-like intonation in Bristol and Cardiff, these are most likely different types of rise. The pervasiveness of uptalk is reflected in its use by non-native speakers, particularly perhaps those with sufficient frequent exposure to native speakers who are uptalkers, such as learners living in Australia, New Zealand or Canada.

5   Origins and spread of uptalk

The focus in this chapter is on the origins and spread of uptalk. In a recent article in the online *BBC News Magazine*, Stokel-Walker (2014) commented that 'the question of how even the UK was infected with this speech pattern has never been adequately answered'. Readers of that article were keen to give their own theories about where uptalk originated, and a follow-up to Stokel-Walker's article lists ten of the most popular opinions expressed by readers (*BBC News Magazine*, 2014). These mainly consist of suggestions concerning its geographic origins, including two sources that have been quite widely reported both in the research literature and in the media: Australia and California. In addition, other correspondents claimed that the source of uptalk is Celtic varieties (e.g., Northern Irish), or the English spoken in and around Bristol in the west of England, or New Zealand English. We have seen earlier that the rises used in Northern Ireland, i.e., UNB rises, are different in form to uptalk rises. Warren (2014b) suggests that the Bristolian rise is part of a more general sing-song intonation typical of that region (see also Section 4.7.1).

Other comments have linked uptalk to the influence of other languages on English. There are three such influences among the ten opinions selected by the *BBC News Magazine*: French, Japanese and Norwegian. Chapter 9 considers uptalk in other languages. The suggestion is made there that uptalk in French, particularly Canadian French, has resulted from an influence from English. Researchers (e.g., F. Inoue, 2006) have also commented on the presence of uptalk in Japanese, without being able to determine definitively its provenance. Some maintain that an intonation pattern like this has existed in Japanese for some time, while others believe that is has arisen or at least become more widespread more recently, following closer contact with English. Andersen (2014: 22) notes that while uptalk has been observed in Norwegian dialects since the 1990s, particularly among younger speakers, it is also most likely due to the influence of English.

Correspondents in the *BBC News Magazine* also identify two possible origins of uptalk that relate to what uptalk might mean. One set of comments, under the umbrella term 'lack of confidence', includes the notion encountered in Chapter 3 that uptalk has a checking function, where it is used to seek confirmation that the listener is still following the speaker. A different set of comments relates to the use of uptalk in sales talk contexts, these comments indicating that the rising inflection is being used to invite the listener specifically to agree with the speaker. This interpretation of uptalk was also discussed in Chapter 3.

In broader geographical terms, and as noted in Chapter 4, Cruttenden (1995) identified two main English-speaking regions that showed more frequent rising intonation patterns than those found in either General American (GA) or British Received Pronunciation (RP). These were the Urban Northern British cities (UNB: Belfast, Derry, Glasgow, Newcastle, Liverpool, Birmingham) and the Pacific Rim (PR: Australia, New Zealand, California, Canada). Cruttenden claimed that usage of rising intonation within each of these two areas was homogeneous, and proposed two hypotheses for the more extended usage of rises, one of which is more relevant to UNB and the other to PR. The UNB varieties, he suggested, could be seen to exhibit a *systemic* difference from RP and GA, in that there is a difference in the ways in which tonal distinctions are used (i.e., there is a intonational form present in one variety that is not found in another). The PR varieties, he believed, showed a more stylistic difference, employing the same 'checking' rise as RP and GA, but using it more frequently. He conjectured, however, that uptalk (or what he calls the 'Australian stylistic HRT') might over time shift from being a stylistic habit to become a systemic intonation pattern like the UNB rises. This might, however, be blocked by universal semantic tendencies for falls to be used to mark definiteness and completeness (Cruttenden, 1995: 171). The fact that uptalk is reported in so many varieties of English and is noted as a common intonational feature of some of those varieties suggests that uptalk may not give up that easily. Indeed, Californian linguist Carmen Fought, a linguistics professor and speaker of Valley Girl dialect, is cited in 2005 as saying that she would not be surprised to find, 20 years later, that uptalk is the unmarked form for statements in Californian English (MacNeil and Cran, 2005: 162–163).

Uptalk certainly appears to have spread very rapidly, like an unchecked infection. Bolinger (1978: 510), commenting on the usage of final terminals at the end of just about every sentence to check that the listener is still following, states: 'It would not be hard to imagine such a habit becoming a contagion, after which, with interlocutors weary of giving the countersign, the language could be said to have a rising intonation as a mark of clause terminals in general.' Various comments in the media and elsewhere similarly use vocabulary that refers to a disease-like spread of uptalk, which is referred to as 'contagious' (Gorman, 1993b; Cave, 1994; Smets, 2000; Horowitz, 2006), an 'epidemic' (DiResta, 2001a; Davis, 2002), an 'ailment that apparently has infected every teenage girl born since 1976' (Edelstein, 1998) or a 'wretched disease' (Wood, 2002), from which speakers 'suffer' (Seaton, 2001), or by which people are 'afflicted' (White, 1995; Guffey and Almonte, 2009).

5.1 Historical and geographic origins

As we will see in Chapter 7, popular notions of where uptalk originated, as reflected in media reports, are fairly evenly divided between the Antipodes (specifically, Australia and New Zealand) and the West Coast of the United States. We will also see that the split depends to some extent on the source of the report, with most British commentators placing the origin in Australia, and most American reports placing it in California. The idea that uptalk originated either in the Antipodes or on the US West Coast is reflected also in Peters (2007) in the background to his report on uptalk in German (see further Chapter 9), where he talks of a Soap Opera theory (uptalk originated in Australian television soap operas such as *Neighbours* and *Home and Away*) and a Valspeak theory (uptalk originated in Valley Girl English in California). Bradford (1996, 1997) challenges the Soap Opera theory as an explanation of uptalk's spread into British English, commenting that it is unlikely that the only feature to have been adopted through television exposure would be this intonational pattern, rather than, say, the vowel system of Australian English which constitutes the main difference with British English. However, my personal experience of encountering British English speakers in the early 1990s who had spent time in New Zealand was that the uptalk intonation pattern was a much more likely pronunciation feature to have 'stuck', compared with the segmental differences.

There are a few rather oblique references to early instances of uptalk in American English (see Ching, 1982). Fought claims that Americans 'pioneered "uptalk," the use of rising intonations for sentences that are not questions' (Fought, 2005). MacNeil and Cran (2005: 38) write that uptalk 'is believed to have spread from California, not just across the United States, but around the English-speaking world'. Writing on the *Language Log*, Zimmer (2006) notes that although uptalk was frequently traced back to Valley Girl English in the early 1980s, it could probably be detected in the speech of southern Californians long before then. This is supported, for instance, in a comment following a short blog on the *Language Log*, where Liberman (2013a) conjectures that the history of Californian uptalk might involve immigrants of Scots-Irish background who arrived in the 1930s during the Dust Bowl era. In a subsequent blog Liberman (2013b) explores this possibility further by checking audio interview data from 1940 with Woody Guthrie, an 'Okie', i.e., one of the many people displaced by the Dust Bowl storms and who consequently moved to California from Oklahoma. The blog presents examples of final rises and other uptalk-like patterns in Guthrie's speech. Liberman points out that final rises existed in English before uptalk was identified as a phenomenon, and that the innovation of uptalk is the frequency with which these patterns are used in certain English varieties and with particular discourse meanings. He notes that to test his hypothesis that Valley Girl uptalk has its origins in Scots-Irish 1930s migration patterns, he would need to show that final rises (in the relevant discourse contexts) were more frequent in the speech of Americans with Scots-Irish backgrounds than generally for American speech, as well as showing a link between Valspeak and the Dust Bowl migrations. Elsewhere in the southern United States, according to an entry in another web log by Beard (2006), uptalk was 'alive and healthy' in the 1950s, and he recalls his cousins using it in rural North Carolina, along with many girls in the city high school.

The earliest systematic analyses, however, are those reported for Australia and New Zealand. As noted in Chapter 4, there are academic references to uptalk in Australia and New Zealand from the 1960s (Mitchell and Delbridge, 1965; Benton, 1966). As observed also by Ladd (2008), it remains unclear whether these earlier academic references to uptalk in Australia and New Zealand than elsewhere really mean that uptalk first emerged in (one or other of) these varieties, or was just researched there before anywhere else. Additionally, it is not clear whether the early development of uptalk in different varieties is independent (Bauer, 2002: 90) or a possible result of contact-induced spread (Bradford, 1996: 23). One thing that does seem likely is that it does not have a British origin. Indeed, as pointed out by Bauer (2002: 90), uptalk is probably 'the first major and demonstrable phonetic effect to go from the colonies to Britain rather than vice versa'.

There has long been a friendly rivalry between Australia and New Zealand in matters linguistic (as well as in sport). For example, both have laid claim to being the source country for the concept of the dessert known as pavlova and therefore providing the origin of the use of the name of the Russian ballet dancer for that dessert (Leach, 2008). For uptalk use, Holmes and Bell (1996) suggest that New Zealand also predates Australia, a claim that they say is supported by Allan (1990), who reports twice the uptalk rate in NZE data compared with that in Sydney, Australia. Similar suggestions of an earlier NZE use can be found in Bauer (1994) and Holmes (1995), with the latter also pointing out that the spread of uptalk usage across all age groups implies that it was more established in New Zealand at that time than in Australia.

In their introduction to the book in which Allan's chapter appears, Holmes and Bell (1990) suggest that uptalk has been present for longer in NZE than in AusE and that its 'form and function seem identical to that in Australian speech, a fact of which Guy et al. (1986) seem unaware'. They suggest (Holmes and Bell, 1990: 8) that it was exported to Sydney from New Zealand. It might indeed be tempting to work backwards from attested levels of uptalk usage in early reports in order to support a single origin in one or other of those countries. So

Allan's (1990) comparison of a 3 per cent incidence level in a dataset collected in 1987–1988 in New Zealand (Holmes and Bell, 1988) with the 1.6 per cent reported by Horvath (1985) for her 1980 Sydney recordings might lead to such a claim for a New Zealand origin. Indeed, Australian researchers Burridge and Mulder (1998) concede that on the basis of incidence data, uptalk may well have originated in New Zealand and spread from there to Australia. However, not only are there differences in the time of data collection in these two sets, but there is a real risk in comparing usage rates whenever different researchers are reporting data from two different datasets. The datasets are liable to differ in terms of the nature of the discourse types that are included (which is clearly important – see Section 3.3). In addition, the researchers are likely to make different judgements about what counts as uptalk (or HRT or AQI), as well as using different criteria for how to determine the units over which uptalk incidence is measured. As an example of this last point, consider that Horvath (1985) reports incidence per tone group, whereas Allan (1990) follows Brown et al. (1980) and abandons tone groups, which can be problematic to identify, and uses instead Pause Defined Units. Britain (1992) similarly points to how such methodological differences make a straightforward comparison difficult.

Further historical evidence from the Mobile Recording Unit data recorded in New Zealand in the 1940s, as cited in Chapter 4, suggests that uptalk-type intonation might have been present much earlier in NZE (Gordon, 1998; Gordon and Trudgill, 1999). It is, of course, possible that similar earlier attestations might be found elsewhere, if comparable recordings were available. Reports of early uptalk-like forms in other parts of the world tend to be found in informal statements; for example, in letters to newspapers. For example, in a 2001 letter to the *Guardian*, Pearson (2001) claims that people in Bristol in the west of England had been uptalking for at least 70 years prior to that date. He maintains that uptalk is used as a polite way of making sure that the listener is following and not getting upset, and that it is 'a far more elegant method of creating an opportunity for conversational negotiation than the tedious and ugly reiteration of "I mean" and "you know" in so much of fashionable contemporary spoken English'.

Ainsworth (1994) entertains the possibility that the exaggerated rising intonation found in child directed speech might be implicated in the development of uptalk. She refers to Sachs et al. (1976), who comment that caregivers of infant children use 'a rising intonation contour similar to that of questions in English (but not in conjunction with a question form)', and which serves to check a child's understanding and whether the utterance should be repeated. Ainsworth's research with four- and nine-year-old New Zealanders indicates that while the older children show a high level of uptalk usage (almost 14 per cent of tone groups had uptalk), the four-year-olds used uptalk in around only 2 per cent of their tone groups. These youngest children, she argues, should be at the stage in their sociolinguistic development where they would be sensitive to the use of linguistic devices to indicate deference and/or solidarity or to check for listener comprehension. It is likely that the lower proportion of uptalk for the four-year-olds compared with the older children is a reflection of the lower incidence of narrative turns from the younger children.

5.2   (Im)migration

One factor, or set of factors, that is often mentioned in connection with uptalk is that its origin and spread might be linked with patterns of migration. Guy et al. (1986) suggested that patterns of migration since World War II may be particularly important. They remind us of Labov's (1980) proposal that linguistic change is often set in motion by the inclusion of new ethnic and racial groups into a speech community, as part of the emblematic function of innovation in language to establish new or revised social groupings. Guy et al. point out that there was massive migration to Australia in the two decades following the war, especially from what were at the time less traditional sources of immigrants to Australia, such as Italy, Yugoslavia, Greece, Turkey and Lebanon. Guy and Vonwiller (1989: 33) suggest that with a sudden influx of immigrants with non-English speaking backgrounds, there was a greater potential need for the use of uptalk as a way of checking that the listener understood what the speaker was saying, a check often made in communities where there are large numbers of non-native speakers. Earlier, McGregor (1980: 2) suggested that the rise of the new form might not have been in the speech of the native speakers communicating with the immigrants but in that of the migrants themselves. McGregor states that 'the notion migrant speakers would make greater use of a form which both reflects uncertainty and prompts confirmation by the listener is intuitively plausible'. While Guy et al. (1986) highlight patterns of migration from southern Europe to Australia following the war, Britain (1992) sees migration to New Zealand from the Pacific as potentially more important, and conjectures that a study of Samoan English in New Zealand might provide a relevant test of Guy et al.'s hypothesis.

A number of authors have suggested that uptalk may have its origin in patterns of Irish migration. For instance, Beard (2006) conjectures that the early forms of uptalk that he noticed in the southern United States (notably in rural North Carolina) may be 'a late development of an Irish accentuation pattern which also tends to go up at unusual points in a phrase'. He suggests that the early influence of Irish (and Scottish) accents on southern accents in the United States was not subsequently 'battered' by an influx of foreign accents as happened in the north. According to this hypothesis, then, patterns of non-native immigration in the northern United States actually dampened the impact of Irish-influenced rising intonation, rather than being the source of uptalk.

However, and as pointed out in Section 4.8, the incidence of rising intonation in Irish and in Irish English is probably not as high as often claimed (Rahilly, 1997), and the UNB rise reported in Belfast and Derry has been shown to be formally and functionally distinct from the uptalk rise (Cruttenden, 1995). What is more, Beard appears to be thinking of rises within phrases ('at unusual points in a phrase') rather than terminal rises.

However, Beard is not the only writer to propose an Irish connection for uptalk. Still in the United States, a report in *USA Today* starts 'So maybe you've heard it somewhere already? An almost Irish, sort of Canadian, not quite Valley-girl intonation that makes declarative statements sound like questions?' (Mendelsohn, 1993). For Canadian English, Paddock (1981) notes that Newfoundland had a strong tradition of Irish settlement early in the nineteenth century. In Australia, Horvath (1985: 39) conjectures that there may be an Irish origin for the high rising terminal, although Leitner (2004: 238) points out that if there is an Irish origin then it is odd that the intonation pattern only started to receive widespread attention from the 1970s, when there was no notable Irish migration to Australia. Seaton (2001) suggests that the fact that uptalk emerges around the same time in a number of different places around the world may relate to 'Irish dialects – and so may potentially pop up anywhere in the world where the indigenous accent has (via two centuries of migration) some debt to Irish ancestry'. Again, this may be based on an unfounded assumption that Irish dialects (it is not clear whether Seaton means dialects of Irish or of Irish English) have a high incidence of terminal rises.

5.3 Origins within the intonational system

The discussion above of the geographical and historical origins of uptalk shows that it is not entirely clear when and where uptalk originated. In this section and the next we consider possible formal origins of uptalk, i.e., its evolution from other intonational patterns or from other linguistic devices. Chapter 3 highlighted the range of meanings that have been associated with uptalk. Against that background, this section starts with a discussion of the origins of this form of intonation in terms of the meanings that it conveys and whether for example uptalk has come to 'stand for' a meaning that might previously have been conveyed by lexical or grammatical means, along with the intonation contour. We then look further at the relationship between uptalk and other intonational forms, before turning in the next section to suggestions that uptalk has developed from tag questions.

McGregor (2005) identifies two main threads in the discussion of the formal linguistic origins of uptalk, or at least of the high rising terminal in Australian English: that it has developed from an existing question intonation, and that it has arisen from the use of rising intonation to mark continuation. The first of these ideas, that uptalk is an adaptation of an existing question rise, is widely believed by the population at large (see Chapter 7), and is often claimed in academic discussions. For example, Guy et al. (1986) suggest that the linguistic evolution of uptalk has involved an extension of the meaning attributed to an existing rising pattern, 'from questioning the propositional content of the utterance, to questioning the listener's understanding of the proposition in the utterance' (McGregor, 2005: 20). Beeching (2007) gives an account of this transfer in terms of a general theory of metaphorical extension of literal meanings to speech act particles. One of her sets of particles is 'interrogation' forms (rising intonation, inversion, tag questions, uptalk, Fifeshire 'eh?' and French 'hein'). These forms have an underlying concept of lack of knowledge or uncertainty. The metaphorical extension to declarative utterances is characterised by Beeching as 'in the same way that I signal I do not know something or am uncertain about it by asking a question or using a raised intonation, my assertion is imbued with "lack of knowledge", "uncertainty", 'openness to negotiation/reassurance"' (2007: 83).

On the other hand, Allan (1984) has suggested that uptalk has evolved both formally and distributionally from a low-rising or level contour used in utterance-medial position to indicate continuation. The formal evolution is that the rise has become a high one, indicating (via the Effort Code, Gussenhoven, 2002) a higher level of deference or of hearer-inclusivity. The distributional change is that the rise is now found in utterance-final as well as utterance-medial position. Allan (1984) thus claims that uptalk rises are high-key versions of the continuation rise, and disputes the notion that they have their origin in question rises. Further, while Guy et al. (1986) suggest that the meanings associated with early instances of uptalk rises, such as uncertainty or deference, derive via a process of social evaluation of early uptalkers (typically young and female) by other speakers, Allan argues that the meanings derive systematically from the meanings of medial rises to indicate continuation and, via conversational implicature, to show that there is 'something relevant to follow' (see also Collins, 1989: 12; Fletcher et al., 2002a: 231).

Cruttenden (1997: 129) argues that uptalk is in fact an innovative combination of two types of rise usage. One is the intonational form traditionally used for particular kinds of questions – echoes or repeat questions, where the speaker is checking that they have heard correctly (hence 'pardon questions'; his example is *You're going a'way?* in response to *I'm going a̗way*). The other is the use of high-rises to give a casual flavour to non-finality. Cruttenden argues that the new usage combines these two uses in sentence-final position to mean 'I'm being deliberately non-assertive and checking that you are following me'. Importantly, the innovation of the new usage 'lies principally in the fact that it is presenting new information'.

Tench (2003) also considers the semogenesis of uptalk. Like Allan, Tench concludes that the formal origin of uptalk is through a process of blending a rising tone with a raised pitch level. Tench, however, aligns himself with Guy et al. in believing that the rising tone has its origins in question intonation. What Tench adds to the discussion is the notion that the raised pitch (compared with what would normally be found for questions) indicates a new section of discourse, much like the raising or 'resetting' of pitch that is used to indicate new 'paragraphs' or turns. In addition, Tench points out that this blended intonation is used on a declarative utterance that keeps its function of declaring new information. As such it therefore differs from the rising intonation found when declaratives are used as questions (see also Chapters 2 and 3). The latter is used to question a statement that is contrary to evidence or to our expectations (*What? You live in Wellington?*). Frequently, the information in the question is already 'given' information, i.e., it is knowledge shared by speaker and hearer, and the question is sometimes used as an incredulous echo of a preceding statement. Even when not used to show incredulity, this questioning pattern is usually in response to what someone else has said. Uptalk therefore differs from question intonation on declaratives on three counts: 'Its function is to provide information and simultaneously check the addressee's comprehension; the information is new; and transactionally, it is not a response, but part of the ongoing discourse' (Tench, 2003: 217). As Tench notes elsewhere, as a result of the blending, uptalk is 'a clever and efficient way of doing two things at the same time: giving information and checking on comprehension' (Tench, 1997: 17).

Tench's semogenesis analysis is predicated on the notion that the 'high-rising terminal' is distinguished from other rises, especially question rises, by the pitch height of its starting point – i.e., 'high-rising' should be interpreted as meaning that the pitch rises from a high level to an even higher level. The blending of a rising tone and raised pitch can thus be seen as a formal development from existing pitch patterns, as well as a semantic innovation. This formal description is appropriate for the examples chosen by Tench to illustrate his analysis (from Watt, 1994, for Toronto English; Britain and Newman, 1992, for New Zealand English; and Bradford, 1997, for British English), but discussion in Chapter 2 has shown that it is not always the starting height of the rise that distinguishes uptalk from question rises. For instance, in the New Zealand studies cited in that chapter, a crucial difference is alignment in time and not in pitch level of the starting point of the rise. Other studies referred to in that chapter indicate that Australian and British uptalk rises frequently have low onsets, or are the second elements of fall-rise patterns that include a relatively low pitch value. These patterns may of course indicate changes in the patterns associated with uptalk that have occurred subsequent to an earlier adoption of a high-onset high-rising terminal, although the comparison in Chapter 2 of rise alignments in statement and question rises in New Zealand English suggests that it is the onset of the rise in questions that is changing, rather than the onset of statement rises.

5.4   Tags and uptalk

A number of researchers have made a connection between uptalk and tag questions and other particles. For example, Beeching (2007), cited above, grouped a number of such elements together as types of interrogative that have a pragmatic function that is a metaphorical extension of underlying concepts of lack of knowledge or uncertainty. Earlier, James et al. (1989: 16) claimed that there is evidence for a parallel between the use of uptalk and the Canadian *eh?* tag, while others have pointed out the functional similarity of uptalk to pragmatic particles such as *you know* or *an(d) that* as well as to tags like *eh* (Allan, 1990: 125; Holmes, 1995:102). Allan (1990) observed that speakers may combine uptalk with such items, and gives the example *they've like ye- four five six in a car ↗you know*. Stubbe (1998) groups together uptalk, *you know*, and *eh* as addressee-oriented devices. Holmes (1995), referring to Britain (1992), comments on how the association of both uptalk and *eh* with the New Zealand Māori population reflects a tendency in Pacific cultures to adopt a more cooperative conversational style (see also Warren and Britain, 2000).

Tottie and Hoffmann (2006) provide a corpus analysis of tag questions, and find nine times as many tags in British English as in US English. They conjecture whether US English may make more use of invariant tags such as *right*, *okay*, *hunh*, which might not show in their analysis, but they also consider the role of intonation. The difference between the two varieties might – they suggest – relate to more extensive use of uptalk in US English.

There may be other similarities between uptalk and tags. Liberman (2005a), referring to McLemore (1991), writes of how tag questions, which were once seen to be seeking approval (and were therefore used by the less-dominant conversational partner), have more recently been shown to be used by the authority figure in a conversation. He points out that uptalk rises show a similar distributional pattern.

Tench (2003) noted how Watt's (1994: 99–101) uptalk contours on sentences with and without tags can be contrasted with the examples he gives of rises on questions. The interesting point here is the parallelism of the contours for non-questions with and without tags. Tench observed that the tag has a checking function and that the same function can be conveyed by intonation for the statement without the tag. 'At times, this … is verbalized separately accompanied by the raised tone as, for example, with *eh? right? know what I mean?* But at other times, the speaker … relies solely on the raised rising tone. Its meaning can still be glossed as "do you know/

understand/appreciate the significance of what I am saying?"' (Tench, 2003: 224). In terms of the evolution of uptalk, Tench's suggestion, also made by a number of other researchers, is that what was a rising intonation on tags has remained when the tags are no longer explicit. Crystal and Davy (1975: 94) pointed out that in final position with a high rising tone, *you know* 'invites the listener to agree with what has been said, or at least express[es] the speaker's assumption that the implications of what he has been saying have been understood' as in (14).

(14)   so then we | all 'went to the 'office by the 'main ⬊GATE | you | ⬈KNOW |

I suggest that if such a meaning became associated with the intonation, so that the lexical material over which it was uttered became redundant, then Crystal and Davy's example might evolve into something like (15), where the rise on the now-elided *know* has been combined with the fall on *gate* to provide a fall-rise, or (16), where the rise replaces the fall. In terms of autosegmental phonology (Goldsmith, 1990), a sequence of HLH tones associated with *gate you know* becomes realigned with just *gate* in (15) and the leading H is subsequently deleted in (16), perhaps as a consequence of tonal crowding (Ladd, 2008).

(15)   so then we | all 'went to the 'office by the 'main ⬊⬈GATE |
(16)   so then we | all 'went to the 'office by the 'main ⬈GATE |

Earlier, McGregor (1980: 1) similarly conjectured that uptalk may have 'arisen spontaneously as an instance of linguistic abbreviation by which the rising intonation sometimes associated with the conversational tag "you know" has simply been mapped onto a preceding element and the tag itself deleted'. Other researchers make similar suggestions. Guy et al. (1986: 48) talk of the Australian Questioning Intonation as 'an elliptical expression of a tag question with the same meaning, such as "You know?" or "Right?" from which all formal content save the intonation has been omitted.... By this view, the innovation which gave rise to AQI was a simple ... ellipsis of the lexical content of the tag, leaving its marked intonation to be carried by the main clause.' Guy and Vonwiller (1989: 33) point out that uptalk is a more efficient device than the tags, since it 'takes less time and effort, and can more easily be attached to the particular word or phrase whose comprehension is being questioned'. Danesi (1997: 458) calls uptalk 'a tag question without the tag', and includes it as part of what he refers to as Emotive Language Programming, being used by adolescents to ensure the participation of their conversational partners (see also Danesi, 2003). Bradford (1997:35) points out the similarities of uptalk functions to those of 'fillers' such as *Right?* or *You know what I mean?*, which are also used to check for listener comprehension and/or agreement, as well as to those of tags like Canadian *eh?* or South African *ya?* She observes:

such fillers are pronounced with a steeply rising pitch movement and are located at the end of a falling tone declarative, the declarative-filler combination producing a fall-rise contour which terminates with a steep and high rise. This leads us to conclude that the phonological form of upspeak, described earlier as a fall-rise with a steep and usually high terminating rise, is the conflation of a standard falling tone with the steep rise of a filler of the 'Right?' kind. In this way, the communicative force of the interrogative filler is intonationally incorporated into the declarative, making the filler itself redundant and reducing syntactic complexity.

The evolution of uptalk via the elision of a tag in what used to be a tag-plus-tune arrangement, leaving just the tune, would seem more plausible if the relevant tags were predominantly realised with rising tunes. Holmes (1982) provides a taxonomy of tags in English. These include reverse polarity tags (*There aren't many, are there?*), same polarity tags (*It's still bubbling away, is it?*), and invariant tags (*It's disappeared, eh?*). They occur with declarative, imperative and interrogative clauses, and the tags themselves can have rising or falling intonation. These are not equally represented in Holmes' corpus. Most frequent is a reverse polarity tag with falling intonation, following a declarative (*That's really strange, ＼isn't it?*), followed by the same with rising intonation (*It's paper or rocks, ／isn't it?*), and then declaratives with invariant tags with falling intonation (*I wish we had a better photo, ＼eh?*). In Holmes's data, same-polarity tags always occur with rising intonation, as do invariant tags after interrogative clauses. Reverse-polarity tags with rising intonation (*Ray had bad luck ／didn't he?*) 'express the request for confirmation with greater strength' (Holmes, 1982: 50–51) than equivalent forms with falling intonation. That is, the rising intonation on the tag indicates less certainty and more tolerance for disagreement. This kind of tag may 'express uncertainty whilst also soliciting agreement or reassurance' (1982: 57).

   Most of the suggestions explicitly linking the idea that uptalk evolved from an intonational pattern formerly found on tags discuss this in terms of the invariant tags. Invariant tags with rising intonation certainly seem to have similar meanings to those attributed to uptalk. Holmes (1986) gives examples of *you know* as a final tag with rising intonation used to seek reassurance or validation of what the speaker is saying. Invariant tags such as *right?* and *ok?* are used to check that the addressee is following or has understood. More recently, Stirling and Manderson (2011: 1590) have suggested that a rising intonation on a final *you know*, when used by pairs of speakers who share common membership of a group (post-mastectomy patients in this case), forms part of an 'overtly signalled appeal for engagement and alignment of the addressee'. These examples suggest that rising intonation on a tag has a general function of seeking some sort of acknowledgement from the listener, while also expressing uncertainty (see Sections 3.3.2 and 3.1 respectively for such meanings associated with uptalk).

A survey of invariant tags across varieties of English reveals a number of cases where these tags are linked with rising intonation, and often also as part of the evolutionary story behind uptalk. A British expat in Canada comments on how Canadian uptalk was preceded historically by *eh* followed by a 'question mark' (Parr, 1995), and an opinion piece by McGillivray (1994) suggests that uptalk caught on in Canada 'because of our widely reported tendency to end every sentence with "eh?" as if seeking the agreement of the person to whom we're speaking: "I headed west, eh? And I hit the TransCanada.[sic] eh?"'. Psychologist Steven Pinker comments that 'Young Californians' uptalk (sentences that sound like questions) is no more pusillanimous or noncommittal than Canadians' habitual "eh?"' (Pinker, 2000).

In the Channel Islands it is claimed that *eh* with rising intonation is used to elicit feedback (Ramisch, 2008), while if it has level intonation it performs the phatic function of keeping contact between speaker and hearer. For Scottish English (specifically Fifeshire English), Beeching (2007: 95) presents the following example, overheard on a train, where the incidence of *eh?* parallels uptalk patterns observed in narratives in other varieties (see Section 6.6) *My daughter had her birthday yesterday eh? we went to the zoo eh? it was fantastic eh? there were all they bears eh?* Also in Scotland, Miller (2004) reports an overheard conversation from 2002 in which a male speaker of around 30 said *I like Sambuca e?* with interrogative pitch on *e? (Sambuca* being the name of a bar). Miller interprets this as equivalent to *I like Sambuca ken (ken* = 'you know', 'you see') or to *I like Sambuca* with a high-rising terminal. For Irish English, McNally (2005), responding to an opinion piece by Irish teenager Conor Behan (2005) argues that uptalk in that variety has come not from America, but from an earlier use of *hi?* in the Border region, with the effect of turning statements into 'implied questions', as in *Yesterday I stubbed my toe, hi(?) It was really painful, hi(?).*

One way in which such a development might be explained is suggested by the work of Calhoun and her colleagues (Schweitzer et al., 2010; Calhoun and Schweitzer, 2012) on the lexicalisation of intonation. On the basis of corpus analyses, this team has identified that there are stronger probabilities than might otherwise be expected of the combination of certain intonation patterns with particular words and short phrases; for example, of a mid-range rising accent with *I guess*, especially when used as a downplayer, or with hedges such as *and stuff* or *like that* when used to mitigate what the speaker is saying. In judgement tasks, native listeners gave higher acceptability scores to collocations of a particular tune both with frequent and with low frequency items that have a similar discourse meaning to the high frequency items than they did to collocations of the same tune with low frequency items with different discourse meanings. The authors explain this in terms of an exemplar approach: on the basis of their experience speakers accumulate over time a set of exemplars or memory traces which contain patterns of co-occurrence of lexical and intonational material. These exemplars conspire to influence the subsequent production and perception of intonation patterns with the lexical items in question. While Calhoun et al. claim that this shows that the form of intonation is not independent of the words used, I would argue that at the same time it allows for the strengthening of the connection between a certain meaning and an intonational pattern, such that the meaning can become associated with that pattern in the absence of the specific lexical content.

5.5   Summary

Uptalk is a contagion, of an unknown precise geographic origin, that has possibly been transmitted through the media. Possible precursors to uptalk can be found in the intonational systems of the English varieties in which is it found, and system-internal explanations of its origin might involve refocusing of the existing meanings of particular tunes. In addition, uptalk has much in common with tag questions, both formally and functionally, and tag questions provide a plausible alternative source for uptalk. The spread of uptalk has been relatively rapid, which has probably been made possible by global communication through the media and through the increasing mobility of English speakers from the mid-twentieth century onwards.

Finally, in addition to the spread of uptalk in speech of English-speaking communities (and in other languages, see Chapter 9), we can also observe a spread into written English. That is, some writers now use question marks to indicate uptalk in the speech of, for instance, characters in fiction. For instance, Donna Tartt in her 2013 novel *The Goldfinch* renders the speech of her young protagonist Theo in the following way: 'they sent him postcards when they went on vacation to places like the Virgin Islands? to our home address? which was how we found out about it?' (Tartt, 2013: 137). This practice has been condemned by at least one commentator (Beachcomber, 2013), who refers to it as the SQM (tongue-in-cheek, on a parallel to HRT and other TLAs [three letter acronyms]), or supernumerary question mark. Beachcomber notes that such SQMs have appeared in emails.

6   Social and stylistic variation in uptalk use

In a summary of the main early sociolinguistic studies carried out in Australia (McGregor, 1979; Horvath, 1985; Guy et al., 1986; Guy and Vonwiller, 1989), McGregor (2005: 34) comments that the linguistic situation at the time of those studies provided a typical starting point for a change in progress based on social distributions. In particular, uptalk was at that time a recent innovation and 'a feature of the speech of young adolescent females ... generally associated with the low prestige, broad variety of Australian English'. Similarly commenting on the spread of uptalk, Bradford (1996: 23) writes about how uptalk was 'initially a peer group activity, creating a speech community' among young women, before it began 'permeating the speech of men and older members of society only after becoming well established in a community'. There is in fact a broad consensus that uptalk is primarily and initially associated with younger and female speakers. In addition, variation in uptalk use has been linked with sexuality/sexual orientation, ethnicity, socioeconomic grouping and a range of other speaker-related factors, as well as with discourse-related factors such as text type. These factors have not been studied equally for all varieties of English, so the following sections will draw from sources from a number of regions. Until further research has been carried out, it will remain unclear whether each of these factors affects each variety in the same way.

6.1   Speaker sex

The most commonly made claim concerning the distribution of uptalk is that it is a feature of female speech. This claim needs to be considered however in the context of more general intonational differences between the sexes.

Differences between women and men in their patterns of intonation have been widely studied (for reviews see, among others, McConnell-Ginet, 1978; Henton, 1989, 1995; Daly and Warren, 2001). For physiological reasons involving the relative size of the larynx, females have higher and wider pitch ranges than men, though the two ranges overlap, covering a range of approximately 50–250Hz for men and 120–480Hz for women (Laver, 1994: 451). The

relationship between acoustically measurable frequencies in Hertz and perceived pitch is not linear, however, with changes at lower frequencies having a
stronger perceptual effect than the same absolute changes at higher frequencies.
This is often dealt with through the use of a transformation, such as the ERB
(equivalent rectangular bandwidth) scale, which is based on psychoacoustic
studies of speech perception (see for example Hermes and van Gestel, 1991).
There are various calculations of ERB scales, for different purposes. The version recommended by Hermes and van Gestel results in ERB value ranges of
4.4–15.4 and 9.1–22.7 for men and women respectively, using Laver's Hertz
ranges quoted above. Clearly the ranges still differ, but a 50Hz inflection at
the top of the male range (200–250Hz) is – on the ERB scale – equivalent to a
80Hz inflection at the top of the female range. All else being equal, then, uptalk
contours or high-rising terminals are expected to be larger in Hertz terms for
the same effect in female compared with male speech.

An early observation that female and male speakers may have different patterns of pitch use comes from Brend (1975: 86), who notes that 'men … very
rarely, if ever, use the highest level of pitch that women use'. She concludes
that men use three contrastive levels of pitch while women have four. Note that
these are abstract levels, rather than actual Hz or ERB ranges. Brend (1975)
also noted that, in American English at least, women made greater use of rises
than men, although a later study by Wolff (2000) found very little difference
in rise incidence between men (4.1 per cent of tone groups were rises) and
women (4.6 per cent) in her sample from Portland, Oregon. Other researchers
have concluded that – in certain speech communities at least – women's intonation patterns tend to be more dynamic, with more frequent and more dramatic
changes in pitch (Daly and Warren, 2001).

One of the earliest researchers to suggest that uptalk is one of a set of features that characterise women's speech was Lakoff (1973, 1975). She argued
that the use of high-rises on declarative answers to questions is a feature of
'women's language', and she comments (Lakoff, 1973: 56) that 'these sorts
of speech-patterns are taken to reflect something real about character and play
a part in not taking a woman seriously or trusting her with any real respon-
sibilities, since "she can't make up her mind", and "isn't sure of herself"'.
This claim and other researchers' responses to it were discussed in Chapter 3.
For example, McConnell-Ginet (1975: 45) emphasised the positive aspect of
uptalk, as the use of an open intonation pattern with a possible goal of 'establishing a communicative encounter'. If it is used more by women than by
men, she writes, then this may be because 'personal interaction is probably
a more important behavioral goal for most women than for most men, so that
women will generally seek to increase interactive opportunities'. Elsewhere,
McConnell-Ginet (1978: 554–555) notes that men also use uptalk and that
'there is no evidence that such uses are heard as effeminate or even particularly

hesitant or indecisive'. She concludes that if there are sex differences in the amount of uptalk use then this is not an issue of 'femininity', but rather that 'one sex has more need or liking than the other for this particular communicative ploy: accompanying one explicit speech act (roughly, declaring) with another, which is implicit questioning, or more generally, requesting some additional input from the other party to the exchange'.

Edelsky (1979) tested one specific claim made by Lakoff (1973), namely that more women than men use a simple rising contour when giving an answer that only they – of the participants in the interaction – could know (e.g., telling an interviewer where they were born or their favourite colour). From a survey that involved asking such questions of a sample of 154 men and 165 women, Edelsky found no sex-related differences in the production of rises, and very few rises overall.

Regardless of the possible function of uptalk, a greater incidence among women than men has been reported for a wide range of speech communities. Thus, in Canada, Shokeir (2008) notes that women in southern Ontario use rising contours more than men (she compares the incidence of the rise patterns L*H-H% and H*L-H% with falls H*L-L%), and Talla Sando (2009: 10) reports that uptalk specifically is more widespread in the speech of Canadian women than in that of men, especially in spontaneous speech and across a range of regions.

For the United States, Barry (2007, 2008) found more uptalk use among women in Southern California. She also reports phonetic differences between the sexes, with wider pitch ranges and later alignment of the low pitch accent (L*) that provides the starting point of the rise in female uptalk. Pratt-Johnson (2006) found that African American women, although infrequent users of uptalk, were more likely to use it than African American men, particularly when interacting with other women. The use of rising intonation patterns more generally is reported by Clopper and Smiljanic (2011) to be higher for women than men (in read speech) in the midland and southern accent regions in the United States. These authors also report that females are more likely to use a bitonal L*H pattern than H*, compared to males, which they conjecture may be due to different frequencies of variant realisations of the same phonological category.

In Britain, Barry's (2007, 2008) study found that the higher use of uptalk that she noted for women in Southern California was also reflected in patterns of usage in London, and Bradford (1997: 35) noted that while 'upspeak in British English appears to cut across gender, the available evidence indicates that it is most prevalent among and first displayed in the speech of young females'.

In Australia, it has similarly been reported that uptalk forms are more likely in female speech (Bryant, 1980; McGregor, 1980; Horvath, 1985; Guy et al., 1986; Courtney, 1996). For instance, Guy et al. (1986) report uptalk in 1 per cent of tone groups for males, but in 2.2 per cent for females. Guy and Vonwiller (1989: 29–30) comment that the greater use among Australian women supports the suggestion that this is a recent and ongoing innovation, as women typically show new forms before men. Given such linkage between uptalk and female speech, it is plausible that a more recent comment that Julia Gillard was the first Australian prime minister to use uptalk (Sussex, 2010) reflects more the fact that Gillard was the first female Australian prime minister than any well-documented aspect of prime ministerial speech patterns.

Across the Tasman Sea, uptalk has been observed more in the speech of New Zealand women than in that of New Zealand men (Britain, 1992; Britain and Newman, 1992; Warren and Britain, 2000; Warren, 2005b), and has been coded as feminine in New Zealand speech (Holmes and Schnurr, 2006). Britain and Newman (1992) found that 3.9 per cent of female intonation groups exhibited uptalk compared with 1.8 per cent for men. The largest sex difference was among the younger adult speakers in their sample (20–29 years of age). Meyerhoff (1996) suggests that this may be a stage when sex differences are more salient or more significant in people's lives. Elsewhere (Warren, 2005b; Warren and Daly, 2005) it has been reported that female rises start later, are larger and more rapid, which is undoubtedly part of a generally more dynamic use of pitch by New Zealand females (Daly and Warren, 2001). In a study of very young speakers, Ainsworth (1994) found that among four-year-old New Zealanders, the girls in her sample had an uptalk rate of 3.6 per cent, compared with that of the boys at only 0.7 per cent. Note that the speech of children at this age is not characterised by absolute pitch range differences according to speaker sex, which suggests that the intonational differences between females and males are social rather than biological. In a study of audience design, i.e., of the impact on speech behaviour of the speaker's (perceived) audience, Bell and Johnson (1997) found that uptalk is more likely in speech directed to women as well as in speech produced by women, in New Zealand.

Not all studies observe higher uptalk incidence among women. In his early study of American English, Ching (1982) used a sample consisting predominantly of female speakers (12 of his 14 informants were female), but both of the male speakers he studied used uptalk. More recently, Loviglio (2008), in an analysis of sex/gender differences in public broadcasting in the United States, commented on an increase in male speakers' use of uptalk. Ellingsæter (2014) reports more uptalk among her young male informants (from Surrey in south-east England) than from her females, although this is largely due to very high levels from one male in particular. In research that considered uptalk use in different speech tasks and with different discourse functions by speakers in Southern California, Ritchart and Arvaniti (2014) report that while females use more uptalk with a floor-holding function, females and males have an equal incidence of uptalk in other types of statement. This is in interesting contrast with the results reported by Barry for the same region (Barry and Arvaniti, 2006; Barry, 2007, 2008), although Barry's data on speaker sex appear not to distinguish floor-holding from other statement types.

In a study of ethnic groups in London, Pennington et al. (2011: 189) found more uptalk use in the English of Chinese males than in that of Chinese females, and in some of the later studies of Australian English, equal numbers of uptalk patterns are reported for female and male speakers (Fletcher and Harrington, 2001; McGregor, 2005).

In New Zealand, Britain (1992) reported that among speakers of Māori English there was no difference, with males showing similarly high levels to those of females. Szakay (2007) found that Māori females produced more uptalk than Māori males, but that Pākehā males produced more than Pākehā females. She conjectures that this may be due to the conversational topic given to the participants – rugby – which might have got the men in her sample more excited than the women. This suggests that the speaker's level of involvement in the topic is a significant factor in determining uptalk use.

With the spread of uptalk we also see changes in its use, which may have affected its acceptability amongst a range of speaker groups. Lowry (2011) reflects earlier comments by Eckert and McConnell-Ginet (2003: 195) that uptalk is heard much more often now than when it was commented on by Lakoff in the earlier 1970s, and that its semantic and pragmatic connotations may have changed, reflecting a change in women's position in society. A consequence of this may be its more ready adoption by male as well as female speakers. Perhaps somewhat trivially, Fisher (1997) comments that since men tend not to ask a large number of questions, uptalk 'does have a redeeming quality. An upspeaking man who has stopped asking questions might not appear a fool.' If this is the case, then uptalk is clearly no longer associated only with uncertainty or lack of authority.

6.2   Sexual orientation

Language features that are typically associated with differences between the sexes, such as uptalk, are frequently 'appropriated' (not always consciously) as markers of sexual orientation. A few recent publications, both commentaries and research studies, have considered intonation patterns such as uptalk in this light. As an example of the former, consider Perry (2005) who, in a review of a television programme about lesbian sex, comments that uptalk is typically associated with feminine traits, and is also used by some of the women featured in the show. In particular, it is used to signal that the speaker 'is neither threatening nor overbearing. It is a conciliatory rather than an aggressive mode of communication, and as such is typically associated with women and girls, most of whom are socialized from an early age to refrain from presenting themselves as aggressive.'

Hancock et al. (2014) report that male-to-female transgender speakers who passed as female (i.e., were rated by naïve listeners as female) were likely to use more rising intonation and less falling intonation than those who did not pass as females. They state that this 'is consistent with the stereotype that females use more "upspeak" but does not necessarily support the notion that men are more monotone' (Hancock et al., 2014: 206).

Corwin (2009) observes that nine of the 13 'genderqueer' individuals that she interviewed for her research combined a narrow pitch range (which she describes as a masculine characteristic) with the frequent use of uptalk (a feminine characteristic), and that this combination is a linguistic device that 'is used to construct a gender presentation that does not fall along strictly binary gender lines'.

Hazenberg (2012, 2013) asks how transsexual speakers make use of uptalk to construct and perform their gender. He notes that transsexual speakers generally tend to have a high level of metalinguistic awareness and to actively use available language features in their performance of gender. Accordingly, Hazenberg finds that female-to-male (FtM) transsexuals in his data set tend to avoid uptalk, presumably because of its association with women and with notions of femininity, while male-to-female (MtF) transsexuals are more likely to embrace uptalk. Interestingly, he finds that both FtM and MtF transexuals comment on negative aspects of uptalk (uncertainty, lack of confidence), but the 'feminine' aspect of this feature seems to outweigh the negatives for the MtF.

6.3   Age

Along with speaker sex, speaker age is a variable frequently associated with uptalk use. In the media and popular press we read that uptalk is 'a primarily youthful practice' (Feschuk, 2009), used predominantly by the under 35s (Parkin, 2005), and employed by teenagers as part of a 'pubilect' (Danesi, 2003). Unsurprisingly, it is seized on as a marker of age: 'she seems far older than a girl who still can't rent a car. She doesn't uptalk or giggle' (Jacobs, 2005).

A dramatised television documentary investigating a UK murder case (*Trail of Guilt: Betrayed – The Murder of Sandra Pool*, broadcast 5 August 2002) reveals how uptalk use was at the time of the case (2001–2002) predominantly associated with younger speakers. The investigation featured a forensic phonetician who was able to help police catch a killer using, amongst other evidence, 'her knowledge of ... how younger people have adopted the Australian question intonation (saying a statement like it's a question?)' (reviewed by McLean, 2002).

The research on uptalk largely agrees with this observation that younger speakers are more likely to exhibit this feature. Thus, it is more likely among teenagers and 'extreme youth' in Australian English (Horvath, 1985; Courtney, 1996; Fletcher and Harrington, 2001). In numeric terms, in one of the early Australian studies McGregor (1979) reported that 56.5 per cent of his adolescent speakers were uptalkers, but only 35.8 per cent of his adults. In addition, McGregor (1980) reports age effects within each group. For instance, in his adult group a higher proportion of the under 25s used uptalk than of the over 25s.

McGregor's observations relate to the likelihood of speakers being uptalkers. Using Horvath's (1985) data, Guy et al. (1986) computed the actual use of uptalk contours by speakers in a range of age groups. When all ethnicities are pooled, teenagers use uptalk in 2.29 per cent of tone groups, while adults have a considerably lower rate of 0.23 per cent. A finer age distribution is found when Anglo-Celtics alone are considered (11–14 years old: 1.6 per cent, 15–19: 2 per cent, 20–39: 0.5 per cent, 40+: 0.2 per cent). On the basis of this pattern, Guy et al. conclude that uptalk probably began in Australia some 20–25 years before the collection of their data, placing its onset in the late 1950s. This would seem to be supported by an incidence of approximately 0.3 per cent in a subsample of Mitchell and Delbridge's adolescents from the 1959–1961 period (Guy et al., 1986).

In contrast to other intonational features, Halford (2007: 27) suggests that the high incidence of uptalk among adolescent Canadians is a difference of degree from the pattern found from adult Canadians, rather than a categorical distinction. Wolff's (2000) study of uptalk in Portland, Oregon also showed an age gradation, with 11–14-year-olds using uptalk in 9.5 per cent of their tone groups, falling to 2.8 per cent for 15–19, 4.5 per cent for 20–39 and 2.3 per cent for the over 40s. The higher level for the 20–39 group than for the 15–19 group is the result of higher levels for the males in the two older groups, especially in the 20–39 group. Note, however, that Wolff had a small sample of only two speakers in each of her eight (four age by two sex) groups. In England, however, the distinction is much more categorical (Ellingsæter, 2014), with values of 8.8 per cent for younger informants (17–23) and 0.4 per cent for older speakers, although with an age range of 66–87 these are much older than the older speaker groups in most surveys.

Warren and Britain (2000) similarly report higher uptalk incidence in younger speakers. Figure 6.1 is based on data reported there, and shows uptalk use from three sources, as indicated against the age groups. While there is variation according to sex and ethnicity, age is clearly a key predictor of the likelihood of uptalk.

Eckert (2008) points out that adolescence is a time when a great deal of identity work is being done. She also notes that the 'construct of inarticulate

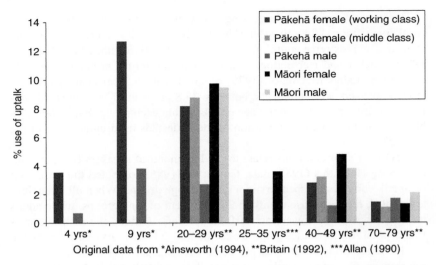

Figure 6.1 Uptalk use by age, sex and ethnicity, in New Zealand English (based on Warren and Britain, 2000: Figure 7.1).

female/adolescent language is popular in the media', and that this includes the description of uptalk as a signal of 'adolescents' lack of concern with precision, or unwillingness to take responsibility for their statements' (2008: 394). However, Eckert also reports a class project at Stanford University where 300 people were observed ordering drinks at a juice stand during a parents' weekend. The female undergraduate server asked customers to give their name. The group that was most likely to use rising intonation in their responses were middle-aged men, which would typically not be the group most likely to be identified as insecure.

Liberman's *Language Log* commentaries on uptalk give plenty of examples of older speakers. In one contribution, Liberman (2008e) acknowledges that he includes such examples in part to debunk the myth that uptalk is a youth phenomenon. In an effort to redress the balance and give some stereotypical examples, that blog includes a series of dramatic examples from prepubescent girls.

Elsewhere, it is noted in a letter to *The Times* that uptalk is used by some older speakers in the United Kingdom (Miskin, 2008), and Pratt-Johnson (2006) reports that adolescent (15–18-year-old) African Americans are in fact less likely to use uptalk than African Americans in the age range from the low 20s to the low 30s. In at least one study, age is claimed not to be a factor in uptalk use in Canada (Shokeir, 2008). Rather, it is claimed that use is stable in Southern Ontario, as indicated by a comparison of 19–25 and 45–55 age groups. Tomlinson and Fox Tree (2011: 59) take Shokeir's findings to be an indication that the incidence of uptalk is not an ongoing linguistic shift (although they do also say that this needs to be replicated with a larger sample). However, Shokeir lumps continuation rises (L-H% in her description) together with what seem more likely to be uptalk rises (L*H-H%). If only the latter is included, then there is a clear age difference as well as a higher incidence among females than males. This age difference reflects better Talla Sando's (2009: 10) finding that uptalk is more likely from younger than from older speakers across other Canadian provinces.

6.4   Ethnicity

Language features are regularly associated with ethnic groups as well as with sex and age groupings. This is also the case for uptalk, with comparisons on racial and/or ethnic dimensions found in a number of English-speaking countries, including the United States, the United Kingdom, Australia and New Zealand.

In the United States, an early study by Tarone (1973) found that black adolescent speakers of American English used a greater pitch range (extending into higher pitch levels) and more rising pitch contours than white adolescents, although it is unclear whether the rises described by Tarone are examples of uptalk. She does note, however, that the black speakers were more involved than the white speakers in verbal competition and may have had greater expectations of some sort of response to their utterances. We have seen earlier (especially in Chapter 3) that these are fairly typical contexts in which uptalk can be found. Toon (1982: 227) makes a similar statement concerning the greater use of rising contours by black Americans, and refers to work by Wolfram and Fasold (1974: 147–148). In Michaels' (1984) study of 'sharing time' (she studied interactions in four primary schools in the Boston area), rising tones are found more frequently in the speech of white children (more than 60 per cent of tonal contours) than in the speech of black children (37 per cent). Pratt-Johnson (2006) reports a more recent investigation specifically into the use of uptalk by African Americans. She notes that while uptalk has undoubtedly become a fixture of American English, it is not used as much by African Americans as it is by white Americans. African Americans were more likely to use uptalk when speaking with white Americans who use uptalk than they were when speaking with other African Americans. This effect interacted with sex, so that black women were most likely to use uptalk when talking with white women, and least when interacting with black men.

In a study of uptalk use in two adolescent ethnic groups in London, Pennington et al. (2011: 188–189) found a higher incidence among those of Chinese ethnicity (around 19 instances per 10,000 words) than from those of Bangladeshi ethnicity (one per 10,000 words). They argue that the use of uptalk primarily by the Chinese adolescents supports its stronger association with middle-class speakers than with working-class speakers (see below), a distinction that they claim is appropriate for differentiating their Chinese and Bangladeshi groups. They also point out that this finding is compatible with Cruttenden's (1997) claim that uptalk is more favoured by New Yuppies (upwardly mobile young speakers) than by working-class speakers. In addition, they conjecture that their Bangladeshi group may not be as strongly listener-oriented as their Chinese group and may have engaged less with the interactional tasks required in the research, which were constructed peer-to-peer conversations as well as interviews with the researchers. Further, they suggest that the Bangladeshis may identify less with speech communities that use uptalk.

In Australia, uptalk use in Italian, Greek and Turkish communities has been compared with that in Anglo communities, and rising pitch has also been given consideration as a potential feature of Aboriginal English. Guy et al. (1986) observed what appeared to be higher rates of uptalk use by Italian and Greek speakers, but in fact there turned out to be only minor variation between speakers of Italian and Greek background on the one hand and those of Anglo-Celtic extraction on the other, once age differences were taken into account. Warren (1999: 92) notes that high-rising intonation on phrase-final syllables is a salient feature of what she refers to as 'wogspeak' and cites examples from a 16-year-old second generation Turkish girl in Australia. Citing Horvath (1985: 122), she also notes, however, that the high-rising tone is associated with 'teenagers, females, lower working-class and either Greeks or Anglos', a quote that makes it somewhat odd that Warren sees the high-rising tone as a marker of ethnicity. Kaldor and Malcolm (1991: 76) note a 'sustained pitch rise in narratives' as a phonological feature of Aboriginal English in Australia, but comment that there has been little systematic work on this. In a related observation, Eades (1991) comments on 'Aboriginal indirectness' as a linguistic strategy used when seeking information, and that this involves the presentation for confirmation of known or assumed information (*You been to town?*). There is no certainty, however, that these features are in any way a distinctive aspect of Aboriginal English compared with other varieties in Australia. More recent research by Jespersen (2014) makes more explicit claims concerning the existence of uptalk in Aboriginal speech. Jespersen analysed the speech of six Aboriginal Australians from Sydney (three males, three females) during radio interviews, and found high-rising terminal intonation patterns in just over 25 per cent of intonational phrases. Of these 79 high rising terminal contours, the majority (65 per cent) were high-rises from a low pitch accent (L*H-H%), with the remainder equally distributed between high pitch accent rises (H*H-H%) and high-range fall-rises (H*L-H%). These patterns are similar to those noted by other researchers on Australian English as discussed in Section 4.1, such as Fletcher and Harrington (2001). Jespersen found indications that uptalk was more likely in a more 'dialectal' speech style. She concludes that the instances of uptalk in her small sample are used to engage the listener and ask for his cooperation, i.e., with functions similar to those identified in Chapter 3.

The principal comparison between ethnic groups in New Zealand is between Māori and Pākehā. Allan's (1990) study explicitly examined NZE speech for effects of ethnicity on uptalk usage. He controlled for possible effects of sex, socioeconomic status and age by selecting participants who were all females in the same age range (25–35) and from the same socioeconomic group. Allan's results indicate more uptalk from Māori women (with 3.6 per cent of pause defined units having uptalk contours) than from Pākehā women (2.3 per cent), although he did acknowledge firstly that the small number of participants (five Pākehā and four Māori) gave the research the status of a pilot study, and secondly that the ethnic division may have disguised socioeconomic variation. However, Allan's findings were subsequently supported by other studies of NZE. Britain (1992) investigated uptalk use in a total sample of 75 speakers, and found a significantly higher rate of uptalk use by the Māori speakers in the sample (5.1 per cent versus 3.5 per cent of tone groups). Allan's and Britain's data are reflected in Figure 6.1. Other research, such as that by Bell and Johnson (1997) indicates not only that Māori use more uptalk than Pākehā, but also that uptalk is more general among Māori, i.e., is not as clearly sex-differentiated in Māori English as in Pākehā NZE (see also Warren and Bauer, 2004). Bell and Johnson's audience design study also found that uptalk in interviews was particularly likely when the interviewer was Māori, especially a Māori woman.

Bell (2000) included uptalk as one of his 'suggested features' of Māori English, in the category of discourse features along with *eh*, *y'know* and tag questions. The functions of these features is to establish interactional empathy, to check comprehension, to make sure that the listener is paying attention, or to confirm shared knowledge. Bell found that the particles *eh* (non-questioning, also found in other regions such as Canada and Guernsey – see Section 5.4) and *y'know* were much more frequent in Māori English than in Pākehā English (per 10,000 words: *eh* 46 versus 0; *y'know* 128 versus 29). Uptalk usage was less markedly different, with 31 per 10,000 words for Māori and 23 for Pākehā. More recently, Szakay (2007) has also found greater uptalk use among Māori, but interestingly she found that ethnicity interacted with sex in the prediction of uptalk use in her study. While the most frequent use was by Māori females, she found that Pākehā males were more likely to use uptalk than both Pākehā females and Māori males. She suggests that this result may indicate a recent change in the patterns of uptalk use among Pākehā males, though the topic of conversation (rugby) may also have had an influence (as noted in Section 6.1).

Britain (1992: 94) suggests that the greater use of uptalk by Māori than by Pākehā may be because non-Western cultures show greater emphasis on 'creation of involvement' in informal discourse. Use by Māori may be because it serves an important interpersonal function as a politeness marker and to indicate cooperation, and non-Western cultures emphasise more involvement in informal discourse (Britain, 1992; Warren and Britain, 2000; Holmes, 2005).

6.5   Socioeconomic grouping

As noted in the preceding section, socioeconomic grouping is often confounded with ethnic or racial divisions. Nevertheless, a number of uptalk studies have used a measure of socioeconomic status as a possible predictor of likely uptalk use. As we have seen, uptalk has frequently been linked to notions such as powerlessness and insecurity (see Section 3.1). In the popular press it has been associated with a lack of professionalism, and – conversely – the absence of uptalk with a professional approach; for example, the implication is clear when Fiorito (2005) describes a poetry reading: 'Seven readers, all pros, no uptalk.'

Conley et al. (1978) investigated language in US courtrooms and in particular noted a style of language used by witnesses that included frequent use of hedges, hesitation forms, polite forms, and question intonation, defined as 'making a declarative statement with rising intonation *so as to convey uncertainty*' (Conley et al., 1978: 1380, emphasis added), along with the overuse of intensifiers. This style was most likely to be used by witnesses of low social status, and was used more by women than by men. O'Barr and Atkins (1980) termed this 'powerless' language, rather than using the previously used term 'women's language' (Lakoff, 1973) because it became clear to them that it was not only women using these forms and that when women (and others) did use them it was because of the relative powerlessness of their status.

While the connection between uptalk and powerlessness or insecurity is hotly disputed in much of the uptalk research, it does lead to a prediction that speakers from lower status groups might be more inclined to use uptalk. Equally, an observation that lower social groups do not use uptalk might be taken as evidence for an avoidance strategy, which in turn supports the notion that uptalk indicates powerlessness. Thus Eckert (1989: 257), referring to work on Australian English by Guy et al. (1986), argues that low use of uptalk by working-class men in their study is 'an avoidance of the linguistic expression of subordination by men in the socioeconomic group that can least afford to sound subordinate'. Eckert bases this claim on Guy et al.'s finding (1986: 37) of a 'curvilinear' function for uptalk use by men across social groups, i.e., it is used most by the upper-working-class group and less by both lower working class and middle class. This contrasts with a linear function for women, with uptalk usage highest for the lower working class, followed by upper working class and then middle class (see Figure 6.2, which shows probability values for uptalk use derived by Guy et al. from their VARBRUL statistical analysis). Overall rates reported by Guy et al. are that uptalk is found in 2.5 per cent of

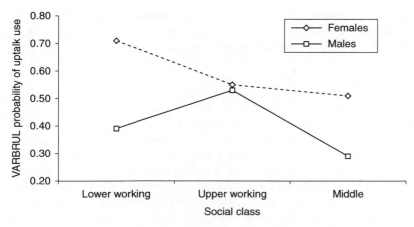

Figure 6.2 Australian uptalk use by social class and sex (based on Guy et al., 1986: Figure 2).

tone groups from lower-working-class speech, with values of 1.7 per cent for upper-working-class speech, and 0.7 per cent for middle-class speech. Guy and Vonwiller (1989) argue that the greater level of use among working-class speakers supports the suggestion that uptalk was at the time a recent and ongoing innovation, as an example of a 'change from below' (Labov, 1966). Later studies (Fletcher and Harrington, 2001; McGregor, 2005) show clear evidence of uptalk in general Australian, suggesting a spread from working-class speakers to the general population.

In his study of adolescents, McGregor (1980: 7–8) found that uptalk was more likely among students from state schools than those from independent or church schools. While he was unable to state precisely why this was the case, he did note that the data showed a relationship with the occupational status of the students' fathers. The distributional pattern also matched that of the estimated proportions of the school roll filled by students from a migrant background, which he argues is consistent with a view that uptalk is a result of migrant influence on native speaker intonation patterns. McGregor had raters allocate his Australian English samples to five sociolectal categories (Broad, Lower General, General, Upper General, Cultivated) and found fewer uptalk users towards the Cultivated end of the spectrum. It should be noted, however, that there is a potential circularity here, in that the incidence of uptalk may have contributed to how the speech samples were classified into the sociolectal categories.

As noted in the preceding section, Allan's (1990) finding that Māori women use more uptalk than Pākehā (NZ European) women could be a socioeconomic feature rather than a marker of ethnicity. However, although uptalk use has sometimes been described as stigmatised in NZE (see Warren and Britain, 2000: 153 and references given there), it does not appear to be strongly stratified on social dimensions. For instance, Britain (1992) found more uptalk use among young women, but largely regardless of class.

In contrast to the general pattern of findings in Australia and New Zealand, studies elsewhere have reported less uptalk use among working-class speakers than in other groups. For instance, in the United Kingdom, Cruttenden (1997: 130) has linked uptalk use with New Yuppies (see also Foulkes and Docherty, 2006), and Pennington et al. (2011: 190) argue that its use by Chinese adolescents in London reflects the association of uptalk with middle-class status. In the United States, Liberman (2008f) acknowledges that the social distribution of uptalk is unclear, but gives some clear examples of the phenomenon from a doctor, i.e., a medical professional. In Portland, Oregon, Wolff (2000) found higher levels of uptalk among middle-class (6.4 per cent of tone groups) than working-class speakers (2.3 per cent). More recent work by Ritchart and Arvaniti (2014) reveals no effect of socioeconomic status on uptalk use. The authors suggest that this is because uptalk is so widespread in the Southern California community that they examined and is no longer a feature that attracts attention. The fact that social stratification of uptalk is also not particularly clear elsewhere suggests that the same may be true in other regions, in contrast with earlier observations mentioned above.

6.6   Text types

Chapter 10 presents an overview of task comparisons that highlights the varying speaking requirements of different speech events. But even within one speech event, such as responding to interview questions or telling a story, there are different types of text that are being produced. Horvath (1985) categorised the responses that participants gave to interview questions in her Australian data into different text types that were defined by the nature of the question being asked. The responses were labelled as descriptions, opinions, explanations, factual texts or narrative texts. This is, of course, a somewhat crude division, since answers to questions of a particular type, such as an opinion-inducing question such as *What do you think about X?* need not be restricted to texts of one expected type. For instance the response to such a question might also include some descriptive or explanatory texts as well as a statement of opinion. Overall, however, Horvath reports that narrative and descriptive texts were the environments most likely to produce uptalk. Guy et al. (1986) report Horvath's result in terms of a scale: narrative > description > explanation > opinion > fact. This hierarchy supports the interactive nature of uptalk, where 'listener involvement during the stage-setting and plot-development is vital' (Guy et al.,

1986: 43). Allan (1990) also found (for NZE) that narrative texts in particular favour uptalk. In an analysis of interactions in a New Zealand courtroom, Innes (2007) similarly noted a high incidence of uptalk in narrative sections; for example, when defendants or witnesses were telling their version of the events that led to the charges before the court. Only a small handful of opinion texts were accompanied by uptalk. Innes (2007: 252) concludes that uptalk relates to the speaker's 'awareness of the other party(–ies) in the interaction and hence their own goals vis-à-vis those others'.

Ainsworth (1994) reports that four-year-old New Zealanders used uptalk in explanatory talk only, while nine-year-olds patterned more with adults, with highest uptalk rates in narrative contexts. But the finding for the younger children may be linked to the paucity of narrative texts in their recordings. Michaels (1984) identified the use of high-rises (which she calls 'sharing intonation') in 'sharing time' speech events in a study of interactions in primary school classrooms in the Boston area in 1981–1982. The context is one where children are called upon to talk about some past or future event or about an object they have brought into school. The contour is 'a high rising tone with vowel elongation, stretching over the last word or two of a tone group (or complete intonational phrase), resulting in sharp pitch modulations' (Michaels, 1984: 220). These sharing time contexts result in narratives similar to those of Ainsworth's nine-year-olds, and result in similar uptalk-like contours. Michaels also observed that these contours typically occur in sequences as the narrative unfolds. Both Horvath (1985) for Australian English and Allan (1990) for New Zealand English found that multiple clause utterances strongly favoured uptalk, and many researchers and lay commentators have noted the tendency of uptalk to occur in sequences of narrative clauses.

Not all studies of uptalk have found the distribution by text type just noted. One of Podesva's (2011) informants used uptalk primarily when providing explanations or issuing instructions, contrasting with the findings in other research such as Guy et al. (1986), where explanations disfavour rising intonation. This particular informant, however, was using the other-oriented characteristic of uptalk in a professional context as a doctor to put his patient at ease (Podesva, 2011: 245). Podesva notes that this is salient use of uptalk not only because of the interactive context in which it is used, but also because uptalk is otherwise only infrequently used by this informant.

Uptalk researchers have commented that a broad distinction between narrative texts and other text types is not detailed enough to reveal fully the nature of uptalk. For instance, Steele (1996) criticises earlier work on uptalk in Australian English for failing to fully explore narrative structure. For her own analysis of 15 narrative texts, Steele employs Labov and Waletsky's (1967) analysis of narrative structure for narratives of personal experience (see also Warren and Britain, 2000). The recordings were analysed into their narrative components

Table 6.1 *Uptalk rate by narrative component, based on data reported by Steele (1996).*

Narrative component	Orientation	Complicating action	Internal evaluation	External evaluation	Total
Uptalk rate	32%	16%	12%	46%	22%
Total count of 'idea units'	102	186	66	26	380

using Labov and Waletsky's approach, and each component was broken down into 'idea units' (roughly equivalent to intonational phrases or tone units). Her results show that the highest incidence of uptalk is in the orientation and external evaluation sequences (see Table 6.1). Orientation sequences are where the speaker sets up the 'who, where, what and when' of the story. The evaluation sequence is where the speaker gives the point of the story, and the external evaluation is when the speaker steps out of the narrative and explains to the hearer what the point of the narrative is. Steele does not include the resolution and coda elements in her report as uptalk use there was minimal.

Warren and Britain (2000) present an analysis of both narrative and opinion texts from 25 young New Zealanders (the dataset first presented by Britain, 1992). Uptalk usage was much lower in the opinion texts than in the narratives. Like Steele, Warren and Britain analysed the narratives into structural elements based on Labov and Waletzky (1967), although they did not distinguish internal and external evaluation. Warren and Britain (2000) report similar findings to Steele's, with higher rates of uptalk use in orientation and evaluation sequences than in complicating action and resolution/coda (see Figure 6.3). In a study reported by Eckert and McConnell-Ginet (2003), Kortenhoven (1998) found that in recordings from adolescent boys almost every utterance in the development of a narrative had uptalk, but the introduction and conclusion never did.

Steele's closer analysis of orientation elements shows that not all elements within an orientation sequence have uptalk. Elements that do have uptalk tend to be more prominent as a result. With complicating action elements, she finds that uptalk similarly highlights more important aspects of the narrative action such as the major event or a dramatic turn in events, and/or they pick out which of two simultaneous actions is more important. Steele argues that a speaker's use of uptalk is selective.

In a student project, Brown (2000) explored the use of uptalk in two groups of age- and sex-matched speakers (four males and four females in the age range 19–23 years). One group was university students, and the other was a group who had joined the workforce. The groups were all from middle-class backgrounds and were all New Zealanders of European descent. Data were

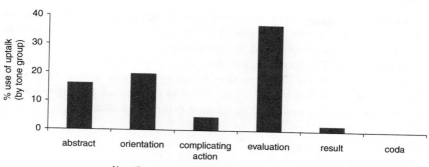

Figure 6.3 Uptalk rated by narrative component (based on Warren and Britain, 2000: Figure 7.6).

from formal interviews, a reading passage and informal prompted discussion. Brown found an effect of *linguistic marketplace*, in that speakers from the group of workers used much less uptalk (7.05 per cent of pause-defined units) than the students (10.31 per cent). As reported by other researchers, more of the uptalk contours were in narrative texts than in other text types, and more in multi-clause turns than in shorter turns. Brown also found that females showed the greatest difference between the two 'marketplaces' – female students used more uptalk than male students, but female workers used less uptalk than male workers. Brown argues that these young workers accommodate to the linguistic demands of the workplace, and that females are more likely than males to make such accommodation.

6.7   Summary

This chapter has presented an overview of the links between uptalk use and social and stylistic variation. Not surprisingly, a major focus has been on uptalk as a marker of young and female speech, both in the research literature and in public opinion. Following on from this, we also noted that uptalk is a linguistic marker that has relevance to the expression of sexuality and sexual identity and orientation. It is less consistently clear how uptalk usage relates to ethnicity and/or socioeconomic grouping, despite some early observations that it was more frequent among working-class speakers, which were possibly linked to the once widespread notion that the questioning nature of uptalk indicates relative powerlessness. In terms of text types, there is consensus that uptalk is most likely in narrative-style talk, which is commensurate with its use to maintain listener involvement in the discourse.

Finally, a recent Master's thesis (Ellingsæter, 2014) that includes uptalk as a sociophonetic variable in the analysis of the speech of people from Surrey in south-east England emphasised the more informal nature of speech in which uptalk is found. Ellingsæter noted that some of the male informants, interviewed in a pub, showed an increasing frequency of uptalk as they drank more beer. She attributes this to the relaxing effect of the alcohol, leading to a more informal elicitation context and an increase in the vernacular.

7 Credibility killer and conversational anthrax: uptalk in the media

'Uptalk' has been commented on in the popular press for quite some time, and journalists periodically return to it as a significant phenomenon in society (for recent examples see *BBC News Magazine*, 2014; MailOnline, 2014; Stokel-Walker, 2014). In this chapter I present a survey of English-language media items over a 20-year period (1992–2012) that include some mention or discussion of uptalk under one or other of the labels discussed in Chapter 1. This survey is based primarily on sources available via online search engines and library resources, and is unlikely to be comprehensive; hopefully it is representative.

The sample consists of 183 items, of which approximately half (88) use the term 'uptalk', with another 52 preferring 'upspeak', along with 21 using 'HRT/high-rising terminal', nine using 'AQI/Australian Question(ing) Intonation', and a small selection of other terms. Of the 183 items, only 42 cited experts (although the expertise covered a range that included phoneticians, linguists, speech therapists and speaking coaches). A (somewhat subjective) categorisation of the stance taken by the items showed that a little over half of them were neutral, but a sizeable minority (78) were clearly negative or condemning of uptalk. A negative approach was much more likely for items where the use of the intonation pattern itself was the central topic, compared to when it contributed more marginally to the discussion, for example, as just one of many behavioural characteristics of a certain individual or group.

Around half of the pieces made mention of speaker age, with discussion of uptalk predominantly in articles about young adults or teenagers. If speaker sex was mentioned, then it was almost always to indicate that uptalk was a typical female trait. Less than a third of the sample made any type of reference to any geographic origin or centre of influence for the phenomenon, and these were fairly evenly split between the Antipodes (mainly in British articles) and the West Coast of the United States (mainly in American articles). Thirty-nine items commented on whether uptalk was spreading or not – only four of these suggested that it was on the way out. The types of media pieces in the survey sample included opinions, letters, advice columns, profiles and reviews, as discussed in the sections below.

Media reports on uptalk, especially opinion texts, show many of the characteristics discussed in studies of language ideology (e.g., Irvine and Gal, 2000; Lippi-Green, 2012). That is, the positioning of the author and the emphasis on particular features of uptalk serve to reinforce the writer's views of uptalk and/or uptalkers. In language ideology research, the emphasis is on discussing and exposing attitudes towards language use, including discrimination on the basis of language, and on providing the understanding and tools to redress language-based inequities. In my discussion of media representation of uptalk, I will refer mainly to the work of Lippi-Green, who bases her analytical framework on two starting points: first, that '[t]here is something deeply inequitable and unacceptable about the practice of excluding the few from the privileges of the many on the basis not of what they have to say, but of how they say it', and, second, that one can and should not demand 'that the disempowered assimilate linguistically and culturally to please the empowered' (Lippi-Green, 2012: xx). What makes Lippi-Green's approach particularly relevant is that she highlights the powerful influence of the media in communicating social values and in promulgating language-based discrimination. Of course, the positioning of the media with regard to uptalk rarely has the severe consequences discussed in the context of language-based discrimination (Lippi-Green, for instance, examines attitudes towards African American Vernacular English, Latino English and Asian English). Nevertheless the stances projected in what Lippi-Green refers to as a 'standard language ideology', i.e., a bias towards an idealised form of language, can often be seen in how uptalk is treated.

As an analytical tool, Lippi-Green (2012: 70) proposes a 'language subordination model'. Here she identifies eight elements, some of which we will see emerging in media reactions to uptalk, particularly in the opinion pieces under discussion in Section 7.1. The first is that the properties of language tend to be mystified. That is, it is assumed that the complexities of language are beyond the understanding of the 'ordinary' native speaker. This is connected with the second element, that commentators claim access to authority on language use either as experts themselves or through their privileged access to experts. Third, there is a tendency to generate or promulgate misinformation about language, often built around what appear to be common-sensical notions, but that are generally based on misunderstandings or inadequate comprehension of the linguistic facts. A classic example is the perhaps trivial but misguided claim that because 'two negatives make a positive' anyone who says 'I didn't see nobody' actually means 'I saw someone'. (Some powerful language myths are exposed in Bauer and Trudgill, 1998.) Fourth, the languages, language varieties or specific forms of language that are under consideration (or attack) are frequently trivialised and made the object of humour. Such trivialisation seems to be particularly frequent in the media. The fifth and sixth elements are related to one another: speakers who conform to 'mainstream' language use are held up as positive examples, while those who use stigmatised forms are vilified or marginalised. The final two elements also form a related pair: promises are made to those who conform, and threats to those who do not. In an employment context, for instance, opportunities will be made available to those who use mainstream varieties but are less likely to arise for those who do not.

Lippi-Green (2012) also points out that much language-based discrimination relies on arguments to do with miscommunication. For instance, the argument that certain language patterns of minority or sidelined groups are inferior is based on the fact that those in a position of authority or in the majority mainstream group claim that they cannot understand what is being said to them. Often these arguments can be seen to be empty and nothing more than an excuse for prejudice – it is unlikely that a speaker saying 'I didn't see nobody' will genuinely be misunderstood in the way often implied, or that a New Zealand English speaker supposedly talking about a car with 'ear-bags' will be understood to have meant anything other than 'air-bags' (there is an ongoing merger of the 'ear' and 'air' vowels in this variety, frequently discussed in the media, where it is criticised as indicative of sloppy communication on the part of younger speakers; see Warren, 2006). In discussing miscommunication, Lippi-Green invokes the notion of 'communicative burden', and points out that all too frequently it is actually the listener rather than the speaker who is ultimately responsible for a breakdown in communication.

In other language ideology research, Irvine and Gal (2000) present a theoretical framework that involves the three notions of *iconisation, fractal recursivity* and *erasure*. Iconisation is when a linguistic feature that indexes a social group becomes an iconic representation of that group 'as if a linguistic feature somehow depicted or displayed a social group's inherent nature or essence' (Irvine and Gal, 2000: 37). Fractal recursivity is when an opposition or partitioning of linguistic features at one level (e.g., between groups or linguistic varieties) is perceived – rightly or wrongly – to recur at other levels (e.g., within groups), and erasure occurs when facts inconsistent with the ideological scheme go unnoticed or are explained away. We will see similar features to these in the opinion pieces on uptalk, to which we now turn.

7.1   Opinion pieces

The largest group of media items mentioning or discussing uptalk is made up of opinion pieces, interpreted here rather broadly to include commentaries, features and retrospectives, as well as items explicitly labelled as opinions. Of these 91 items, roughly half take a negative view, the others being neutral. As in the whole sample, there is a stronger tendency for a negative stance in those pieces that include uptalk as a central topic. The elements of Lippi-Green's (2012) language subordination model that seem to emerge most clearly are the use of authority, misinformation (deliberate or unintentional), the highlighting of the consequences of (non-)conformity, vilification and the use of trivialising humour.

7.1.1   Authority

Many of the media items in this category make use of authority to support their arguments. Sometimes this is the authority of the writer themselves. For instance, Hank Davis, a psychology professor, writes in the Toronto *Globe and Mail* (Davis, 2002), of how uptalk was hardly evident in the early 1990s, and of how by 2002 he has for years 'been getting on my students for this need-less vocal tic that devalues what they have to say'. He writes of how he was questioned about this speech habit by a British colleague at an international conference, and of how he hears uptalk from other professorial colleagues. Not only is there an explicit acknowledgement in the piece of Davis as a professor (albeit of psychology, not linguistics), but he also makes reference to his international status and to his students, reaffirming his position of authority, so that the reader assumes that he is an expert in what he is writing about.

The position of expert is also asserted by Rosewarne (2009) in the *Times Educational Supplement*. As a postgraduate student in applied linguistics at Birkbeck College in the University of London, Rosewarne in 1983 coined the term 'Estuary English' for a variety of English found in the south-east of England (Maidment, 1994). He first published an article on Estuary English in 1984 in the *Times Educational Supplement*. Twenty-five years later he reminds us of this, thereby lending authority to a newer description of this variety that includes discussion of how uptalk can add tentativeness to a statement of new information.

The authority of other experts is also used by writers to support a negative stance towards uptalk. For instance, Daum (2007) cites the claim of speech coach Bob Corff that uptalk 'signifies a lack of accountability for one's words'. The presence of an expert voice lends credibility to Daum's inaccurate description of uptalk as 'declarative sentences turned into questions'. White (1995) similarly uses a speech coach, Dennis Becker, as her source of expert opinion for a negative reaction to uptalk in the *Boston Globe*.

Not all expert views expressed in opinion pieces are negative, however. Linguistics professor Carmen Fought points out for instance that when a student leaves a voicemail message 'This is Heather? From your Linguistics 10 class? I have a question about the homework?' then this student is not showing uncertainty about things to which she (the student) surely knows the answer, but is establishing common ground; she wants to check that Fought knows who she is (Fought, 2005). Psychology professor (and Canadian) Steven Pinker writes in the *Wilmington Star News* in North Carolina that 'young Californians' uptalk (sentences that sound like questions) is no more pusillanimous or non-committal than Canadians' habitual "eh?"' (Pinker, 2000).

Fought and Pinker are clearly writing as experts on language issues. Many of the journalistic pieces are similarly well-informed and make claims that are largely in line with the findings of academic studies. For instance, Dominic Kennedy (1996) cites academic Barbara Bradford in *The Times*, who points out that uptalk is used to indicate shared knowledge and 'gives the impression of a sort of bonding'. BBC News education reporter Sean Coughlan presents an interview with linguist Yvonne Pratt-Johnson (Coughlan, 2005) in which the latter's analysis of uptalk in different speech groups, including its lack of currency amongst black Americans, is objectively presented. Linguistics professors Bert Vaux, John Singler, Walt Wolfram and William Labov are all consulted for an article on 'City girl squawk' in the *New York Observer* (Horowitz, 2006), along with psychologist Steven Pinker and speech coach Sam Chwat. The spread of uptalk in New York is attributed to 'the young career women who are constantly out on the town, armed with cocktails and a seemingly inexhaustible gift of gab'. Chwat's expertise was earlier called on by the *Orlando Sentinel* (1995) to point out a common disparity between the intended and received message of uptalk: 'Though your intent may be to convey the thought "Don't you agree?" or "Shall I go on?" the message you send is "I don't really believe what I'm saying," Chwat says.' It is Chwat, too, who is called on to comment on Monica Lewinsky's performance once secretly recorded tapes of her phone conversations with her friend Linda Tripp were released (Morris, 1998). Lewinsky uses 'classic late teen-ager upspeak patterns' and is 'looking for reassurance ... for verification'.

Robert Fulford (1995) also cites experts in the Toronto *Globe and Mail*, including Cynthia McLemore and Deborah Tannen. And in the *Toronto Star*, Judy Gerstel (2006) cites sociolinguist Sali Tagliamonte, who responds to the assertion that uptalk shows female insecurity and a quest for approval and attention by questioning how you measure insecurity. At the same time, she points out, if language usage is linked with a particular social group that is undervalued, then their intonation, along with other aspects of their language, will be scorned. As Gerstel summarises, 'it's not the rising voice that makes the speaker seem inadequate, it's the expectation that the speaker is inadequate that is reinforced by the rising voice'. It is easy to see how this connection could lead to or encourage the iconisation (Irvine and Gal, 2000) of uptalk as a representation of inadequacy.

In Australia, linguist Jean Mulder is cited in the *Herald Sun* (Bruce, 2007) as claiming that uptalk was a passing trend, 'just a teen phenomenon'. A number of other press items comment on change in the use and incidence of uptalk, but without reference to expert opinion. In a series of articles over a ten-year period, Rob Kyff notes the spread of uptalk as the 'worst linguistic trend' of the year 1994 (Kyff, 1995), then somewhat prematurely celebrates the decline of 'this insidious upward intonation ... popular among teenagers and college students during the early 1990s' (Kyff, 1998), before then regretting its continuing survival: 'the annoying uptalk that infested young women's speech during the *late* 1990s, but which, unfortunately, still lingers' (Kyff, 2004, emphasis added). In the *Irish Times*, Adams (2009) commented that he was noticing uptalk less, and hoped that it was on the way out, this phenomenon 'where sentences end with an upward intonation, so that every utterance sounds like a question posed by an Australian'.

In the *Denver Post* (Briggs, 1994), local psychologist Andrea Van Steenhouse is quoted as saying that before uptalk became 'cool' it indicated a lack of confidence and that it still shows that the speaker is 'passive' or 'intimidated'. It is likely that this change in meaning is in fact a change in perception by non-uptalkers. Stefanie Marsh, writing in *The Times* (Marsh, 2006), also comments on a change in its meaning. Formerly, she says, referring to research by speech coach Diane DiResta (in fact from a media release put out by DiResta's company: DiResta, 2001b), uptalk indicated low self-esteem or self-doubt. By 2006, however, Marsh is able to cite work by Liberman (2005a, 2005b) in order to claim that uptalk allows speakers to establish common ground with their interlocutors. I suspect that the apparent change in usage is more likely a difference in the perspectives of the authorities Marsh cites; a speech coach is her source in the first instance and a linguist in the second. This parallels a tendency in the opinion pieces cited above for the more negatively oriented items to cite speech coaches and the more positively-oriented ones to cite linguists. These two groups of experts clearly have different orientations and expectations.

7.1.2   *Misinformation*

The use of misinformation in justifying a negative view of uptalk and of uptalkers, another aspect of Lippi-Green's (2012) language subordination process, is quite widespread in the media reports in the survey. However, when misinformation is given in a media article it is sometimes difficult to determine whether this is a deliberate act by the writer, a genuine error or perhaps a case of the writer simply not being in a position to know any better. An example might be the description by Daum (2007) of uptalk as questions. This oversimplification contrasts with the results of linguistic research cited in Chapter 3 that points to a positive set of meanings associated with uptalk as a mechanism by which interaction is maintained, an interpretation that is rarely presented in the media. Fergus (1997) identifies three college students he encounters as being from California because 'they all spoke that "upspeak" lingo that involves a rising inflection at the end of each sentence, which makes every remark sound like a whiny question'. Nussbaum (2007) reports meeting three 15-year-old girls from Kansas City who speak 'in a tangle of uptalk' – it is not clear how uptalk results in a tangle. Page (1996) reports a phone interaction with a clerk in Newark, New Jersey, who 'responded in that extremely unreassuring uptalk manner in which every statement sounds like a question'. We saw in Chapter 2 and will see further evidence in Chapter 8 that not every uptalk statement sounds like a question. Somewhat less negatively, another Fergus, writing in Illinois, maintains that uptalk is likely to be heard from a teenage female 'asking for your opinion on what she has just said' (Fergus, 1994).

In his *Globe and Mail* article referred to above, Davis (2002) wishes to focus on the place of uptalk in Canadian English. To do this, he argues that uptalk, as a characteristic of 'Valley Girl Talk', did not really catch on in the United States:

Its tentative, unsure nature never really fit the American psyche. So it moved north in search of different values. And what did it find? It found a culture known for politeness. A place where 'If you have nothing nice to say, say nothing' is printed on restaurant placemats and embroidered on our souls. Here, in Canada, uptalk found a home.

Given the incidence of uptalk in English varieties discussed in Chapter 4, and especially the documentation of its presence in United States English, the view that uptalk found a natural home in Canada because it did not catch on in the United States is misinformed, if not actually misinformation. It seems that there has been some 'erasure' of inconvenient facts of the type mentioned by Irvine and Gal (2000). This contrasts with the writing of other Canadians, who specifically denigrate uptalk as being an American (i.e., US American) mannerism. For instance, Canadian travel writer Taras Grescoe (2002) writes of his encounter with a Canadian who adorned her possessions with maple leaf flags in order not to be thought of as American, but who – to Grescoe's dismay – liberally used uptalk. Grescoe was left thinking that if she indeed did not wish to be considered American then she should 'stop talking like a Valley Girl'.

The social stigmatisation of uptalk is potentially accentuated by misinformation provided (deliberately or otherwise) by Kerwin (1997), who complains about the spread of certain fashions of dress and speech in San Francisco. These fashions include uptalk, which he claims is spreading from the lower classes, a trend that has not been widely claimed for uptalk, as pointed out in Section 6.5. Kerwin concludes by exhorting speakers to 'like, get a language' – the truth is that they already have a language, marginalised though it may be by comments such as this.

Waterhouse (2000), commenting on the spread of uptalk in British English, claims that it 'used to be the exclusive lingua franca of Ulster,

New Zealand and certain parts of the United States, particularly Manhattan. Essentially it is a defensive speech pattern, where the speaker is uncertain how what is being said will be received. You know?' The use in the quoted passage of the technical term 'lingua franca' lends a sense of authority to the piece, but is largely inaccurate, since uptalk is just one feature of language, not a common language in its entirety. In addition, the linking of the UNB rises of Ulster with the uptalk rises of New Zealand and Manhattan together with the omission of other uptalk regions such as Australia, Canada and California is misinformation, which perhaps downplays the relevance of uptalk (by limiting its geographic scope) while also accentuating its threat to British English (by finding it in Ulster).

In what looks very much like another case of misinformation, because it seems to lack any support in the research literature, Howard (2001) complains in *The Times* about the use by young people in Britain of 'mobile phone speak', which he considers to be cognate with uptalk, and which he labels a 'new dialect that is emerging in America'. He explains that to his mind 'mobile phone speak' is the native British variant of uptalk, featuring rising intonation because users of mobile phones are continually needing to check whether they are coming across loud and clear to the person at the other end of the phone. Rather than seeing it as a mode of speaking in its own right, he somewhat oversimplifies by characterising it as 'changing the "intonation contour" at the end of a sentence to a rising tone. This makes any declaratory statement sound like a question.' Howard charts the progress of uptalk from an origin in upper-middle-class female Californian adolescents, across the United States to Canada, spreading much the way fads in slang language do, i.e., simply because teenagers want to sound like other teenagers. Howard states that uptalk may originally have been a 'dialect of insecurity, wimpishness or spanielling to be petted on the part of the speaker', but wonders whether it is now showing deference, or is a means of being 'cool'. Perhaps, he says, uptalk 'echoes the lack of a core of shared knowledge in society. Nobody knows any more whether another person has the faintest idea what one is driving at.'

7.1.3   Trivialisation

A further element of Lippi-Green's (2012) language subordination process that frequently emerges in opinion pieces is the trivialisation of uptalk (and uptalkers), usually through references that are intended to be humorous. For instance, the piece by Davis (2002) referred to above uses a certain amount of trivialising humour in his description of uptalk as though it were a disease. Observing that uptalk is more prevalent among young women but is spreading to older speakers and is found among his professional colleagues, particularly the younger ones, he states that 'adults who never talked that way before have become prime agents of the virus' and that it is 'threatening to infect all of us like some sort of conversational anthrax'.

Tomkins (2004) pokes fun at uptalk while also showing the strength of his feelings, through his suggestion of a system of social credits. His idea is that antisocial behaviour could be limited by issuing people with a limited number of such credits, which can be spent as the user wishes on activities that others would find antisocial. He suggests that while driving a large uneconomical car might cost just one credit in his system, using uptalk would cost 1,000 credits. We should note, however, that just a year later Tomkins (2005) has changed his tune somewhat, stating that uptalk, 'diffident and consensual, is much more polite than the bull-necked and dogmatic speech patterns of old'.

Humour is also used to denigrate uptalk by Daum (2007), who complains that it was once used exclusively by 'actual Valley Girls (and anyone who worked at a tanning salon)', before noting that it is now 'infiltrating a host of unlikely venues', such as Ivy League campuses and workplace conference rooms.

Uptalk is also trivialised when we see it featuring on people's lists of most irritating things, as in Jill Thielmann's 'Top 10 irritating things people do' in the *Edmonton Journal* in Canada (Thielmann, 2005), where it is attributed to California, and seen as part of a style of speaking: 'Valley Girl Upspeak … like, like, totally, like, like, ya know?'

To an extent, the frequent association of uptalk in British English with the influence of Australian soap operas also trivialises uptalk and downplays its potential significance. As pointed out by Chambers (1998), it is also unlikely to be the complete story. It was noted in Chapter 5 that Bradford (1996, 1997) similarly concluded that it was improbable that soap operas alone could account for the spread of uptalk. In a chapter that aims to debunk the myth that television has a major influence on the way in which we speak, using a range of examples, Chambers emphasises in particular the global nature of the spread of uptalk, and points out that 'the one social context where uptalk is almost never heard is in broadcast language' and that 'it is also not a regular, natural (unselfconscious) feature of any character's speech in sitcoms, soap operas, serials or interview shows anywhere in the world. Undoubtedly it soon will be, but that will only happen when television catches up with language change. Not vice versa' (Chambers, 1998: 127–128).

Nevertheless, British speakers in the 20s–30s age range are criticised for their speech habits by Koch (2012), who comments on a range of features and notes that '[e]ven inflection is changing. Misspent childhoods watching antipodean soaps such as Neighbours and Home and Away have given twenty and thirty something Brits a speech habit in which their voice rises at the end of a sentence.' Mark Lawson (1998) had earlier made similar attributions in *The Guardian*. While admitting that there was an alternative linguistic theory that uptalk is a sign that 'a fretful generation is seeking validation and reassurance with everything they say', Lawson prefers the soap opera explanation. The same soap-opera source for uptalk in British English is given by Bathurst (1996), it is blamed for 'Slop English' by Norman (2001), and it is also apparently in the mind of Mesner (2001) when he criticises electrical retailer Currys for using a new slogan 'Currys ... no worries'. Mesner suggests that the company might have been better advised to avoid the Australian phrase ('no worries'), asks whether we should 'assume all Currys customers are hooked on teatime soaps and Australian questioning intonation', and questions the claim of Currys' marketing director that the slogan was intended 'to create more confidence and enhance our reputation'. For a general overview of the influence of *Neighbours* on British culture, see also Henning (1996).

The *Daily Mail's* Jill Parkin variously describes uptalk as showing that you want someone else to make up your mind for you (Parkin, 2005), and as being an infuriating singsong (Parkin, 2006), while she has more recently stated that when a service provider calls, 'I actually tell them I don't understand them. They speak a rapid sing-song, high-pitched and going up at the end of each sentence' (Parkin, 2008). This, and her wish that she could live in uptalk-free Cranford (in reference to a television series set in the 1840s and based on novels of Elizabeth Gaskell), clearly pokes fun at uptalk(ers).

Lusher (2010) sees an almost self-deprecating new ironic use of uptalk, as he reports in *The Guardian*. Whereas once it was, he writes, a 'tedious habit of speaking in a rising cadence, with, like, an especially perky uplift in tone at the end', there has since been an increase in its deliberate and humorous use 'to deflate any awkward sentiment accompanying the words, a sort of preemptive apology'.

7.1.4   (Non-)conformity

One of the oppositions in Lippi-Green's (2012) language subordination process is that those speakers who conform with mainstream use are held up as positive examples, while non-conformers are vilified or marginalised. Each finds an example in Canadian politics. In the Toronto *Globe and Mail*, Cernetig (1997) writes of how Canadian politician Preston Manning 'used to be prone to the rising inflection known as upspeak' but is according to an aide 'a much better speaker now, much more statesmanlike'. Later, a Canadian government minister's communications director in her mid-20s is berated for partaking of the 'primarily youthful practice in which one's voice rises to make a sentence sound, oh so annoyingly, like a question' (Feschuk, 2009). In Lippi-Green's terms, conformity has produced a better speaker in Manning, but the non-conformist use of uptalk by the communications director is evaluated negatively, and elsewhere in the article it is pointed out that she has lost her job, although it must be said that this is not only or even primarily because of her uptalk.

It is also frequently to be found that non-conformity, through uptalking, will result in doors being closed. On Canadian television, voice instructor Michael Connolly notes in an interview that 'if your voice suddenly goes up two notches, you've lost your own sense of power' (Edenson, 1996). Indeed, teenagers, stereotypical users of uptalk, have themselves spoken out against it. An Irish teenager writing in a teen's column in the *Irish Times* (Behan, 2005) deplored the use of uptalk, saying that 'it completely perverts our natural accent' by making 'questions out of sentences that really shouldn't have been questions in the first place'. This despite the fact that Irish English, particularly but not exclusively in the north, makes extensive use of rising intonation – not just uptalk – on statements (see also Sections 2.1 and 4.8, and the response to Behan by McNally, 2005). It is interesting that young people interviewed in the media are often cited as being aware of the possible negative impact of uptalk, i.e., of the fact that uptalk as an instance of non-conformity presents a negative image and can result in lost opportunities for advancement (Lippi-Green, 2012). On the east coast of the United States, another teenager was cited by Cave (1994) as acknowledging that uptalk does not make the speaker sound very intelligent. In Utah, a commentator who is herself a former ESOL teacher, noted that the use of uptalk by Californian Valley Girls meant that '[e]very conversation with them sounds like a game of 20 questions with no answers' (Fisher, 1997). In *The Ottawa Citizen*, Mason (2007) complains of younger speakers – tweens (10–12-year-olds) – who 'are incessantly perky and energetic. They giggle constantly and talk in upspeak, an assault on English diction that makes every factual sentence sound like a question.'

White (1995) quotes her expert, speech coach Dennis Becker, as saying that after their late 20s, speakers should avoid uptalk, since in work situations 'if you end your sentences in uptalk, you're saying that you're not sure what you're doing, that you have doubts about whether you're qualified to do the job'. This also presents an example of a message that non-conformity in language use can result in doors being closed, the implication being that using uptalk can make someone unsuitable for employment.

7.1.5 *Vilification*

There are many examples in the opinion pieces of strong condemnation of uptalk and the vilification of uptalkers. In an early piece in the sample, Jim Gorman, a science writer for *The New York Times* and a journalism lecturer at New York University, noted how contagious uptalk was, noticing it entering his own speech patterns, where he judges it 'to mark a character flaw' (Gorman, 1993a). Other items written around the same time take a similarly negative stance towards uptalk and uptalkers. An editorial item in the *Orange County Register* in California (*Orange County Register*, 1993) not only makes a suggestion about the origins of the 'irritating cadences' of uptalk, but in an extreme form of vilification of language users it also attributes criminal characteristics to its speakers: 'It's, like, we have a theory? That it all started in the South? You know, where they try to sound so gracious? Even when they're knifing you between the shoulder blades? Even when they're being totally demagogical?' At the same time, of course, the rapid repetition of these question marks indicating rising intonation adds to the supposed humour of the piece, i.e., they provide an example of how such forms of language are trivialised. The Massachusetts *Telegram and Gazette* cites dialect coach Bill Wadsworth, who points out that when speakers constantly uptalk 'they actually sound vacuous' (Anthony, 1993). In *The Commercial Appeal* from Tennessee, Kevin Cowherd writes that if he were given the opportunity to talk with the young people who use uptalk, then he would point out that it makes the sound 'kind of ... dumb' (Cowherd, 1995).

In Australia, an opinion piece in the *Sydney Morning Herald* (Deane, 2001) lists a number of features of language, including uptalk, which, it is claimed, is 'particularly popular among younger rural folk and guaranteed to make them sound like yokels'. In a more extensive 'opinion piece', Australian Don Watson, who was a speechwriter for former Australian prime minister Paul Keating, links uptalk to the decay of language and describes it as a 'fiendish contrivance' and suggests that there 'is a theory that the tendency developed among baby boomers when they lost God and took to marijuana and sociology' (Watson, 2003: 157–158).

Despite the rich array of negative views expressed in the media items cited above, we have seen that not all opinion pieces are condemnatory. In a more balanced item in the *Guardian*, Seaton (2001) considers a range of issues concerning uptalk, including its spread and its possible origins (focusing on California and Australasia, but also suggesting a possible Irish influence). On its meaning, he states 'uptalk is close to the spirit of postmodernism, concerned with advancing relativistic, provisional statements – in contrast with the classic discourse of modernism, pronouncing absolute truths'. In Canada, McGillivray (1994) had earlier commented that uptalk is 'non-confrontational and so more suitable to the gentler, less-aggressive 1990s than the "in- your-face" lingo of the 1980s'. There is similarly something positive to be taken from Dunn's (1999) profile of a group of teenage Connecticut girls. Dunn comments that they have a 'fear of offending' that 'extends to their speech, which has a noncommittal, nonconfrontational, questioning intonation'.

A 2011 blog entry on a Canadian site (VoicetowordBlog, 2011) acknowledges that '[t]here is nothing wrong with uptalk and it tends to sound friendly and casual'. But the item also sounds a warning that resonates with the language ideology frameworks, particularly with the idea that certain usages will mean that no one will take you seriously: 'if you want to sound professional, it can work against you. The constant upward intonation makes it sound like you are seeking approval and that you are not quite sure if what you are saying is okay.'

7.2 Letters

The collection of letters included in the media sample is probably an underestimation of the amount of correspondence on this topic. Not all letters are published, and not all newspapers and magazines are included in web- and library-based search engines.

Of the 21 letters in the sample, more than half are negative, and their comments often contain trivialisation of or misinformation about uptalk, thus fitting the patterns of marginalisation noted in Lippi-Green's language subordination model. For instance, Calo (1993), writing to the *New York Times*, observes that uptalk is used to avoid offending, and asks if it should be referred to as 'sheeptalk'. Letter-writers frequently use the same arguments as were noted above in opinion pieces. The misrepresentation of uptalk as questions is perpetuated by an online dater (White, 2007), who writes that the next step after making contact online, the first phone call, can be a turn-off if the date uses the 'dreaded upspeak' to end each statement with a question. In the United Kingdom, a correspondent complains in the *Sunday Times* (Robinson, 2010) about the 'Australian question intonation', which she also refers to as 'the moronic interrogative', and asks what can be done to teach young people to talk properly. A writer to *The Times* (Room, 2002) bemoans the use of quotative 'like', which he believes shows uncertainty and which he therefore links to the use of uptalk among 'young, unconfident speakers'.

Many of the letters contain heavy negative rhetoric and imagery. In the Toronto *Globe and Mail*, a correspondent praises a columnist's standard of English and bemoans the fact that 'the English language is under siege from the inarticulate masses' whose speech habits include uptalk (Hawkins, 2004). Four years later, another writer to the same newspaper celebrates the fact that this 'annoying habit' is becoming less common, while complaining about the rise of a new rhetorical question form 'How ... is that?' as in 'How annoying is that?' (Kotyk, 2008). Also in the *Globe and Mail*, a correspondent (Sucharov, 2002) applauds a columnist referred to earlier in this chapter (Davis, 2002) for exposing what he sees as the 'national linguistic scourge' of uptalk.

Experts are sometimes disparaged. In New Zealand, a letter to the Christchurch *Press* (McKerras, 2010) refers to earlier articles in the same newspaper by linguist Elizabeth Gordon (2010) and commentator Joe Bennett (2010) who use the terms 'high rising terminal' and 'imbecilic interrogative' respectively, and asks 'Whom do we believe? Surely Gordon is joking? Who speaks like that?'

In addition to these negative views, there is a surprising amount of positive commentary in the letters, with some interesting additional information being provided by correspondents in response to articles from journalists. One correspondent (Parr, 1995) recalls hearing uptalk-like intonation being used some 50 years earlier with the Canadian tag *eh* (see also Section 5.4), and notes that this undermines journalist Robert Fulford's (1995) idea that uptalk originated in the context of phone answering machines. Responding to Matt Seaton's (2001) article in the *Guardian*, one correspondent (Kill, 2001) makes an interesting claim of having first encountered uptalk in an army barracks in Exeter, where it was used by the toughest of young men who would not have been bothered about whether they were getting agreement, nor would they have experienced television soaps, since this was in 1959. Another (Pearson, 2001) responds that 'talking-up' has existed in Bristol for at least 70 years as a polite check that the listener is still following and not being upset. See Section 4.7.1 for discussion of uptalk in the English West Country.

A letter to *The Times* charts the progress of uptalk from Australian soaps, through call centres and customer service desks (Miskin, 2008). The correspondent sees that its spread through these channels is related to its non-threatening means of eliciting a response to a statement, 'to gauge whether the speaker is being understood'. He points out that while it was originally used by young female speakers, it is no longer restricted in this way, and that some of his own contemporaries, in their 60s, use it.

Finally, a small collection of letters in a *Times* question and answer item (*Times* Q&A, 2002) reveals a number of interesting purported facts. As well as Tom Cunliffe's comments that uptalk came via Australian soaps and is used by teenage girls faced with otherwise being ignored by young men, we find David Malaperiman claiming that it started in the United States in the 1950s, and Susan Persaud noting that 'Belfastmen and Bristolians have been speaking like this for ages?' Aran Wood links uptalk to lack of confidence in the under 30s, and contrasts its presence in responses to a moral question with its absence when the speaker is recounting their weekends (contrast the opposite pattern found in linguistic work discussed in Chapter 3). Wood also sees parents inheriting uptalk from their children. Finally, John Scrivens reports receiving a sports equipment catalogue accompanied by the message 'We also do mail order?', showing that uptalk is influencing the written form of sentences (see also SQMs mentioned in Chapter 5).

7.3   Advice columns

Seventeen items in the sample can be classified as advice columns. They all take a negative stance towards uptalk. To these 17 we can add several other items mentioned in the section on opinions, since many of these quoted public speaking coaches or guides to business communication, and similarly urged speakers to avoid uptalk. In addition, there are articles in business-related journals that carry similar advice. In an item outside the time frame of the original media survey, Grant and Taylor (2014: 82) recommend that female executives should '[a]void uptalk because the higher tone of voice at the end of sentences produces tension in the body. An even tone that allows the voice to drop keeps the body and voice relaxed.' While it is the case that higher pitch is associated with greater vocal cord tension, and that this most likely involves muscles both in and around the larynx, the suggestion that this is linked to more general body tension is another example of misinformation.

The language ideological features (Lippi-Green, 2012) in most of the advice columns are that using uptalk means that no one important will take you seriously (and conversely, avoiding it will help to open doors to employment and other opportunities) and that using uptalk marks you out as stupid, ignorant or deviant. A feature article in *Redbook* magazine, published in New York, warns against excessive use of uptalk as it can make you 'start to sound like a ditz' (*Redbook*, 2007). In Toronto, a *Globe and Mail* writer warns young workers that if they want older colleagues to take them seriously then they have to avoid youthful jargon and the 'aggravating habit of inflecting up at the end of sentences' (Gray, 2007).

Advice columns also frequently cite experts, and this use of authority also contributes to the subordination of uptalk. One the biggest pet peeves of communications expert Betty Cooper is 'the Canadian habit of putting a rising inflection at the end of each sentence as if each thought was a question'. It makes each thought seem incomplete and allows the listener to take control, an undesired outcome for a public speaker (Stevenson, 1995). Her views are shared by Barbara Tannenbaum (Rau, 1996), Nancy Austin (Zielinski, 1998) and many other experts on public speaking and business presentation skills.

A frequently heard expert is Diane DiResta. She states that uptalk 'renders the speaker weak, tentative, lacking conviction and authority' (DiResta, 2001a), and that anyone using uptalk when asking for a salary increase will not get one. Similarly, sales staff using uptalk are unlikely to make a sale (DiResta, 2001b). In a success guide for business women, DiResta (2010) talks about ten ways in which she believes that women in business weaken their image. The second is the use of uptalk (the first is too much head-nodding), and DiResta states that uptalk is 'tentative' and 'a real credibility killer. Women will not be taken seriously with this vocal pattern.' Her prescription is that 'American intonation patterns use a downward inflection to declare or demand and a rising inflection to question or indicate uncertainty'. We have seen in Section 2.1 that the falling versus rising division is not generally true for English declaratives versus interrogatives, so while DiResta presents herself as an expert, she is not providing the complete picture. She does however concede that this generalisation is not true for all cultures: 'In Canada, India, Pakistan, France and China it is more commonplace to hear the voice rise at the end of a sentence.' Explicitly listing countries where – it is claimed – the voice typically rises at the end of a sentence suggests again some expert knowledge, but it is not clear what the evidence is that supports this grouping, nor which languages are involved of the many spoken in those countries.

Similar sentiments are expressed in guide books for professional speaking. Thus Guffey (2006: 4) identifies uptalk as an unprofessional speech habit, comparable to 'using *like* to fill in mindless chatter, substituting *go* for *said*, relying on slang, or letting profanity slip into your conversation'. Guffey and Almonte (2009: 297) observe an increase in uptalk in the workplace, with the negative consequence that speakers seem weak and their messages lack authority. 'If you want to sound confident and competent, avoid uptalk.' Hustad (2008) points out that a 'successful self-deprecating remark also has a particular inflection – it ends with a falling intonation (not the "uptalk" that suggests a question, or implies you have no idea what you're talking about)'.

In a guide for graduates new to the job market, Graham and Reidy (2009: 109) claim that speaking in uptalk will diminish credibility: 'If you listen to any executive or well-known person', they write, 'you don't hear qualifiers, uptalk, or clichés.' They continue to claim that 'uptalk ... implies youthfulness, insecurity, and uncertainty. Using uptalk can make you come across as unprofessional and longing for acceptance' (Graham and Reidy, 2009: 110). In conclusion, their advice is 'ask your friends and family to tell you if they catch you using uptalk. Work to realign your speech to be affirmative, to say sentences with strength, and to portray yourself as able and confident. Who knows, maybe you'll even get the job you're after!' (Graham and Reidy, 2009: 111). A similar sentiment is expressed in the *Chicago Tribune* by Kapos (2004), who reflects the emphasis put by business communications expert Barbara Pachter on performance in interviews, where uptalk should be avoided because it 'shows you are uncomfortable and it takes away from your credibility'.

Under the heading 'Maturity', a guide to how to file for divorce mentions that uptalk is something to avoid during negotiation, stating that 'upspeak is passive, as though the speaker is looking for validation. Practice speaking assertively by dropping your voice before you enter any negotiation' (DeSimone and Haman, 2005: 84).

In *Seventeen*, Annemarie Conte urges young women not to use uptalk with their boyfriends because 'it will seem like you're asking for permission (which you're not)' (Conte, 2007).

Outside of the survey sample period, and writing in a blog published by the Bernard L. Schwartz Communication Institute based at the City University of New York, a blogger (Young, 2014) notes that she feels obliged to tell her students that when they use uptalk (a trend 'so common that it often goes unnoticed, particularly among millennials') they make statements sound like questions and that they sound like they are asking their audience whether what they are saying is correct, whereas in fact 'they have done the research and therefore they are the experts'. The blogger is reacting in a way that the language subordination process discussed earlier would predict – if the speakers want to be taken to be experts then they need to avoid the negatively stereotyped speech habits.

On the other hand, a recent blog entry by a biology professor (terHorst, 2014), while opening with the observation that when students give practice conference presentations they are advised not to use uptalk, proceeds then to provide a more considered reaction, and comes to a different conclusion. One female student pointed out to terHorst the relationships between ways of speaking and power dynamics. To his credit, terHorst followed up by considering some of the literature on the uses and meanings of uptalk. He concludes that '[i]nstead of telling female grad students to use less upspeak, maybe we should be telling the male grad students to use it more. If we're really serious about increasing the number of women in science, it should be less about telling women "you need to do this", and more about changing the system into one that's less dominated by male values.'

Finally, note that when a linguist (Liberman, 2008a) was asked for advice from the concerned parent of an uptalking psychology PhD student, his advice was quite different from that of DiResta et al. Citing analyses of uptalk and proposals concerning its origins, he hopes that looking at the evidence for how uptalk is actually used 'will help you to make linguistic peace with your uptalking daughter and her professional friends'. That is, his advice is to use authoritative sources appropriately, rather than selectively.

7.4   Profiles

In contrast to opinions, letters, and advice columns, very few of the 17 personal profiles that mention uptalk portray it in an explicitly negative light. Instead, the mention of uptalk, which is generally just one of many characteristics being explored in such items, tends to be neutral and non-judgemental. Even the negative comments are rather oblique, such as in this description of designer

Clodagh (McQuillan, 2004): 'Apart from occasional "uptalk" intonation, she's a beguiling storyteller with a keen sense of humour.'

A frequent effect (intended or not) of mentioning uptalk in many of the profiles is to endear the profiled person to the reader. Yet this continues to belittle uptalk, providing further examples of what Lippi-Green referred to as trivialising non-mainstream language, 'Look how cute, how homey, how funny' (Lippi-Green, 2012: 70). Canadian Major Meagen McGrath, climber of the world's highest peaks, and competitor in the 243km, seven-day Marathon des Sables across the Sahara, has a 'curiously girlish tendency to uptalk everything into dangling questions' (Beun, 2009). Film director Sofia Coppola has 'gentle, lilting tendency to uptalk and a semi-articulacy, like a super-intelligent version of Valley-Girl speak' (Bradshaw, 2010). Cancer researcher Franziska Michor uses 'a rising stress – an echo of American uptalk – that emphasizes … her youth, her blond beauty, her occasional awkwardness, and her supreme confidence' (Junod, 2007). Canadian model Meaghan Waller 'speaks in a quiet, wispy voice peppered with uptalk' (Kopun, 2009). As a child, Irish singer-songwriter Sharon Murphy was sent to a school for orphaned or abandoned children. The presence in her speech of uptalk, 'the mark of today's youth-speak in Ireland, was actually the strongest indication that Murphy had survived' (McCarthy, 2001).

A few items in this group also note the absence of uptalk. For example, a profile of actor Jessica Beal notes that she seems older than she actually is, and suggests that one reason for this is that she does not use uptalk (Jacobs, 2005).

Almost all the profiles in the sample are about women. This may reflect a greater proportion of profiles of women than of men more generally, but is likely to at least in part reflect the stronger association of uptalk with female than with male speech.

7.5   Reviews

Uptalk and related terms get a number of mentions in reviews, not only where it would be expected, in the context of the spoken media (television, film and theatre reviews), but also in connection with the written word (book and poetry reviews). Of the 32 mentions in reviews in our sample, discussion of uptalk is central only to one. Nine of the 32 take an overtly negative view of uptalk.

One review of a new television news show hosted by Connie Chung notes that she vowed in the first show that she would not speak in uptalk like a Valley girl, to which the reviewer retorts 'Gee, why bring that up? Has uptalking been a problem lately on cable news? I hadn't noticed' (Buckman, 2002; see also Johnson, 2002). Most of the television reviews that mention uptalk, however, confirm the stereotypes of its origin and use. A review of television movie *Quarantine* mentions 'bratty teenage daughters who chatter on in an insufferable upspeak about how their busy parents don't make time for them' (McDonough, 2000). In a review of a documentary about then editor of *Marie Claire*, Joanna Coles, uptalk is associated with 'well-groomed women and camp men' (Wollaston, 2009). When the spoof fly-on-the-wall television series *The Office* first screened on British television, one critic commented on how Ricky Gervais' character David Brent, the boss who wants to be matey, 'ends his sentences with an upspeak "yeah" or "all right"' (Freedland, 2002; see also Section 3.4). American reality series *Making the Band* is summarised as 'a bizarre look at male socialization in a world where everyone talks locker-room upspeak' (Thomas, 2000). An Australian origin of uptalk is claimed in a review of an episode of arts programme *Arena* in which British model Lily Cole comments on her portrait by Rolf Harris, 'doing that uptalk thing which, like Rolf, came from Australia' (Mullaney, 2010). A review of television series *Simple Life 2* (Heffernan, 2004) comments on actress Nicole Richie's use of questioning intonation (referred to as 'upspeak'), and makes the standard link to 'insecurity in young women'. In this case, however, these really are questions. The absence of the 'insufferable uptalk of most teen series' from the series *Undeclared* is highlighted to point out how the series does not pigeonhole characters into obvious stereotypes (McDonough, 2001).

Similar stereotypes feature in film reviews. Gwyneth Paltrow in the movie *Proof* uses 'hipsterish high rising terminals' (Smith, 2006). A review of the 2005 movie version of *The Hitchhiker's Guide to the Galaxy* comments that when the original radio series appeared in 1978, character Zaphod Beeblebrox's mid-Atlantic accent 'seemed hilariously pretentious. Now, sadly, our daughters all upspeak (like this?)' (Clarke, 2005).

In a book review, a comment made about Carrie Snyder (in connection with her short story collection *Hair Hat*) is that she rarely uses question marks since she 'has such an allergy to the interrogative even her teenagers fail to upspeak' (Andrew, 2004).

7.6   Popular culture

Given its spread and the attention it has received in media commentary, it is not surprising that uptalk has also infiltrated popular culture. In a 2006 episode of *Family Guy*, entitled 'Whistle While Your Wife Works', the character Stewie comments how Brian's somewhat idiotic girlfriend talks 'like ↗this. You know, where everything has a ↗question mark at the end of it. With an upward ↗inflection.' In *Room 101*, where celebrities get a chance to banish their pet peeves to the room of that name, comedian Stephen Fry condemns uptalk, referring to it as Australian Question Intonation, and 'the language of the Sunny Delight generation', although he does concede that it is not simply an indicator of lack of confidence, and that it is not a feature solely of Australian speech (Fry, 2001). *Grumpy Old Men* is a British television series narrated by actor Geoffrey Palmer in which the 'old men' (British celebrities in the 35–54 age bracket) talk about things that they find highly annoying. The first episode, broadcast on 10 October 2003, included uptalk (Palmer, 2003). Comedian Harry Hill's CD *Funny Times* includes a track called 'I Wish My Brother in Law's Voice Didn't Go Up at the End of Every Sentence' (album reviewed by Price, 2010).

Cruttenden (1995) cites examples of fiction that make reference to high-rising intonation. He mentions Dick Francis' *The Edge* (Francis, 1988) set in Canada and David Lodge's *Paradise News* (Lodge, 1991) set in Hawaii, to which we can add John Updike's *Marry Me* (Updike, 1976), set in Connecticut but featuring a speaker originally from Seattle.

As the melody of speech, intonation is often linked to music. This connection is made by at least two musical artists. In 1995, the British composer Michael Nyman (well-known for composing film scores for Peter Greenaway films such as *The Draughtsman's Contract*, as well as for the film *The Piano*) wrote a piece called *HRT* for the Relâche Ensemble in the United States, having noticed 'how Australians especially – and some Americans – when they get to the end of a sentence, their inflection and intonation rises, so that every sentence turns into a question' (as quoted in a preview by Wilson, 1995). The composer's intention 'was to write a piece in sentence form, with each sentence ending with a little rising, melodic tag'. Jazz musician Brian Lynch has a track on the album *Conclave Vol 2* called 'The Downside Of Upspeak'. The sleeve notes (Hogan, 2010) include the following explanation:

The Downside of Upspeak alludes to a recent trend in the modern vernacular that finds many youth ending their spoken phrases with a rise in pitch. Adding to the tune's derivation, Brian simply says, 'You really know when you're getting older when certain things about contemporary culture irritate you as opposed to becoming something you identify with.'

7.7   Summary

The clear impression of uptalk that arises from commentary in the media is a negative one. The complaint tradition (Milroy and Milroy, 1999) is alive and well when it comes to this form of intonation. As is typical of linguistic complaints, particular groups (the young, particularly females) are 'blamed' for the introduction of uptalk. As is also typical, a perceived decline in linguistic standards is frequently associated with a decline in other aspects of behaviour. The complaints are revealing – they show that the incidence of uptalk has led to a level of awareness that means that it can no longer be ignored. Importantly, the complaints are for the most part readily interpretable in terms of the discussion in earlier chapters of the meanings of intonation and in particular in terms of the different layers of such meaning, and of how different speaker and listener groups will ascribe different significances to meanings on these different layers. For the most part, the writers of opinion pieces and of letters to the editor are members of the 'out-group' as far as uptalk is concerned, and naturally have a different interpretation from that of the uptalkers themselves. This is reflected in the fact that many of the media pieces lend themselves to analysis in terms of language ideology models such as Lippi-Green's (2012) language subordination process. We have seen in particular that authorities are cited to support the negative views of uptalk, and that a certain amount of misinformation is propagated or that some sort of erasure (Irvine and Gal, 2000) of inconvenient truths is carried out. Uptalk and uptalkers are frequently trivialised, but also marginalised and warned that they will not be taken seriously. On the other hand, non-uptalkers are praised as positive examples of language users, and the avoidance of uptalk presented as part of a pathway to success.

8   Perception studies of uptalk

With respect to uptalk, Cruttenden (1997: 129) pointed out that just 'a small amount ... can mark out the speaker very noticeably for the listener'. In this chapter we consider studies that have focused on the perception of uptalk, and on how uptalk is noticed and interpreted by the listener. With regard to the interpretation of uptalk, House (2006: 1555) noted that the high boundary tone (H%) is tantamount to an instruction to the listener to interpret the phrase ending in that tone as part of a larger structure. As a consequence, that phrase remains 'open-ended', indicating a wider context, and so the listener needs to work out what that wider context could be and what, therefore, the speaker's intentions were in using that particular intonation contour. Using the framework of Relevance Theory, House proposes that the listener will select the first interpretation that is sufficiently relevant. Since relevance depends on the context of use, including the prior experience of the listener, uptalk may be ambiguous, interpreted by some listeners as conveying the affective functions of high pitch, such as deference or powerlessness, by others as having a linguistic function such as the indication of a question, and by a further group as being used interactively and collaboratively to maintain involvement of both parties to the conversation.

Three aspects of the perception of uptalk will be considered in the chapter. The first involves the question of whether listeners can distinguish between statement rises (uptalk) and question rises. We have seen in Chapter 2 that a number of studies have found differences between the two types of sentences in some of the phonetic parameters of the rises. The second aspect concerns the interpretation of and attitudes towards uptalk. The third considers other speaker- and listener-related factors that have been claimed to influence the interpretation of uptalk.

8.1   Perception of high-rise forms

Anecdotally, Benton (1966: 71–72), in his study of the New Zealand English of Māori school children, notes that 'confusions related to question intonations were frequently encountered'. Specifically, utterances with declarative word order intended by him as questions were interpreted by the children as statements. Benton presents *He'll be coming tomorrow?* as an example of ambiguity in the perception of high-rise forms. This utterance was intended as a question but interpreted as a statement. The likelihood of such a misunderstanding is probably not very high. For Australian English, McGregor and Palethorpe (2008: 173) have claimed that while uptalk utterances are 'generally not perceptively different from yes/no and declarative question rises', there is very little confusion between these utterance types because cues from the utterance context generally make the speaker's intention clear.

In Chapter 2, we learned of a number of claims to the effect that there are differences in the forms of question and statement rises. A number of studies have addressed experimentally the basic question of whether questions and statements can be reliably identified on the basis of these different rise shapes. Most of these have asked participants to listen to utterances that could be either statements or intonation-only questions and to decide which they were. Such tasks are problematic, in that there can be considerable variation in participants' interpretations of what is meant by 'question' (or 'statement', though possibly less so in this case). Šafářová (2006) usefully problematises this notion of what is a question. She found wide disagreement among informants concerning which of a large selection of utterances from a corpus of free conversation should be labelled as questions. Twenty-six participants assessed transcriptions of a total sample of 875 utterances from three speakers. Of these transcribed utterances, 218 were identified as a 'question' by at least one participant and only six by all participants. More than 60 per cent of the utterances categorised as questions were labelled as such by only five or fewer judges. Not surprisingly, the presence of subject–verb inversion and the use of a wh-word were the most important features determining the 'question' response. Recall that Šafářová's participants were judging written versions of the utterances and had no access to the intonation patterns that would have been produced with the utterances (although they may have 'heard' intonation contours while reading the utterances to themselves, via implicit prosody – see Fodor, 2002). Nevertheless, such high levels of disagreement about what constitutes a 'question' are potentially problematic, since 'in categorization tasks designed to investigate the interpretation of contours, it cannot be taken for granted that subjects employ the same definition of the term "question"' (Šafářová, 2006: 57).

An early study of the interpretation of intonation contours was carried out by Uldall (1961). American English listeners gave ratings on a number of semantic and attitudinal scales to a synthesised version of the utterance *He'll be here on Friday*, with a range of different synthetic intonation contours. Unsurprisingly, scores on a seven-point scale ranging between 'very strongly indicating a question' to 'very strongly indicating a statement' showed that versions synthesised with rises were preferentially identified as questions, and those with falls as statements. However, responses to four falling-rising contours synthesised by Uldall depended on the extent of the final rise. Uldall's schematic drawings of the fall-rise contours suggest that the size of the fall and the point at which the rise started were held constant (though the schematics do not make it clear where this point was relative to the content of the utterance), but the size of the rise component differed. At one extreme it went back to the top pitch level, and at the other extreme it was a low-rise. The other two forms had rises at intermediate stages between these two. The fall-rise with the highest rise component was unambiguously scored as a question, those with the two smallest rises were most likely to be interpreted as statements, and the remaining fall-rise with a rise to a fairly high pitch was ambiguously labelled sometimes as a question and sometimes as a statement. While there is insufficient detail in her study to determine the most appropriate intonational analyses of Uldall's materials, the rise components of the unambiguous question and statement forms seem likely to correspond to the question and statement rises much more recently suggested by Ritchart and Arvaniti (2014) for Southern Californian English, i.e., L* H-H% and L* L-H%, respectively.

In an Australian English study, Fletcher and Loakes (2010) asked participants to listen to a series of stimuli with rises that varied in terms of pitch level and range, and to indicate for each one whether it was a statement or a question. They found significant effects of the pitch levels both of the onset and of the endpoint of the rise. Most statement-like were contours where the rise onset was at a low level and had a narrow range for the rise component, i.e., contours that were most like L* L-H%. Participants were most confident of their 'question' answers for H* H-H% and of their 'statement' answers for L* L-H%, with L* H-H% in-between. For American English, in contrast, Levis (1999: 41) refers to claims based on his thesis (Levis, 1996) that 'listeners do not distinguish changes in meaning between high-rising contours that begin at a high pitch and those that begin at a relatively low pitch' (i.e., H* H-H% and L* H-H%).

In her thesis referred to above, rather than labelling them as 'questions', Šafářová (2006) asked participants to consider whether utterances expected an 'evaluative response', i.e., 'the speaker stops talking and expects that the addressee will confirm or negate what has just been said'. She found that participants were most likely to label declarative utterances as being of this type if they had contours that were non-falling and that had a boundary tone higher than the pitch accent, i.e., L* L-H%, L* H-H% and H* H-H%. She also found that none of these contours were interpreted as indicating continuation.

A small-scale identification task was carried out by Zwartz and Warren (2003), using manipulated intonation contours on the utterance *He'll be at the*

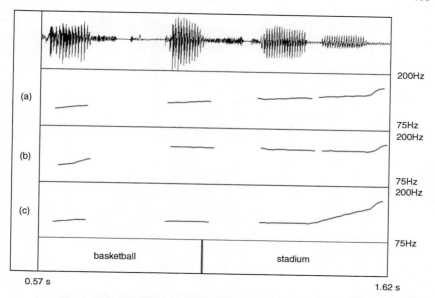

Figure 8.1 Waveform and example pitch tracks from materials used by Zwartz and Warren (2003).

basketball stadium (see also Warren, 2005b). The re-synthesised stimuli were based on two original utterances, one produced by a young male and one by a young female speaker of New Zealand English. The utterances had a nuclear accent on the first syllable of *basketball*. The contours selected for the utterance were based on other studies of production data which had indicated an earlier starting point in New Zealand English for the rise in uptalk statements than in questions, as noted in Chapter 2, as well as earlier rises for male speakers than for female speakers (Warren, 2005b; Warren and Daly, 2005). In addition to altering the starting point of the rise, so that it ranged from being on the accented syllable to being on the final syllable of the utterance, Zwartz and Warren (2003) also manipulated the shape of the rise, so that F0 either rose on a straight line to a high point at the end if the utterance (creating a set of gradient rises), or it rose sharply to a high point that was maintained to the end of the utterance (creating a series of rise-plateau contours). Examples of three of the manipulated contours are given in Figure 8.1, where (a) shows the pitch track from a gradient stimulus with the rise starting on the accented syllable, (b) shows a rise to a plateau from the accented syllable, and (c) shows a rise on the final syllable of the phrase. The results of a forced choice task indicated that the stimuli with earlier rises were more likely to be reported as questions and those with later rises as statements, reflecting the observations from the

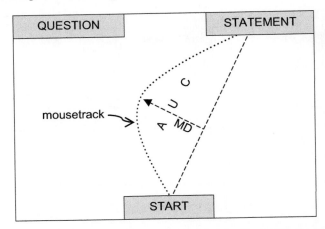

Figure 8.2 Screen layout for mousetracking study, showing measures taken from the task.

production studies, but also that the rise-plateau contours were more likely to be reported as questions than gradient rises with the same rise starting point. This suggests that it is the overall amount of high F0 material that influences whether the utterance is perceived as a question or as a statement. Or conversely, that a contour with a dramatic late rise is most likely to be interpreted as an uptalk statement. There were no significant differences in the response patterns to the male and female utterances in this study.

In a more recent study (Warren, 2014a), it was similarly found that early-aligned rises resulted in a higher level of question responses in a forced-choice task (80.6 per cent versus 68.4 per cent for late-aligned rises). An example stimulus sentence is given in (17). The early-aligned rise started on the accented syllable of *animals*, and the late-aligned rise started on the final unaccented syllable.

(17)   John's mother cared for stray animals

In this case the task was a timed task and an additional finding was that question responses were faster for early-aligned rises. The task involved moving the mouse from a starting point in order to click on a question or statement response box. By allowing the tracking of the movement of the mouse, this task provides a more qualitative analysis of the response than a simple yes/no choice.

Figure 8.2 gives an indication of the layout for the task, and overlaid on that is an example mousetrack with two of the measures taken in the mousetracking paradigm – the Area Under the Curve (AUC) and Maximum Deviation (MD), both of which reflect the degree of (un)certainty in the participant's decision (Freeman and Ambady, 2010).

A further permutation of the experimental materials to which participants were responding was that they contained a word with one of two variants of the SQUARE vowel, in the first half of the utterance. In the example in (17) this word is *cared*. The vowel was manipulated so that it had either the more open starting point appropriate for SQUARE or the closer starting point of NEAR. This manipulation reflects an ongoing merger in New Zealand English of the SQUARE and NEAR vowels, towards NEAR. Older, more conservative speakers are more likely to have a SQUARE vowel in a word like *bear*, while younger speakers are more likely to have a NEAR vowel, resulting in homophony of *bear* (and *bare*) with *beer*. In the experiment, SQUARE words such as *cared* that had no counterpart with the NEAR vowel were re-synthesised so that the vowel had either an open SQUARE-like starting point or a more closed NEAR-like starting point. The results showed a more direct movement of the mouse to the question response for the early rise stimuli, but only if the SQUARE-word had a NEAR vowel, i.e., only for utterances that were more likely to have been produced by a younger, less conservative speaker. This suggests that listeners' sensitivity to the phonetic markers of question versus statement in intonation contours is affected by whether they perceive the speaker to be a younger rather than an older, more conservative speaker, which was signalled in the utterance by the nature of the SQUARE vowel.

Geluykens (1987: 484) found that the interpretation of utterances with declarative form but rising intonation depends not simply on the nature of the intonation pattern but importantly also on pragmatic-contextual cues. This was supported experimentally, with the finding that sentences like *You're not feeling very well* and *You like apples a lot* were interpreted as questions 53 per cent of the time, seemingly regardless of intonation pattern, whereas *I'm not feeling very well* and *I like apples a lot*, as well as *He's not feeling very well* and *He likes apples a lot* were more likely to be interpreted as statements, with rising intonation bringing a slight increase in question responses. This difference between the second-person sentences and the others reflects the fact that it is less likely that a speaker will make a statement about the listener's feelings and desires than about their own or those of a third party (and conversely are more likely to ask questions about the listener's desires or feelings). The type of rising contour used did not seem to make much difference. (For further discussion see also Batliner and Oppenrieder, 1988; Geluykens, 1989.)

Tomlinson and Fox Tree (2011), in a paper based on Tomlinson's doctoral thesis (Tomlinson, 2009) present the results of a comprehension study that is based on the assumption that rising intonation is ambiguous between a backward-looking function indicating the speaker's uncertainty about the truthfulness of the propositional content of what they have just said, and a forward-looking function that indicates that further information is to be provided. (Note that this ignores the other functions of uptalk discussed in Chapter 3.) Tomlinson and Fox Tree distinguish two utterance types with uptalk, those that have 'delay' in the form of prolonged utterance-final syllables (prolonged, that is, beyond what would normally be expected in terms of pre-pausal lengthening), and those that do not have delay. They found that uptalk on an utterance that does not have delay will signal a backward-looking function of either seeking confirmation from the listener of the relevance of the utterance or simply shifting responsibility to the listener for determining the truth of the utterance. The presence of delay, however, is associated with extra time being needed to contemplate either the utterance currently being executed or (in terms of 'planning time') the next utterance. So uptalk with delay should be associated by listeners with the forward-looking functions. This is what they found in a word-monitoring study, with words after the uptalk being recognised more rapidly when the uptalk was on prolonged syllables. The authors argue that when the rise at the end of the first utterance was accompanied with prolongation, then the listener's attention is drawn towards the next part of the utterance, facilitating faster word monitoring times. The slowest responses were for rises without prolongation, and conditions in which the utterances had falling intonation were between these two. Note though that the presence or absence of delay was a between-item variable, so there could have been other item-differentiating factors involved in this result.

Tomlinson and Fox Tree also included an experimental design where listeners were told that the speakers were either non-experts or experts in the field being talked about. They found a replication of the basic effect of 'delay' only in the non-expert condition, and claim that this is 'strong evidence that listeners establish relationships between linguistic form [patterns of intonation and prolongation] and function by first presupposing speakers' mental states' (Tomlinson and Fox Tree, 2011: 66).

8.2   Attitudinal studies of uptalk

It would not be surprising, given the range of functions identified for uptalk (see Chapter 3), to find that there is frequent misperception or misconstrual of the speaker's intentions, and this of course will contribute to the negative interpretations of uptalk that we saw in abundance in the review of media reports in Chapter 7. At the most obvious level, speakers who are not themselves uptalkers are likely to interpret uptalk in the speech of others as indicating a questioning and/or doubting, insecure attitude; 'since non-uptalkers often think that uptalk rises are really meant as questions, and assign low status to the people they associate uptalk with, it's natural to conclude that uptalk must be a signal of self-doubt and need for reassurance' (Liberman, 2006b).

In addition to such negative connotations, a number of studies have found that rising intonation such as uptalk can at the same time convey a positive signal. In her early study of intonational meaning, Uldall (1964) noted that listeners associated high-ending rises not only with 'submissiveness', but also with 'pleasantness'. Guy and Vonwiller's (1984) study of Australian English found that uptalk users were rated lower for job suitability, confidence and forcefulness, but higher for friendliness, attentiveness and expressiveness, as well as being deemed younger. Guy and Vonwiller used a total of 97 participants, who listened to short passages of about 30 seconds of interview speech in a matched-guise task, i.e., using two passages from each of the same three speakers, one passage with and one without an instance of uptalk. When speakers used uptalk they were also deemed less suitable for higher status professions (e.g., as a judge or university professor), which matches the finding that in early Australian English production studies that speakers from lower socio-economic groupings are more likely to use uptalk.

However, Steele (1995, 1996) replicated Guy and Vonwiller's study some 11 years later, again for Australian English, and found no differences in the level of occupation that would be ascribed to use and non-use of uptalk, and no differences in the semantic differential scales for confidence, forcefulness, friendliness and attentiveness. The only scale to show significant results was that for expressiveness – uptalk users are seen to actively engage the listener in the conversation. Steele argued that this change compared with Guy and Vonwiller's original study showed the wider social acceptance of uptalk in Australia by the mid-1990s.

Guy and Vonwiller's study was also partially replicated by Borgen (2000) for New Zealand English. While Guy and Vonwiller used only female speakers, Borgen used both female and male. The passages she selected were of similar length to Guy and Vonwiller's but the passages containing uptalk had between two and five instances, compared with Guy and Vonwiller's single example of an uptalk contour in their uptalk passages. Borgen used the same questionnaire as Guy and Vonwiller. She presents her study as a pilot, since she had a relatively small set of participants (17), which included both native speaking listeners (eight) and non-native speaking listeners (nine). The native speaking listeners showed a pattern of responses that partially reflected that reported by Guy and Vonwiller – the passages with uptalk were rated lower for job suitability and higher for friendliness, as well as being associated with younger speakers. The other ratings, while generally showing more negative responses for uptalk passages, were less consistent across the samples. While Borgen's result appears to indicate a difference between Australian English in the 1980s and New Zealand English in 2000, it should be remembered that her sample was relatively small, with only eight native speaker raters. Interestingly, Borgen's non-native raters tended to give higher ratings to uptalk users than to non-users. This could be because the non-native speakers did not share the same stereotypes about uptalk use as the native speakers, or alternatively because the non-natives' experience of New Zealand English was primarily from younger speakers, where uptalk was in more widespread use.

Employability was also an issue in Spindler's (2003) survey study conducted in South Dakota. Spindler discussed uptalk with a total of 81 students and then presented them with a short questionnaire that included a question about whether they would employ an uptalker. Thirty-four said they would not, 24 said they would but eight of this set stipulated that this would only be for a low-paid, low-status position. Only one student thought that uptalk would be of possible benefit, claiming that it could indicate a non-threatening and helpful person. The heavy bias against employing uptalkers echoes the sentiments expressed in opinion and advice columns reviewed in Chapter 7. In addition, 21 of Spindler's informants found uptalk annoying, 32 openly condemned its use and 25 claimed that it made a speaker seem less intelligent. Geenburg's (2009) study with participants from the Cornell University student community similarly found that uptalk users were rated as less intelligent, as well as less confident.

Intelligence was also one of the features explored by Conley et al. (1978), using four versions of materials based on recordings of witnesses made in a North American courtroom. Two versions were recorded by each of two actors, one female and one male. One version recorded by each actor was as direct a copy as possible of the original tape. This was referred to as the 'powerless' version, as it included features that were typical of the style used by the witnesses, who were from lower social groupings. The other version omitted these features, as far as possible. In the powerless version the recordings had more uptalk than in the powerful version. A panel of 96 undergraduate listeners responded to each of the four versions, giving ratings for questions such as 'how convincing in general was this witness?'. Compared to the 'powerful' style, both speakers in the 'powerless' style were rated as significantly less intelligent, as well as less believable, less convincing, less competent and less trustworthy. These ratings could, however, be due to any one or a combination of the features of 'powerless' speech, not just uptalk.

A lower level of conviction in the speaker's voice was also related to the presence of rising contours in research using students as listeners at Northwestern University in Illinois, all native speakers of American English. Gravano et al. (2008) used utterances such as *That would be my roommate* and *That is my roommate*, i.e., versions with an epistemic modal (*would*) and with a main verb *be*. These were recorded with three intonation patterns: declarative (a simple fall, H* L-L%), downstepped (!H* L-L%) and yes–no question (L* H-H%). Note that the yes–no question contour is one, as we have seen in other research reported above, that is frequently used as uptalk on statements in American English and other varieties. The researchers found that versions with the yes–no question contour were rated as significantly less 'certain' both than utterances with a standard declarative intonation and than utterances with a series of downstepped pitch accents.

In a further study equating rising intonation with lack of confidence, Barr (2003) exploited the fact that we perceive colours not in terms of their continuous distribution across the colour spectrum, but in terms of a 'centre' for each colour and less clear boundary areas. So there would be high agreement that a red colour near the centre for red is actually 'red', but there is a boundary area where there is less confidence whether a colour might be 'red' or 'orange'. Barr asked participants to learn new concepts by listening to new colour terms, using made-up names such as *riallo*, presented in association with colour patches. Learning took place in two conditions. In the consistent condition, hesitation and rising prosody were used when the speaker was naming instances of the colour that were in a boundary area between two colours, but these pronunciation features were absent when the instances were closer to the centre of a colour category. In the inconsistent condition, the relationship between the pronunciation features and the colour instances was switched. The results showed that learning was slower when rising intonation and hesitation were used when naming colours in the centre of the category than when naming boundary area colours. This is compatible with the notion that rises, along with hesitation, indicate uncertainty or lack of confidence.

Another aspect of confidence is explored in research that investigates the notion of 'feeling of knowing'. Smith and Clark (1993) commented on the fact that answers to questions serve at least two functions. On the one hand, they provide an exchange of information. On the other, they allow the respondent to present something of themselves, including their confidence in the information they are providing. Smith and Clark asked participants to indicate their confidence or 'feeling of knowing' for answers to questions that they had previously answered. They found that feeling of knowing was lower for questions that the participants themselves had previously answered with a rising intonation. Nevertheless, the same participants' recognition of correct answers in a subsequent multiple choice test was no worse for questions they had answered with rising intonation. In a follow-up to this study, Brennan and Williams (1995) found that when answers to questions are conveyed with final rising intonation the speaker is judged by others to be less likely to know that the answer is correct. Note that 'final rising' intonation is not further qualified.

8.3   The influence of speaker and listener factors on uptalk perception

The studies outlined in the preceding section show clearly that uptalk contributes to listeners' perceptions of certain behavioural characteristics of the speaker and can influence the attitudinal stance taken by listeners towards speakers. In earlier chapters we have seen how the incidence of uptalk has been linked to speaker demographics, typically but variously (depending on regional differences) to young women. In this section we consider briefly how the resulting association of uptalk with certain speaker characteristics might influence the perception of uptalk.

Some perceptual evidence that rising contours are associated with female speakers comes from a study by Edelsky (1979). Although she does not specifically refer to uptalk, the rising contours used in her experiment are described as the type of intonation that speakers use when only they have the information needed to answer a question that has been asked of them, with reference to Lakoff (1973). Lakoff was, of course, providing one of the earliest descriptions of what has become known as uptalk, and she also claimed that this is a characteristic of women rather than men. Edelsky asked participants to listen to place names produced by three male and three female speakers using simple rise, simple fall and rise-fall-rise contours. They were told that these names had been produced by delegates at a convention as answers to a question about their birthplace. The listeners' task was to rate the individual responses using a set of scales independently developed as being related to sex stereotypes (e.g., dominant-submissive). Although Edelsky found no differences in production data between men's and women's use of the rising contours, the ratings showed that simple rises were more strongly associated with stereotypically feminine attributes.

In her study of intonation patterns in Southern Ontario, Shokeir (2007, 2008) asked participants to rate certainty, finality and confidence conveyed by speakers with utterances produced with falling contours (H* L-L%) and rising contours (L* H-H% and H* L-H%). Shokeir found that the sex of the listeners was important, with men more likely to interpret falling contours (H* L-L%) as markers of certainty and finality and one of the rising tunes (L* H-H%) as showing uncertainty and continuation. Her female participants on the other hand were less likely to perceive the contours as having these traditional meanings, suggesting that for these listeners they have other social functions. However, it should be noted that Shokeir (2008) conflates sex and age in her perception study, in that her male listeners were older than her female listeners.

Some of the studies reported in the preceding section showed that speakers were rated as younger when their speech contained uptalk (Guy and Vonwiller, 1984; Borgen, 2000). The age factor is undoubtedly significant in determining how uptalk is perceived. For instance, Di Gioacchino and Crook Jessop (2010) reflect that the reactions to uptalk found in younger and older listener groups provide a parallel to the ways in which native speakers perceive the phonemes of their native language and those of a foreign language. The younger listeners fail to hear uptalk as extraordinary, while the older speakers 'find uptalk to be such a jarring trend because it defies their perceptual boundaries of acceptable and inacceptable contours for statements versus questions in their native language' (Di Gioacchino and Crook Jessop, 2010: 13).

Speaker and listener ethnicity also have an impact on the perception of uptalk. In a study of how prosodic cues might function in the identification of speakers of New Zealand English as either Māori or Pākehā (speakers of European descent), Szakay (2007, 2008, 2012) found that a higher rate of uptalk use by Māori speakers led to a higher rate of identification of those speakers as Māori. There was no effect of uptalk on the identification patterns for Pākehā speakers, leading to the conclusion that uptalk use is a secondary cue to ethnicity, 'unlikely to influence responses alone, but increasing the certainty of the listener if a speaker has other characteristics that make them sound Māori' (Szakay, 2007:66). One of these other characteristics is speech rhythm. In a listening condition in which rhythmic and intonational structure was preserved but segmental information removed, Szakay (2007) found that the rate of use of uptalk contributed to ethnic identification, but only if the speech was stress-timed. Speech that had more syllable-based timing was regularly identified as Māori, but speech that had stress-based timing was more likely to be identified as Māori if there was a high level of uptalk use, but as Pākehā if uptalk was less frequent. Szakay also reports that the slope of the uptalk rise influences ethnicity judgements, with steeper rises leading to a greater likelihood that the speaker is identified as Māori. While she did not find a corresponding pattern in the production data that she collected, Szakay refers to an undergraduate project (Stanton, 2006) that has found that Māori speakers do indeed show steeper uptalk rises than both Pākehā and Pasifika speakers.

Szakay also tested for effects of the ethnicity of her listeners on the identification of the speakers' ethnicity. She found that only the Pākehā listeners showed any sensitivity to rates of uptalk use, with more 'Māori' responses to voices with higher uptalk rates. However, when the speech samples were further manipulated so that they conveyed only intonation (both segmental and time-based rhythmic cues were removed), the Māori listeners identified a speaker as Māori if they used a lot of uptalk, but Pākehā participants now showed no sensitivity to uptalk usage.

Finally, Foulkes and Barron (2000) found that uptalk was not a reliable cue to speaker identity in a forensics study carried out in the United Kingdom. They present data from a speaker recognition experiment involving speakers and listeners from a close-knit group of friends. The group consisted of ten male undergraduates at the University of Leeds, with a range of geographical origins within the UK, and the experiment used telephone-bandwidth speech. The study showed that the group members were surprisingly poor at recognising one another's voices, but that there was better recognition for speakers with more extreme average pitch (either lower or higher than the mean for the group) and with higher pitch variability. Some of the participants commented on intonational features of the other speakers, but the three speakers who were the main uptalk users were not recognised any more reliably than the others.

8.4   Summary

The perceptual studies reviewed in this chapter have shown that rising intonation patterns are reliably linked with 'question' percepts, but that the extent to which this is found to be true depends on the shape of the rise. More 'question' responses were given to fall-rises with higher final targets (as well as to simple rises) in a study of American English, to rises with higher starting points for Australian English, and to rises with earlier starting points for New Zealand English. These patterns all reflect the production data noted in earlier chapters. In addition, a recent study with speakers of New Zealand English (Warren, 2014a) suggests that the interpretation of intonational patterns reflects expectations about which speaker groups produce uptalk, with speaker group membership cued by an independent sociophonetic property. Further perceptual studies have investigated the attitudinal meanings conveyed through uptalk, and found confirmation of many of the meanings discussed in Chapter 3 and that are reflected in media commentary outlined in Chapter 7. Other studies have likewise confirmed the expectation that uptalk will be – perhaps stereotypically – associated with feminine characteristics, but also that female listeners are less likely than male listeners to associate uptalk with some of the more stereotyped meanings such as uncertainty.

9   Uptalk in other languages

While most of the research literature and most of the media reports on uptalk have focused on varieties of English, uptalk has featured in discussion of other languages. A frequent theme in much of this discussion is whether uptalk intonation patterns have arisen through the influence of English, either through contact in bi- or multilingual settings, or via the global impact of English-language media, especially through television and film.

9.1   Germanic languages

Peters (2007) discusses uptalk in German through the example of politician and industrialist Franz Müntefering, with further illustration using material from the satirical television show 'Münte', featuring imitations of Müntefering by broadcaster Harald Wehmeier. Peters presents analyses of speeches from Müntefering (125 intonation units) and from eight other leading German politicians (three female, five male, with a total of just over 1,000 intonation units), as well as from an interview with Müntefering (22 intonation units), together with extracts from the *Münte* television programme (48 intonation units). In the politician's speech the function of uptalk is claimed to be to secure the floor (which might seem odd in the context of a political speech), but the possibility is also entertained that it indicates insecurity. In the satire, uptalk contributes to the identification of the object of the satire by means of exaggerated stereotype. Peters' detailed analysis of the uptalk instances shows that Müntefering typically steps up to a high accent and keeps his voice pitch high till the end of the intonation unit, as in Figure 9.1. The pitch accent in this example is on the third syllable of *informelle* and the high pitch is held to the end of the intonation unit, a feature that also seems to be quite strong in the speech of two of the three female politicians analysed. On the other hand, Wehmeier's caricature of Müntefering uses rises from a low accent, either L* H0% in Peters' system for northern standard German (Peters, 2005), or an exaggerated 'double rise' contour with a rising pitch accent and a high boundary tone, transcribed as L* HH%. An example of one of Wehmeier's rises from L* is shown in Figure 9.2,

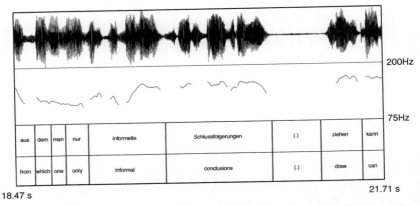

Figure 9.1 Uptalk in the speech of German politician Franz Müntefering (translates as: 'from which we can only draw informal conclusions').

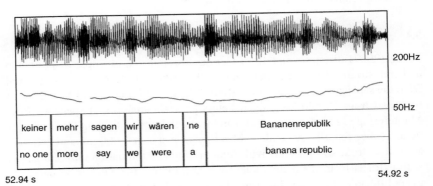

Figure 9.2 Uptalk in the political satire *Münte* (translates as: 'no-one should be able to say any more that we are a banana republic').

where the rise starts from the accented second syllable of *Bananenrepublik* and continues to the end of the intonation unit. Müntefering himself uses this L* HH% pattern in the interview context, but not so much in his political speeches. Peters also comments that uptalk does not appear to have entered German via teenager talk, and that therefore there seems to be little evidence of cross-cultural influence.

Leeman (2009) reports uptalk in interview data in the Alpine Valais dialect of Swiss German. He argues that uptalk here serves the purpose of encouraging the addressee to participate in the conversation, i.e., has a similar function to one of those claimed for English in Chapter 3.

In Scandinavian languages, Hadding-Koch and Studdert-Kennedy (1964: 176) note that 'polite statements in Swedish, though spoken on a lower frequency level than questions, quite often end with a rise'. The *BBC News Magazine* (2014) prints comments from readers that uptalk perhaps originated in Norwegian and that Scandinavian settlement in Minnesota in the United States is implicated in the spread of uptalk (but see Chapter 5). Andersen (2014: 22) maintains, however, that uptalk in Norwegian is most likely due to the influence of English. She notes that it has been observed in Western Norwegian dialects since the 1990s, particularly among younger speakers.

9.2 Romance languages

It has been argued (e.g., Šafářová, 2006) that rises in French are associated mainly with yes–no questions and with topic openings. However, there has been some discussion of uptalk-like intonation in French, which has focused on bilingual Canada, where an influence of English on French is frequently claimed and often bemoaned. Tennant and Rampersaud (2000) considered the use of uptalk in a minority version of Canadian French, as spoken by French-English bilinguals in Ontario. Their data are from students in two French language high schools in London, Ontario, a town where only around 2 per cent of the population have French as their first language. They analysed ten-minute interview samples from 12 bilingual speakers in the 15–17 age range, recorded in 1998. Overall, 10.9 per cent of tone groups had uptalk rises. Discourse and textual factors proved to be the strongest variable in their analysis, with the same rank ordering of different text types as reported for Australian English by Guy et al. (1986) (see Section 6.6), i.e., the highest rate of uptalk use was in narratives and descriptions, and the lowest in opinion and factual texts. Tennant and Rampersaud also found that the presence of a code-switch (i.e., inclusion of English lexical, morpho-syntactic or phonological elements) in a French tone group strongly increased the likelihood of that tone group having an uptalk rise. This supports the claim that uptalk has appeared in Canadian French under the influence of English. In addition, students who reported a high usage of French in a range of situations, including in the home, were less likely to use uptalk. As in many other studies of uptalk usage, it was found that females used it more than males. In addition, there was evidence that working-class students (class being determined on the basis of parental occupation) were more likely to use uptalk than middle-class students.

In a collection of papers on intonational variation in Spanish (Prieto and Roseano, 2010) a type of final rise in Dominican Spanish is documented that 'bears considerable similarity to the High Rising Terminals noted in a variety of English dialects' (Willis, 2010:124). Willis reports finding final rises with broad focus statements as well as with exclamative and emphatic statements.

He suggests that yes–no questions are kept distinct from statements by the use of a rise to a high level early in the tone group, which is maintained until a fall on the tonic, followed by either a low or a high boundary tone. Across his corpus, rises on statements were typically much larger than those on questions, but he finds no common meaning to the statement rises he observes. In the same volume, Armstrong (2010) similarly reports rises on emphatic statements in Puerto Rican Spanish, but not on broad focus or exclamative statements, suggesting if anything a narrower use of uptalk-like intonation in this variety.

Fought (2003: 73) recounts an episode where she asked a Mexican informant in Spanish what wishes he had for his future children. The informant responded *Que tengan todo lo que ne- necisiten ellos?* ('That they have everything they need?', with rising intonation as indicated by the question mark). Interpreting this as a clarification request, Fought followed up with a rephrasing of the question, and only later on listening to the tape realised that the speaker had given a direct answer, a declarative. Note, however, that the reported tonal pattern is not quite the same as uptalk, being more a rise-fall (so-called circumflex) pattern. Fought also notes, however, that as part of a two-way influence between Spanish and English in California (see Section 4.5 for the tonal patterns of Chicano English), the Spanish of some younger speakers has 'Californian intonations' superimposed on it, resulting in uptalk patterns as well as the circumflex pattern (Fought, 2003: 76).

Danesi (1997: 458) points to the use of a tag form as an equivalent to uptalk in adolescent Italian: 'Allora ti piace, eh?' (*so you like it?*) 'No, no, eh, non e mica vero, eh?' (*no, no, uh, it's not true at all?*), although the first example would seem more like a genuine question and the second an exclamation.

Cristina Schmitt (personal communication) has also commented that uptalk is found in Brazilian Portuguese.

9.3   Japanese

Mellow Monk's Green Tea Blog (Mellow Monk, 2006) notes that uptalk is found in Japanese, where, as in English, it is 'a phenomenon of the young, but many older people who should know better are guilty of it, too'.

Inoue (1997, available in English translation as F. Inoue, 2006), notes similarities between an intonation contour found in Japan and those that have been taking root in the English-speaking world. Inoue acknowledges that the extent of the acoustic-phonetic similarity of the Japanese pattern to those found in Australia, New Zealand and the United States is unclear (F. Inoue, 2006: 216). However, the examples given of the functions of the Japanese contour are clearly similar to the functions of uptalk: it is used to show that the speaker has not yet finished their turn, it serves to block interruption by the listener, and it asks the listener for a sign that they are still following the interaction. Elsewhere, Inoue

(1998, 1999) noted two new types of intonation that had recently emerged in young people's speech in Japan. Both have been interpreted as serving the function of holding the speaker's turn in a conversation or drawing attention to it. In addition, the use of these forms signals group membership. One of these new forms (the 'Shiriagari intonation') is a final rise-fall that appeared in the 1970s and was still spreading in the 1990s. The other ('Han-gimon' or 'half question' intonation, also referred to as 'quasi-questioning intonation') is a rising contour that started being noticed among young female speakers in the 1990s, but then spread to older and male speakers. From pitch traces published in Inoue (1998), the term 'half-question' would be misleading if it was thought that it applied to the form of this intonation, as the rises are full and steep. It is not clear whether M. Inoue (2006: 262) is describing the same rising pattern, but she notes a sharply rising intonation pattern that is associated with Japanese women's speech in particular.

The form of the 'half-question' intonation pattern is very similar to uptalk. Inoue (1998) points out that many older speakers interpret the intonation as expressing a genuine yes–no question, and respond accordingly. Alternatively, they think it strange that the speaker uses rising intonation to express something that should be well-known to them. These are the same kinds of responses as those found among non-uptalkers in English. Inoue (1998: 20) suggests that the form may have been introduced from English, and that if this is the case then it is 'a rare case of global dissemination of a suprasegmental phenomenon'.

It has been argued that the basis for an uptalk intonation existed in Japanese before uptalk emerged as a phenomenon, as has been claimed for English (Chapter 5). Thus Abe, writing about rising intonation on statements in Japanese, states (1955: 392) 'the speaker is appealing (strongly) to the hearer or calling for the latter's "participation" in or sympathy with his view or statement'.

Ueki (2005) notes that the use of uptalk in Japanese is similar to that found in English, in that it does not add to the denotative meaning of the utterance on which it is used (i.e., the utterance would have the same meaning if spoken with a less marked contour), but rather has discourse functions. However, in Ueki's data, these appear to be different functions to those of English uptalk. Most of her examples suggest that a rise is being used for prosodic marking of a repair, with other categories including marking discourse structure and listing. As pointed out by Ueki, uptalk in Japanese has been commented on in Japanese newspapers since the early 1990s. The comments are reminiscent of those made in the English press, namely that it is annoying, and a sign of uncertainty or hesitation. There is a similar perception that it is used predominantly by younger speakers.

Maekawa (2011, 2012) also discusses the 'quasi-questioning' intonation, which he claims is the Japanese counterpart of uptalk. He describes a quasi-question as 'an utterance that is interpreted pragmatically as an ordinary statement while the end of utterance is associated with a yes–no-question like rising intonation' (Maekawa, 2012: 993). It is also used, in his data, almost exclusively by female speakers, across a range of ages. In an exercise in automatic classification of speech registers in Japanese (into academic presentations, extemporaneous speech on everyday topics by recruited layman participants, dialogue and read speech [reading aloud the transcripts of one of the first two types]), Maekawa (2011) found that the quasi-question intonation contributed significantly to the differentiation of academic presentations and extemporaneous speech.

9.4   Arabic languages

Al Bayyari (2007) identified three prosodic cues that were most likely to result in back-channels in corpora of Egyptian Arabic and Iraqi Arabic. The Egyptian corpus (of male and female speech) was from long-distance phone calls originating in North America, and the Iraqi corpus (all males) was provided by informal face-to-face conversations recorded in the United States. The most common prosodic cue to back-channels was a steep pitch downslope, and the least frequent a period of low flat pitch with lengthening at a point of disfluency. However, the second most frequent cue, present for 14 per cent of the subsequent back-channels in the Iraqi corpus, and 9 per cent in the Egyptian corpus, was a pitch upturn, which the author tentatively compares (2007: 20) to uptalk, although insufficient detail is given to determine whether this is the case.

Ghada Khattab (personal communication) reports uptalk in Lebanese Arabic, particularly among young people who have experienced English-language instruction at university and/or who have received exposure to English-language media exposure, especially American English.

9.5   Austronesian languages

Western Cham is an Austronesian language spoken in Vietnam. Ueki (2011) provides an analysis of the intonation of this language and notes a use of rises that is similar to uptalk (2011: 144). Ueki suggests that a high terminal on declaratives indicates non-finality, but is unable to state with any certainty whether the rise has the same discourse functions as in English, since the data being analysed are from monologues.

Tuvaluan is a Polynesian language spoken mainly in Tuvalu, a nation consisting of nine small islands in the south-central Pacific. As noted earlier, Britain (1992), among others, has commented on the importance of narrative in Polynesian societies. The variety of Tuvaluan spoken on the atoll of Nukulaelae was analysed by Besnier (1989), who emphasises how the success of Nukulaelae 'gossip' depends on the audience sharing the speaker's own feelings and attitudes to the topic. Britain argues that this entails the use, among other devices, of uptalk. Referring to work by Duranti (1981), Britain claims that uptalk is also common in Samoan narratives. Calhoun (forthcoming), however, argues that final rises in Samoan are stress-aligned boundary markers.

9.6   Other languages

In an analysis of the language used in Greek-language commentaries on Greece's victory in the final of the 2004 UEFA European Football Championship, Theodoropoulou (2008: 337) found uptalk being used in two thirds (2,589) of the 3,864 declarative utterances in her corpus. Since Greece were the rank outsiders at the competition, she suggests that the commentators were using such a high level of uptalk 'probably unconsciously, to index their surprise'. In other work on Greek, Tsiplakou (2012) and Themistocleous (2012) have identified uptalk as a characteristic of Nicosian Greek, and claim that this is one of the distinguishing factors between this urban Cypriot variety and standard Greek.

In a study of conversations between pairs of Finnish teenage girls recorded between 1991 and 1997, Ogden and Routarinne (2005) found final rises occurring at a rate of about two a minute, mainly on declaratives and in narrative contexts. The functions they attribute to these rises are similar to those aligned with English uptalk: 'they provide a place for a coparticipant to mark recipiency, and they project more talk by the current speaker' (2005: 160). Phonetic criteria for this contour used by Ogden and Routarinne are that it starts with an L tone on the last accentually prominent syllable and ends midhigh to high.

9.7   Summary

While uptalk is predominantly referred to as a characteristic of English, it is also found in other languages. If there is truly a universal contrast between high tone indicating openness and low covering a more closed meaning, then this would not be at all surprising, and may indeed account for some of the adoption of uptalk forms in other languages, even if not specifically for its origin. Much more likely, however, is a contact influence from English. As a global language and a language of the media, English is found in many countries where there is a different native language. English is, of course, also a significant language in international youth culture – in television, film and music. It comes therefore as no surprise to discover that the influence of uptalk, still a predominantly youthful trait, is found in the youth culture of other languages. It remains to be seen whether uptalk will take hold in other languages in the way it appears to be doing in English.

10   Methodology in uptalk research

The various studies of uptalk reviewed or summarised in this book illustrate the complexities of the forms, functions and distributions of this type of rising intonation. What is perhaps less clear is that the study of uptalk has involved a range of researchers, including sociolinguists, discourse analysts, phoneticians and intonational phonologists. Not surprisingly, the reported research includes a number of different methodological approaches. This chapter summarises some of the main methodological issues. The purpose is twofold. First, an understanding of variation in methods is crucially important for our understanding of any differences we find in the conclusions drawn about uptalk. Second, it is to be hoped that an awareness of these considerations will be of use to future researchers wishing to investigate this intonational pattern. Issues to be discussed include the way in which speech data are collected (including the use of speech corpora and the selection of the speaking or listening tasks given to informants) and the types of analysis made of the speech data.

10.1   Language samples

Early reports of uptalk have tended to be anecdotal. That is, observers have noted examples of rising intonation in what seem to them to be surprising contexts, i.e., at the ends of what would usually be understood to be declarative statements. For many lay observers (as we saw in Chapter 7), the immediate reaction is to suspect that the speaker had some reason to ask a question, and it is often assumed that this reason relates to uncertainty or insecurity. For the researcher, some important early steps are to explore whether this unexpected use of intonational rises reflects a few isolated cases or is more systematic, and to determine with greater care what meaning or function this intonation pattern might have. These tasks are best supported by a larger dataset than the initial anecdotal observations. While continued informal listening (e.g., to conversations involving speakers suspected of uptalking) may allow more general statements about speaker behaviour, the building of a collection of recordings permits more careful scrutiny of how often and under what circumstances uptalk is produced.

Many of the uptalk studies cited in this book have used spoken language corpora, i.e., collections of speech data that have been put together by researchers. With the advent of increasingly sophisticated computational tools and speech processing software, and the availability of cheaper and larger storage capacity for digitised speech data, it has become possible to construct large speech corpora that can be used to explore and verify linguistic behaviour in ways that would have only been dreamed of 30 or so years ago. Most such corpora have been orthographically transcribed, but many also have time-aligned phonetic transcriptions, and a few have additionally been transcribed for intonation. One of the advantages of an extensive corpus is that it can reveal some of the less common language phenomena as well as the more common ones. Given the relatively low levels of incidence of uptalk (especially in some of the earlier studies), this is an important consideration. In addition, any grammatical descriptions – including descriptions of intonational structure – which result from the study can be based on empirical data, rather than being dependent on the linguist's own introspections or biases. The use of multiple speakers in a corpus should also make it more representative of the speaker group and speech events being considered.

While some more targeted collections have been made – for example, recordings made with the express purpose of obtaining data on intonation patterns – most of the corpus-based studies of uptalk have by and large made use of collections of speech data that have been constructed for more general purposes; for example, as a record of a particular language or variety of a language spoken by particular groups of speakers at a particular time. A few have used existing corpora of different varieties of English in order to compare uptalk forms and incidence in those varieties (see for example Wilhelm, 2015). It is worth summarising a few of the corpora used in uptalk studies, in order to get an impression of the size and nature of such corpora, since the type of language recorded for the corpus will affect its usefulness for the investigation of uptalk.

For New Zealand English, Britain (Britain, 1992; Britain and Newman, 1992) used data collected by Holmes et al. (1991) for a social dialect study. The study involved 60 working-class speakers from Porirua, a city just north of Wellington, distributed across three age groups (20–29, 40–49, 70–79), two ethnicities (Māori and Pākehā) and two sexes. In addition, 15 middle-class Pākehā women were recorded, five in each age group. Speakers were involved in a mixture of formal tasks (reading sentences and word lists) and casual speech events, including responses to the 'danger of death' question often used for speech elicitation (Labov, 1966). Each recording was about 60 minutes in duration, giving a total of some 75 hours of speech. Although the interviewers attempted to keep interactions with the participants as informal as possible, there was no dialogue between pairs or groups of participants.

In Australia, Horvath (1985) based her uptalk analysis on the complete sociolinguistic interviews from each of 130 speakers in the 'core speech community' of her corpus of Sydney English, recorded in 1977 and 1980. The core group (of a total recording sample of 177 speakers) excludes, on the basis of an analysis of vowel variables, a group of peripheral speakers classified as Accented and Ethnic Broad and consisting of most of the Italian and Greek speakers in the original sample. For the uptalk analysis, Horvath used approximately 45 minutes of speech data per speaker in the core group, giving a total sample of just under 100 hours.

Fletcher and Harrington (2001) investigated intonation patterns in a subpart of the Australian National Database of Spoken Language (ANDOSL, see Millar et al., 1994). This corpus was developed in the 1990s and comprises data from a total of 108 native speakers of Australian English in three sociolects (General, Broad, Cultivated), three age groups (18–30, 31–45, 46+) and two sexes. Each speaker carried out a range of speech tasks, including reading out sentences and word lists, as well as two interactive map tasks. Fletcher and Harrington's data come from a small group of ten participants in this interactive task. The New Zealand Spoken English Database (NZSED, see Warren, 2002) is modelled on ANDOSL, and uses adapted versions of the same tasks.

The Hong Kong Corpus of Spoken English (Cheng and Warren, 2005) is a corpus of two million words, or approximately 200 hours, half of which has been prosodically transcribed using a discourse intonation transcription system (based on Brazil, 1997). For their investigation of rise and rise-fall tones, Cheng and Warren (2005) included recordings totalling some 120,000 words, i.e., around 6 per cent of the total corpus, or about 12 hours of speech. This sample included six discourse types: conversations, service encounters, informal office talk, placement interviews, business meetings and academic supervisions. Recordings were mostly between adult Hong Kong Chinese and native English speakers, and so also involve intercultural communicative considerations.

A few corpora have been developed specifically to provide data for the analysis of intonation. For example, the research of Grabe and her colleagues (Grabe and Post, 2002; Grabe, 2004; Grabe et al., 2005, 2007) is based on their Intonational Variation in English (IViE) corpus. The IViE corpus was recorded between 1997 and 2002, and covers seven urban varieties of English (London, Cambridge, Leeds, Bradford, Newcastle, Belfast and Dublin). A total of 108 16-year-old speakers provided 36 hours of speech data on an array of tasks that included reading sentences and the Cinderella story, retelling the Cinderella story, and taking part in two interactive tasks: a map task and a free conversation.

In order to investigate the intonational behaviour of a specific community, McLemore (1991) built a corpus of sorority speech in Texas, including recordings of meetings and social events involving sorority members, as well individual and group interviews with the researcher. The corpus therefore has a mix of spontaneous language related to events in the college life of the participants and recordings from a more formal interview situation. In total it is approximately 25 hours long.

The corpora listed above are variable in length, and the studies of uptalk based on these corpora have tended to use just a subsample of the recorded data, albeit in cases quite a substantial subsample (such as Horvath's use of nearly 100 hours of speech). Some more exploratory studies have used smaller corpora or subsets of corpus data. For her doctoral research, Post (2000) developed a corpus of French consisting of map task data (see below), from which Šafářová et al. (2005) subsequently selected a sub-corpus of two speakers and two dialogues, for a total of 301 speech turns.

Using a corpus originally developed for work on the prosodic naturalness of text-to-speech systems, Carmichael's (2005) doctoral thesis analysed 9,302 intonationally transcribed utterances from a single speaker in a variety of spoken tasks and situations. However, the materials – which included news reports, phonetically rich sentences, chat room messages, emails and instructional prompts – were all based on reading from scripts. Carmichael acknowledges a further disadvantage of using a corpus based on a single speaker, which is that it is not possible to distinguish patterns of speech behaviour that might apply across a linguistic community from individual idiosyncrasies.

As these few examples have shown, the extent and nature of a spoken language corpus can be quite variable, and can depend on the original aims of the corpus. Some corpora rely more on scripted speech than others, and some more on monologue than on dialogue. These properties are important to a researcher's decision about the usefulness of the speech data in a corpus to the investigation of uptalk, and it is important to remember that few collections of speech data have been made expressly for the study of uptalk. The following section will consider some of the tasks that have been used to collect speech that has subsequently been analysed for uptalk, tasks that usually represent a subpart of a larger corpus, but that in some cases provide all the recordings in a sample.

10.2   Speaking tasks

As earlier chapters have made clear, uptalk is more likely in certain discourse contexts than in others. In particular, the significance of the interactional meanings of uptalk means that a researcher is unlikely to arrive at many insights about this phenomenon by looking at scripted tasks, such as the reading aloud of dialogues or of decontextualised sentences. The choice of speaking task used in data collection is therefore crucial for the study of uptalk, and must be taken into consideration when one compares the findings of different studies.

Significant task differences can be found in the comparison of reading tasks and more spontaneous speech tasks. As pointed out by Speer et al. (2011: 38–39), there are a number of issues involved with basing an analysis on data collected in a reading task. The most crucial of these is that readers and speakers have different pragmatic goals. When a participant reads sentences aloud, they are usually doing so in response to instructions to speak clearly, and they will often focus more on a clear pronunciation of the words in the sentence than on getting across the meaning of the sentence as a whole. When the listener is the experimenter, as is often the case in reading tasks, then the speaker can also assume that the listener already knows the intended meaning, since they provided the reading materials in the first place, and this can affect how the sentence is read. The same can often be true of scripted dialogue – although there is an explicit intended listener (the dialogue partner), the context of the recording is often such that the speaker is 'performing' for the experimenter as much as for the listener. In contrast, spontaneous speech usually occurs in a way that is contextually appropriate and the speaker's aim is to achieve their own communicative goals.

Other differences between reading and spontaneous speaking tasks include the fact that in spontaneous speech the speaker has to go through the entire process of planning and producing an utterance, involving the generation of ideas, the selection of words and sentence structures to convey those ideas, as well as determining the prosodic structure of the utterance. On the other hand, the reader is provided with a sentence structure complete with words, and simply has to convert the text to speech that is as fluent as possible (and is often allowed or required to repeat a sentence that contains a disfluency). While for many studies there are clear advantages in providing a script for speakers to use (e.g., when a particular linguistic element or contrast is being investigated that is unlikely to occur with sufficient regularity in spontaneous speech), caution should be used when interpreting read speech as if it were comparable with spontaneous speech.

In the study of uptalk, the use of a scripted or read task will be of limited value compared with spontaneous interaction or goal-oriented interactive tasks. This is because, as pointed out by McGregor and Palethorpe (2008: 174), uptalk rises tend to occur 'in task-oriented discourse, such as a narrative, where the intention is to achieve a common goal' (as discussed further in Section 3.3). It is therefore not surprising that uptalk studies tend not to report data directly from scripted recordings, although some research in this area does refer to additional data from read speech, as in comparisons in New Zealand English between statement rises and those found in studies of intonation-only questions (Warren and Daly, 2000; Daly and Warren, 2001).

Amongst the largely unscripted tasks employed for the collection of speech data used in uptalk studies, we find considerable variation in the likely involvement of the listener. This is highly relevant, given the earlier observations about the functions of uptalk. If a primary function is to check the listener's comprehension of or engagement with the speaker's contribution (Chapter 3), then it is far less likely to emerge in a task where the listener can be assumed to already know the general content of what the speaker is saying. Therefore, tasks that ask speakers to recount something that is already known to the investigator are disfavoured. Instead, the more monologic tasks used in uptalk research ask the speaker to recount from memory something that the experimenter-as-listener might plausibly be not expected to know. For example, McGregor (1980) asked his informants to retell the story of a book or movie they had recently seen. McGregor reports that most of his speakers were able to produce this kind of narrative after only momentary hesitation. Other monologue tasks include the recounting of personal narratives. Thus Webb (2008) asked her participants some topical questions relating to their past experiences and allowed them to speak for a few minutes without interruption, unless they needed prompting with further questions to continue speaking. Such tasks are similar to the structured sociolinguistic interviews used by other researchers looking at various speech features including uptalk (Horvath, 1985; Ellingsæter, 2014), but compared with the sociolinguistic interviews, they involve less interaction from the researcher. In addition, they are not as unmonitored as conversational speech, but after an initial period of self-conscious attention to their speaking, participants frequently relax into the task. The narratives that result from the sociolinguistic interview frequently allow analysis in terms of narrative structure, as discussed in Section 6.6 (and see for instance Michaels, 1984; Horvath, 1985; Guy et al., 1986; Allan, 1990; Ainsworth, 1994; Steele, 1996; Warren and Britain, 2000; Innes, 2007; Podesva, 2011).

Edelsky (1979) took a very specific approach to address the issue of whether uptalk is used more by women than by men. She used a simple interview technique in which experimenters (who did not know the real purpose of the study) approached strangers on the street and asked them either where they were born or what their favourite colour was, i.e., a question to which only the respondent would know the answer. The responses showed relatively few 'straight rises', and no difference between men and women.

In addition to one-on-one interviews, Ellingsæter's (2014) data included group interviews, in which the attention frequently shifted more rapidly away from the recording to the conversation itself. These were also in relaxed social environments, i.e., in restaurants or bars. As well as interviews, Pennington et al. (2011) collected data in much less structured peer-to-peer conversations between participants of the same sex and ethnicity (the study was of Chinese and Bangladeshi communities in London). In these conversations, participants were speaking with their friends about their activities and interests. McLemore's (1991) study of the speech of members of a sorority in Texas similarly provided plenty of opportunity for within-group interactions. Group interviews and peer-to-peer discussions, while less constrained in terms of the direction they can take, are less likely to be influenced by the inhibitions associated with more formal interview situations.

Other researchers have used data from much more goal-oriented tasks. Along with the prompted narratives mentioned above, Webb (2008) had her participants take part in a verbalised tangram task, in which participants cooperate with one another to match geometric shapes. Not only is this goal-oriented, but it is a task that involves collaboration and a considerable amount of checking between participants. Webb found similar numbers of high rising intonation patterns in the two tasks, but in the prompted narratives (referred to by Webb in her results as 'interviews') almost all these rises were on declaratives, while in the tangram task they were more evenly split between declaratives and questions. In addition, all participants used similar numbers of high-rises in the tangram task, but there was much more individual variation in the narrative task. The higher incidence of question rises in the tangram task is not surprising, given the nature of the task, and the more even spread of uptalk (statement rises) across speakers in this task suggests that this is a common checking device, again not surprising given the requirements of the task.

A large number of the corpora mentioned in the previous section make use of one particular cooperative task, namely the map task devised by Anderson et al. (1991). In this task, two participants each have a map, but there are important differences between the maps. Figure 10.1 shows as an example one pair of the maps used in the New Zealand Spoken English Database, NZSED (Warren, 2002), in turn based on the maps used in the ANDOSL project (Millar et al., 1994). There is a route marked on only one of the maps, and the task for the speaker with that map is to describe the route in such a way that the other participant can accurately draw the route on their own map. In addition, some of the landmarks on the two maps have different names, and some are present on only one map. Important features of the map task are therefore that it is dialogic, and that it involves questions, statements of fact and checking for shared information. This combination of utterance types has made the map task quite attractive for the study of uptalk. The advantages of such a task over sentence reading tasks or the reading of a prepared dialogue include the fact that the participants are involved in meaningful discourse. The negotiation involved in the task is similar to that seen in the tangram task, and results in a considerable amount of checking for comprehension and that the other participant is keeping up with the task.

Map task recordings provide the data for a range of uptalk studies. Fletcher and Harrington's (2001) analysis of Australian English focuses on the

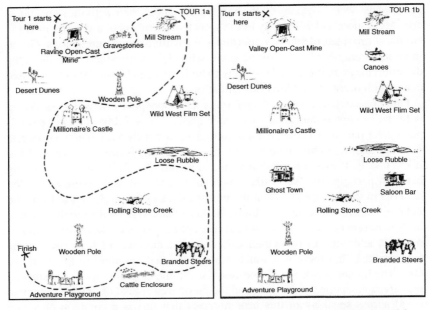

Figure 10.1 Example maps as used in the map task in NZSED, adapted from those used in ANDOSL (see text).

ANDOSL map task data, and uses ten such dialogues, all involving speakers of general Australian English. The dialogues range approximately from six to 11 minutes in length. This relatively small sub-sample of the whole corpus yielded 447 high-rises on statements. Other research using map task samples from the ANDOSL corpus includes Stirling et al. (2001), Fletcher et al. (2002a), Fletcher (2005), McGregor's (2005) doctoral thesis and McGregor and Palethorpe (2008). Many of these studies have combined intonational analysis of the ANDOSL map task data with coding systems for dialogue structure (such as that of Jurafsky et al., 1997).

Map task data have also been used in the study of the intonation of other English varieties including New Zealand English (Warren, 2005b; Warren and Daly, 2005), British English (House, 2007) and Southern Californian English (Ritchart and Arvaniti, 2014). The fact that researchers in different parts of the world have used the same basic task is also promising for comparisons between English varieties, and the map task has been explicitly used in this way by Barry and Arvaniti (2006) in their comparison of the English spoken in Southern California and in London.

Unsurprisingly, a number of researchers have made explicit task comparisons in their study of the use of uptalk. In an analysis of spontaneous and read speech, Ayers (1994) compared participants' contributions to conversations with the experimenter and the same speakers' re-enactment of their contributions. These re-enactments involved a reading aloud of the transcripts of the conversations, with an attempt to make them sound spontaneous. While Ayers does not specifically discuss uptalk, it is of interest that she found that final high rising intonation (to H-H% boundaries in the ToBI system) were found in the spontaneous versions but only rarely in the re-enactments. The re-readings instead employed L-L% or L-H%, i.e., the 'reflections of the dialogue structure of the original conversation were eliminated in the read version …, making the read version more like coordinated monologues rather than a true dialogue' (Ayers, 1994: 28–29).

In a more direct investigation of uptalk in different text types, involving an analysis of spontaneous and read speech across eight Canadian English regions, Talla Sando (2009: 11) found higher rates in spontaneous speech, although he more narrowly argues that 'one of the reasons why "upspeak" occurs more frequently in spontaneous than in read speech may be that in read speech, pauses are clear-cut and there is no room for the reader of the text to hesitate while thinking about what to say next'.

Using Southern Californian speakers, Ritchart and Arvaniti (2014) compared a version of the map task with a reading of the transcript of a scene from a popular television sitcom, a retelling of that scene and the reading of more controlled materials such as isolated questions and statements. They found significantly more uptalk in the map task than in the retelling of the sitcom scene, and the uptalk rises in the map task also had greater pitch excursions. That is, there were more and larger uptalk rises in contexts where the interactional functions of uptalk are more clearly at play.

At least one study has considered how different speaker groups respond to different task requirements. Pennington et al. (2011) found that their Bangladeshi group was less strongly listener-oriented than their Chinese group and therefore less engaged with interactional tasks, and that this was reflected in a lower level of uptake of uptalk.

Of course many of the task differences mentioned above were considered in more detail earlier in this book, for example, in sections dealing with the distribution of uptalk in different text types. These differences are mentioned again here as a reminder that the interpretation of existing studies should keep in mind the tasks being required of speakers and therefore the relative likelihood of uptalk occurring. But they should also serve as a warning that future studies of uptalk should take such factors into account when selecting tasks for speakers to engage in. Depending on the goals of such studies, it might be appropriate to have participants engage in a cooperative task such as the map task or the tangram task. Yet at the same time, these tasks themselves potentially lead to ambiguity, since participants frequently ask direct questions for information ('You have a 'Wild 'West ↗Film 'Set') as well as issuing directions that simultaneously seek confirmation of understanding ('You go 'round the ↗Millionaire's 'Castle'). While the reaction or response of the other participant will often give an indication of whether the utterance was a question or a statement, this will not always be the case.

10.3   Perceptual tasks

Just as production studies of uptalk have used a range of tasks, so too studies of the perception of uptalk have selected listening tasks according to the kind of question that is being addressed (see Chapter 8 for more details). When the issue is whether a particular utterance type is interpreted as a question or as a statement – for instance, when different rise shapes are being investigated – then a simple categorisation task might be sufficient, such as asking listeners to indicate whether an utterance they have heard is a question or a statement (Geluykens, 1987; Levis, 1996; Zwartz and Warren, 2003; Šafářová, 2006; Fletcher and Loakes, 2010). However, such tasks, while seemingly simple, can be rather problematic, since it is not always clear that participants share a common understanding of what is meant by terms such as 'question'.

As mentioned earlier, at least one study has combined a categorisation task both with a response time measure (indicating how long the participant took to make up their mind) and with the tracking of computer mouse movements as participants select their response (showing how strongly they were tempted towards the competing answer before selecting their response). This produces more qualitative information about the decision-making behind the categorisation than is afforded just by the binary outcome (Warren, 2014a).

Tomlinson and Fox Tree (2011) used a word-monitoring study, in which participants had to respond as soon as they heard a target word, which occurred in the second of a pair of sentences, with the first sentence ending in either a rise or a fall and with or without extended duration of the syllables carrying the intonation contour. This task was used to measure whether the function of the rises was backward-looking (related to the preceding utterance material, and potentially indicating uncertainty or tentativeness) or forward-looking, i.e., influencing the subsequent interaction. They found that words that were preceded by longer duration rises were monitored faster than words preceded by non-prolonged rises, suggesting that the duration of the rise affected its interpretation as forward- or backward-looking.

A large number of studies have used listening tasks to determine what meanings or values are assigned to intonation patterns, including uptalk. In such tasks, listeners typically rate utterances on a number of scales such as friendliness, confidence, likely employment status, employability and so on (Uldall, 1964; Conley et al., 1978; Guy and Vonwiller, 1989; Barr, 2003;

Spindler, 2003; Shokeir, 2007; Gravano et al., 2008; Geenberg, 2009). Guy and Vonwiller (1984) additionally used a matched-guise approach, in which the same Australian English speaker was rated in two conditions – the utterances that were presented contained or did not contain uptalk. This approach has been replicated by Steele (1995, 1996), and for New Zealand English by Borgen (2000). Since uptalk is claimed to be used more by certain speaker groups than others, some rating tasks have used more than one listener group, to see if the same group characteristics, such as age (Di Gioacchino and Crook Jessop, 2010) or ethnicity (Szakay, 2007, 2008, 2012) influence listeners' reactions to uptalk.

10.4 Speech analysis types

In addition to task differences, the results of research on uptalk are influenced by the fact that studies utilise different types of analysis of the speech data that have been gathered. In the majority of cases, researchers report auditory or impressionistic analyses. The more sophisticated of these can involve a transcription system such as those described in Chapter 1. Often, however, the purpose of the study can be fulfilled by marking on an orthographic transcript the points at which an uptalk contour has been heard, or even more simply by counting the number of uptalk rises and working out frequency of occurrence statistics for different speakers or different texts. More detailed analyses of the shapes of uptalk rises frequently also employ acoustic analyses of pitch contours, as shown in Chapter 2. These analyses can be important for determining the phonetic characteristics of uptalk, such as the pitch levels involved or how the beginning and end of the rise are aligned with the text being spoken.

To a certain extent the distinction made here between auditory and acoustic analyses coincides with one between broad and narrow analyses of intonation patterns (Warren and Daly, 2005), or between phonological and phonetic studies. However, these two types of analysis are frequently now combined in the ToBI (Tones and Break Indices) approach, and more and more research studies, as well as textbook descriptions, are based on this framework (see papers in the collections by Jun, 2005, 2014). An increasing number of localised ToBI descriptions are also being constructed for other languages, such as JToBI for Japanese (Venditti, 2005), GToBI for German (Grice and Baumann, 2002), or SpToBI for Spanish (Beckman et al., 2002).

It is not appropriate to provide a full description here of how to carry out a ToBI transcription. The document *Guidelines for ToBI Labelling* (available at www.ling.ohio-state.edu/~tobi/ame_tobi) continues to be the definitive reference for labelling in ToBI. This guide has for a long time served a dual role as both a reference manual and a tutorial tool, but there are many additional tutorial sites available online with detailed examples that can help researchers

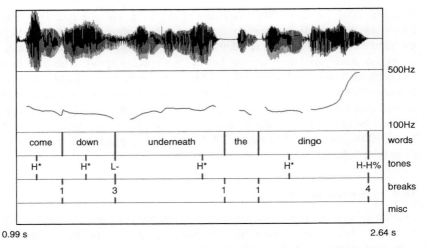

Figure 10.2 ToBI transcription of an Australian English map task utterance, adapted from Figure 14.2(b) in Fletcher et al. (2005).

familiarise themselves with the ToBI system and acquire the relevant transcription skills. ToBI transcriptions are usually carried out using computer-based speech processing packages with annotation possibilities, such as Praat (Boersma and Weenink, 2014). The analysis involves listening while also considering the acoustic evidence from the speech waveform and from the pitch track (i.e., a record of fundamental frequency or F0).

As the name indicates, a full ToBI transcription involves marking not only the H(igh) and L(ow) tone or pitch events (including bitonal accents), but also break indices, which indicate the strength of the boundaries between words, ranging from 0 (the two words are run together and involve connected speech processes across the boundary, as in 'gonna' for 'going to'), to 4 (for a boundary between intonational phrases). An index level of 1 is the default inter-word boundary, and 3 indicates the end of an intermediate phrase. Level 2 shows a strong rhythmic disjuncture that is not also marked by tonal patterns. For most of the transcriptions reported in this book the Break Index representation has been ignored, since our focus is on the high rising tonal patterns. In Figure 10.2, however, annotations for both breaks and tones are shown.

This figure shows the annotation of an extract from a female Australian English speaker, taking part in a map task. The example previously appeared in Fletcher et al. (2005). The first three panels are as in previous examples in this book, showing the speech wave, the pitch track and an orthographic transcription at the word level. Below that are three further tiers in which tones, breaks and other miscellaneous information is represented. Pitch accents (marked with *) are placed in the tones tier in alignment with the accented syllable. Any syllables that the transcriber does not mark with an accent can be assumed to be unaccented. Phrase accents (shown by H or L with a trailing -) and boundary tones (H or L with %) are marked at the end of the relevant phrase. A break index is marked at the end of each word in the breaks tier.

The utterance in Figure 10.2 consists of two intermediate phrases, which together make up a single intonational phrase. While all the pitch accents in the utterance have high pitch, note that in the first intermediate phrase the second pitch accent has a lower absolute pitch than the first one, as a consequence of declination (described in Section 1.3). As explained in Chapter 1, the intermediate phrases are terminated by a phrase tone. The first intermediate phrase ends in a low tone and a rhythmic break, with the latter marked by the 3 on the breaks tier. The sequence of H* L gives a falling intonation pattern over this first phrase. The entire intonational phrase ends additionally in a boundary tone, so that the utterance ends in a combination of a high phrase tone and a high boundary tone (H-H%). Together with the high pitch accent, this gives a H* H-H% sequence, one of the tonal sequences associated with uptalk in Australian English.

In addition to the annotations in Figure 10.2, other information can be provided in further tiers, for instance to indicate the discourse structure of an utterance. Fletcher et al. (2002a), for example, used a separate tier to add dialogue act labels from the SWBD-DAMSL system (Jurafsky et al., 1997). This system distinguishes between a range of discourse functions, including forward communicative functions such as information requests and other types of communication that influence the subsequent interaction, and backward communicative functions reflecting the preceding discourse, such as responses and acknowledgements. Combining this annotation with a ToBI transcription allows the researcher to ask more systematic questions about the relationship between intonation and discourse structure.

A database of recordings that have been transcribed using the ToBI system can subsequently be searched for specific sequences, such as H* followed by H-H%, from which appropriate statistics can be derived for the study of uptalk incidence. In addition, once those sequences have been located, they can be subjected to detailed acoustic phonetic analysis, for instance in order to determine the point at which the intonational rise starts, or the absolute pitch height of the beginning and end of a rise (see Chapter 2).

The success of such ventures depends of course on the reliability of the initial transcriptions, and so it is important that appropriate training be undertaken, and that collaborators check with one another the decisions that they are making about the labels being used. Speer et al. (2011: 47) present some data on agreement between the three authors of that paper, together with two further experts for a subset of the data, for the transcription of a set of 179 target utterances produced by 13 American English speakers as instructions in a game-based production study. They report more than 90 per cent agreement among the panel of five transcribers on the locations of pitch accents, phrase accents, and boundary tones, with more than 94 per cent agreement between the three authors taken alone. When it came to the type of tone, agreement ranged from 60 per cent for pitch accents to 83 per cent for boundary tones. If the difference between downstepped (!H) and non-downstepped (H) tones is discounted, then these figures rise to 72 per cent and 84 per cent respectively. In other words, intonational transcription is not straightforward – not only is it difficult, but it also gives rise to quite a bit of disagreement between experts. This reflects the large element of subjective judgement that is involved in deciding on the nature of pitch accents in particular. It is important therefore that researchers check and recheck their transcriptions, carrying out blind reanalysis for a substantial portion of their materials, and if necessary calling on colleagues to provide validation.

For many languages and varieties of languages there are existing transcription conventions and examples that can be used in training before embarking on an analysis, or for recalibration of the transcriber's decision criteria during the analysis. However, it will also happen that analysis will involve varieties that have not previously been analysed with respect to their intonation patterns. As pointed out elsewhere (Warren, 2005a), the analysis of the intonation of a hitherto unanalysed variety requires some important decisions to be made, and to be made with some care. For example, the researcher must decide whether to base the analysis on that of an existing variety, tweaking the analysis as necessary to fit the new variety, or to start essentially from scratch, treating the new variety as though it were a language for which no existing analysis is available. Both approaches have disadvantages as well as advantages. Starting from an existing framework, for instance, means that some of the groundwork has been done, but the presence of that framework can be constraining, leading the researcher to expect a pattern that may not be found, or to analyse an intonational feature, such as uptalk, as equivalent to an existing feature in the variety that provides the starting point.

10.5   Counting uptalk

Auditory analysis involves close listening (usually to recordings, so that repeated listening can take place) in order to provide some sort of record of how often uptalk occurs and in what types of speech event it is most likely to be found. However, there are differences in how this counting takes place, and it is worth being mindful of these differences when considering the (often competing) claims being made concerning the relative frequencies of uptalk in different studies. For instance, early studies of uptalk in Australian and New Zealand

English counted instances of uptalk over differing domains. Some used units that were delimited by pauses (Allan, 1990), while others used tone groups (Horvath, 1985). While these can coincide, in that the presence of a pause as a boundary marker helps to identify the edge of a tone group, they need not, because tone group boundaries can also be marked by other properties, without the requirement that a measurable pause be present. Similarly, an intonational phrase or tone group may be interrupted by a hesitation pause without breaking it into multiple tone units. This can make comparison of studies problematic (see further discussion in Chapter 5). One recommended procedure would be that recordings are first analysed into intonation units such as intermediate and intonational phrases based on an accepted prosodic analysis (e.g., using the break index analysis of the ToBI approach), and that the incidence of uptalk is then calculated relative to such phrases.

Quite a different approach was taken by McGregor (1980), who also based his decisions about the presence of uptalk on auditory impressions. However, his main measure was derived from this auditory impression, since he was interested not so much in the frequency of uptalk as in whether or not speakers were uptalkers. His measure of uptalker status was calculated as follows. The average time at which a high-rising terminal first appeared in the speech recordings of adolescents in his sample (excluding those who did not use them at all) was 19.21 seconds, with a standard deviation of 16.72 seconds. A value of 47 seconds represents this average plus 1.66 standard deviations, and represents a 95.2 per cent probability level that an instance of uptalk would have been produced by that point in the recording. McGregor therefore firstly excluded from consideration anyone who had recordings that were shorter than 47 seconds. Of the remainder, anyone who used uptalk within the first 47 seconds was designated an uptalker (or 'HRT user' in McGregor's terms), and anyone else a non-uptalker (even if they subsequently produced uptalk after 47 seconds). There is a certain pragmatism behind taking this approach at a time when large-scale and annotated corpora were not readily available. McGregor wanted to carry out an extensive study of a large number of speakers, so that he could look at the effects of a number of social variables. He reports data based on the recordings of 115 adolescents and 120 adults, considerably more participants than are found in most of the more recent corpus-based studies that have been able to take advantage of computational advances since 1980.

10.6   Summary

As the brief summaries in this chapter have shown, uptalk studies have used various sources, tasks and methods of analysis. The selection made in each of these areas will almost certainly impact on the results of the studies, and such considerations therefore need to be taken into account when evaluating uptalk research. Future students of uptalk would also be well advised to consider carefully the nature of the speaking tasks that their participants are asked to engage in. Often this selection will be carried out with the specific aim of comparing task effects, for example, in order to determine more precisely the meanings or functions of uptalk, such as whether it is more likely in narrative or opinion texts, in interactions or in monologues, etc. However, where the goal is to see whether certain speaker groups are more likely than others to use uptalk, then it will clearly be important to use equivalent or directly comparable tasks for the different groups, whether these are young versus old, male versus female, New Zealanders versus Australians, and so on.

Since uptalk is, for many communities, still a relatively unusual intonation pattern, researchers will also need to anticipate carrying out a large amount of speech data collection before sufficient samples are available for meaningful comparisons. Good use can be made of existing corpora, provided these involve appropriate tasks. The level of intonational transcription and other analyses that are required will depend on the nature of the questions being asked. For a measure of uptalk incidence, marking the recordings into intonation units and counting cases of uptalk might be sufficient. For more detailed analyses, further prosodic transcription and/or acoustic analyses may be necessary.

11   Summary and prospect

The aim of this book has been to draw together in one place a range of research findings and other commentary relating to uptalk. Many questions have been asked of uptalk, including what it is, where it has come from and where it will go.

11.1   What is uptalk?

There are widely held views that uptalk is the use of question-like intonation with declarative statements, and that speakers use uptalk because they have doubts or insecurities concerning what they are saying, and so are continually questioning their own output. Such views are understandable, since uptalk utterances are marked by a rising intonation pattern, and intonational rises are typically associated with questions. The link between uptalk and questions is perpetuated by much of the public commentary, and lies behind stereotyped interpretations of uptalk as signalling uncertainty or insecurity. This is, however, too narrow and blinkered an approach. First, it ignores many of the meanings claimed for uptalk, which were explored in Chapters 3 and 6. Second, there are formal properties both of uptalk and of questions that call into doubt the claimed equivalences of the two.

   With regard to its meaning, it is clear that uptalk is not simply about asking questions. In particular, we find uptalk in contexts where the speaker is the owner of the information being communicated, rather than the seeker of information. This is a reversal of the situations in which we might normally find questions. If there is a questioning aspect to uptalk then it is more an invitation to participate than a request for factual information. It is asking the listener to continue to engage in the interaction, and it does this by checking that the listener is following. For both uptalkers and non-uptalkers, the meanings associated with uptalk are those associated with high intonation, i.e., openness or incompleteness. However, to these different groups, i.e., to the in-group and to the out-group, uptalk can mean different things. The authors of opinion pieces and of letters to the editor who complain about uptalk tend to be members of the out-group. Unsurprisingly, given the form of uptalk utterances, non-uptalkers tend to associate uptalk with a questioning attitude, which in turn leads to claims that uptalkers lack confidence, are submissive, uncertain of what they are saying, and so on. Similarly, it is argued that for uptalkers uptalk also indicates openness, only in this case they are inviting the listener to participate in the conversation, or to indicate their understanding of what has been said. It is used to share information rather than to tell (or to question). We have also seen that intonation conveys meanings on different levels, and some of the differences in interpretation can be related to differences in the level at which the rising intonation is being understood – for instance, does it signal a question (a sentence-level linguistic meaning) or is it a checking device (a discourse-level meaning)?

Given the meanings of uptalk, it is not surprising that it is found more frequently in certain types of speaking than in others, nor that it is often accompanied by feedback or back-channelling on the part of the listener. It is particularly prevalent in narrative texts, such as when speakers are relating a story or an episode in their lives. In addition, it is frequently found in interactive tasks, such as map tasks, where it is important for the success of the talk that the listener remains engaged and keeps track of what is being related. This suggests that meanings that are linked to uptalk's interactional functions of checking for comprehension or for engagement in what is being told are much more likely than the stereotyped meanings of uptalk as an expression of doubt or lack of confidence. A further consequence of these uses of uptalk is that it is frequently found in clusters within a speech event, for example, in particular sections of a narrative where listener comprehension is especially crucial.

The formal linkage of uptalk with question intonation is also too narrow. On the one hand, while there are intonation-only questions that are marked by rising intonation as a signal of openness, there are many questions that do not have a rising intonation pattern. This is especially the case when there is morphological or syntactic marking of a question, such as through the use of a question word or of subject–verb inversion in English. In such cases the preferred intonation pattern is often a falling tune.

Furthermore, closer inspection of the forms of uptalk in many varieties of English shows that they often have distinct shapes from the rising patterns of questions, as shown for production data in Chapter 2 and reflected in some of the perceptual studies reviewed in Chapter 8. Some of these distinctions have been difficult to isolate, in part because there is considerable variation in how uptalk is realised across the varieties of English in which it has been studied. Nor should we necessarily expect there to be consistent distinctions, since the meaning of the intonation is often conveyed sufficiently well by the context in which it is produced. If there is a general property that might serve to distinguish uptalk rises from other rises, then it might be found in the more dramatic nature of uptalk rises. For example, they tend to be rises from a lower starting point than question rises in Australian English, or from a later starting point than question rises in New Zealand English, and they have been described as particularly sharp rises in other varieties. Another, related distinguishing characteristic is the tendency for intonation rises associated with questions to result in overall higher average pitch values than those associated with statements.

In addition, it is important to remember that there are other non-question forms that have rising intonation. In some varieties of English, such as the Urban Northern British varieties, rising intonation on statements is standard and carries different meanings from uptalk. More generally, rises on statements are found across varieties in contexts such as producing lists or showing continuation (so-called comma-intonation). Most of these rises can be distinguished from uptalk on both formal and distributional grounds, and so should not be confused with uptalk, although they often are.

Uptalk is frequently also defined by reference to its practitioners. It is associated with younger speakers and with female speakers. As such, it fits a common pattern found for linguistic innovation. In consequence, however, this association of uptalk with young women has allowed the stereotyped meanings to flourish, since the characteristics of insecurity and lack of confidence are unfortunately all too frequently associated with young women. By extension, uptalk is also often associated with lower socioeconomic groups, despite unclear evidence supporting this. However, we have seen that uptalk is not exclusively linked to young speakers, nor to women. Increasingly it is reported in the speech of older speakers, and in that of men. It would perhaps be more appropriate to consider uptalk's distribution among speakers as a reflection of the functions that it fulfils and of the needs or desires of different speaker groups to express those functions. As a device that serves to maintain interaction by seeking input (verbal or non-verbal) from other people taking part in the speech event, uptalk is predictably heard more frequently from the mouths of certain types of speaker. This includes not only women, but others whose cultural traditions are more strongly focused on engaging in conversational narrative. We have seen, for example, that uptalk is more frequently found in the speech of Pacific and other non-Western communities that emphasise more involvement in informal discourse.

What this shows us quite clearly is that the definition of uptalk as a certain type or pattern of intonation is far too simplistic. A fuller definition requires us to take note not just of its form but also of the contexts in which it is used and of the meanings that it conveys. It is the use of often frequent and usually dramatic rises on statements that serve to maintain interaction by either checking the listener's understanding of the discourse or by inviting the listener to engage in the speech event. Misrepresentations and popular misconceptions of uptalk have often failed to appreciate the contexts in which it is being used.

11.2   Where has uptalk come from?

Uptalk appears to have arisen in a range of English varieties – Australian, New
Zealand, Canadian, United States American – at around the same time, and
came to wider attention in the 1970s and 1980s. It was given different labels
(uptalk, upspeak, high-rising terminal, Australian Questioning Intonation,
among others) that reflected both its phonetic properties and its contexts of
occurrence. It is not clear if there was a single original global source for uptalk,
and it is unlikely that we will ever know if that was the case. Nevertheless,
plenty of potential sources have been suggested, as pointed out in Chapter 5.
It is possible that some of the variation in the shapes of uptalk rises across different English varieties may result from the fact that although it may have been
introduced into different regions from some common source, it subsequently
adapted to the intonational system of each variety. As we have seen, despite the
differences, there is a commonality in the dramatic nature of the rise, resulting from a lower starting point, a higher endpoint or a later starting point. In
many varieties the dramatic nature of the uptalk rise helps to distinguish it from
question rises.

Uptalk did not arise in an intonational vacuum. Intonational rises already
existed in all varieties of English, albeit with different meanings and functions
from uptalk. We can see uptalk as an extension of the existing intonational
system. Critics, however, often fail to do this, and treat uptalk as though it were
fulfilling the functions already attributed to rises. What uptalk has done is build
on existing foundations, combining aspects of the meanings of other rises, as
well as of the meanings of other discourse particles such as tag questions. That
is, the continuation signalled by fall-rise patterns at clause boundaries and by
the rises of listing intonation, as well as the interrogative nature of rises on
yes–no questions, are all compatible with the use of uptalk – and of tag questions – to engage the listener in the continuation of discourse. The different
intonational meanings remain in some sense distinct, and this is reflected in the
responses of conversational participants. In particular, listeners do not generally respond to uptalk by providing answers of the type that they would if they
were responding to questions. Rather, they provide minimal feedback, often
non-verbal, indicating that they are still engaged in the conversation.

Our brief survey of other languages across a number of language families has
shown some evidence that uptalk is not unique to English. The emergence of
uptalk in these other languages is later than in English, although there is some
strong indication that precursors to uptalk also existed in some of these other
languages, such as Japanese. The contexts in which uptalk is found in these
other languages suggests that contact with English is a highly likely explanation for the occurrence of uptalk. This contact might well involve the global
spread of English through the media and through youth culture in particular.

11.3   What does the future hold for uptalk?

Linguists will seldom be drawn on questions about the direction in which the development of a linguistic feature will go, as languages often surprise us in the shape that changes in form or usage can take. There are, however, some pointers in the material covered in this book. One comes from the comparison made by Guy et al. (1986: 41–42) of somewhat older speakers in their sample who would have been of the same generation as the teenagers studied 20 years earlier by Mitchell and Delbridge (1965). Particularly noteworthy is the finding that there are similar levels of uptalk usage in a cohort in their mid-30s as they showed as teenagers. This suggests that uptalk as a linguistic behaviour remains relatively fixed into adulthood. More evidence of this type is needed before we can be confident that uptalk is here to stay.

We have also seen evidence that the incidence of uptalk has increased in more general terms in those varieties in which it has been studied over a longer period, and that it has spread to other varieties, to a broader range of speakers, and to a wider range of contexts. It is no longer true (if it ever really was) that uptalk is the preserve of Australian soap opera characters or of young female Californians (as part of Valley Girl speech). Of course, characteristics of language can go in and out of fashion just as easily as styles of dress. The fact that uptalk is as much the object of media commentary today as it was 20 years ago indicates not only that it remains a feature of spoken English but also that it has not yet become so widely accepted that it is no longer deemed noteworthy.

Another and perhaps more indirect indicator of whether uptalk will persevere can be found in the increasing number of studies that suggest that formal distinctions are developing between uptalk and question intonation, and further studies that indicate that these distinctions are perceptually relevant. At the same time, it is important to remember that there will be relatively few contexts in spontaneous speech where it is not clear whether a speaker's rising inflection is asking a question or doing uptalk. A low level of situational ambiguity not only acts as a brake on the development of alternative intonational forms to distinguish uptalk from other rises, but it also has a permissive aspect, allowing uptalk use to spread rather than being curbed in order to avoid misunderstanding.

References

Abe, I. (1955). Intonational patterns of English and Japanese. *Word*, 11, 386–398.

Aceto, M. (2008). Eastern Caribbean English-derived language varieties: phonology. In B. Kortmann and E.W. Schneider (eds.), *Varieties of English. Vol. 2: The Americas and the Caribbean*. Berlin: Mouton de Gruyter, pp. 290–311.

Adams, C.M. (1969). A survey of Australian English intonation. *Phonetica*, 20, 81–130.

Adams, D. (2009). Attacks on the language are rising, basically. *Irish Times*, 19 August, p. 16.

Ainsworth, H. (1994). The emergence of the high rising terminal contour in the speech of New Zealand children. *Te Reo*, 37, 3–20.

Al Bayyari, Y. (2007). *A Prosodic Cue that Invites Back-Channel Responses in Arabic*. MSc thesis, University of Texas at El Paso.

Allan, K. (1984). The component functions of the high rise terminal contour in Australian declarative sentences. *Australian Journal of Linguistics*, 4(1), 19–32.

(1986). *Linguistic Meaning, Vol. 2*. London: Routledge & Kegan Paul.

Allan, S. (1990). The rise of New Zealand intonation. In A. Bell and J. Holmes (eds.), *New Zealand Ways of Speaking English*. Clevedon: Multilingual Matters, pp. 115–128.

Allsopp, R. (1972). *Some Suprasegmental Features of Caribbean English: and their Relevance in the Classroom*. Cave Hill, Barbados: University of the West Indies.

Andersen, G. (2014). Pragmatic borrowing. *Journal of Pragmatics*, 67, 17–33.

Anderson, A., Bader, M., Bard, E., Boyle, E., Doherty, G.M., Garrod, S., Isard, S., Kowtko, J., McAllister, J., Miller, J., Sotillo, C., Thompson, H.S. and Weinert, R. (1991). The HCRC Map Task Corpus. *Language and Speech*, 34, 351–366.

Andrew, M. (2011). 'The real world': lived literacy practices and cultural learning from community placement. *Australian Journal of Language and Literacy*, 34(2), 219–235.

Andrew, S.A. (2004). Enough of the hair, already; a talented debut collection is marred by one clumsy device. *Toronto Star*, 2 May, p. D15.

Anthony, T. (1993). Uptalk's on the rise? Everybody's doing it? *Telegram & Gazette*, 28 December, p. C1.

Aoki, H. (2011). Some functions of speaker head nods. In J. Streeck, C. Goodwin and C.D. LeBaron (eds.), *Embodied Interaction: Language and Body in the Material World*. New York: Cambridge University Press, pp. 93–105.

Armstrong, M.E. (2010). Puerto Rican Spanish intonation. In P. Prieto and P. Roseano (eds.), *Transcription of Intonation of the Spanish Language*. Munich: Lincom Europa, pp. 155–189.

Ayers, G. (1994). Discourse functions of pitch range in spontaneous and read speech. *Ohio State University Working Papers in Linguistics*, 44, 1–49.

Bansal, R.K. (1969). *The Intelligibility of Indian English*. Hyderabad, India: Central Institute of English.

Barr, D.J. (2003). Paralinguistic correlates of conceptual structure. *Psychonomic Bulletin & Review*, 10(2), 462–467.

Barry, A.S. (2007). *The Form, Function, and Distribution of High Rising Intonation in Southern Californian and Southern British English*. PhD thesis, University of Sheffield.

(2008). *The Form, Function and Distribution of High Rising Intonation*. Stuttgart: VDM Verlag.

Barry, A.S. and Arvaniti, A. (2006). *'Uptalk' in Southern Californian and London English*. BAAP 2006 Colloquium, Queen Margaret University College, Edinburgh.

Barry, M.V. (1982). The English language in Ireland. In R.W. Bailey and M. Görlach (eds.), *English as a World Language*. Ann Arbor: University of Michigan Press, pp. 84–133.

Bartels, C. (1999). *The Intonation of English Statements and Questions: A Compositional Interpretation*. New York: Garland Publishing.

Bathurst, B. (1996). A cute accent? *The Observer Review*, 24 March.

Batliner, A. and Oppenrieder, W. (1988). Rising intonation: not passed away but still alive: a reply to R. Geluykens. *Journal of Pragmatics*, 12(2), 227–233.

Bauer, L. (1994). English in New Zealand. In R. Burchfield (ed.), *The Cambridge History of the English Language Vol. 5: English in Britain and Overseas: Origins and Development*. Cambridge: Cambridge University Press.

(2002). *An Introduction to International Varieties of English*. Edinburgh: Edinburgh University Press.

Bauer, L. and Trudgill, P. (eds.) (1998). *Language Myths*. London: Penguin Books.

BBC News Magazine (2014). 10 theories on how uptalk originated. *BBC News Magazine*, 18 August, www.bbc.com/news/magazine-28785865.

Beachcomber (2012). 95 years old and still training dolphins. *Express*, 17 January, www.express.co.uk/comment/beachcomber/373352/95-years-old-and-still-training-dolphins.

(2013) 96 years old and STILL apostrophic with rage. *Express*, 10 June, www.express.co.uk/comment/beachcomber/406401/96-years-old-and-STILL-apostrophic-with-rage.

Beal, J. (2008). English dialects in the North of England: phonology. In B. Kortmann and C. Upton (eds.), *Varieties of English. Vol 1: The British Isles*. Berlin: Mouton de Gruyter, pp. 122–144.

Beard, R. (2006). The lowdown on uptalk. *Dr. Goodword's Language Blog*, www.alphadictionary.com/blog/?p=26.

Beckman, M.E., Díaz-Campos, M., McGory, J.T. and Morgan, T.A. (2002). Intonation across Spanish, in the Tones and Break Indices framework. *Probus*, 14, 9–36.

Beckman, M.E., Hirschberg, J. and Shattuck-Hufnagel, S. (2005). The original ToBI system and the evolution of the ToBI framework. In S.-A. Jun (ed.), *Prosodic Typology: The Phonology of Intonation and Phrasing*. Oxford: Oxford University Press.

Beeching, K. (2007). A politeness-theoretic approach to pragmatico-semantic change. *Journal of Historical Pragmatics*, 8(1), 69–108.

Behan, C. (2005). Leave upspeak to the, like, Americans? *The Irish Times*, 16 August, p. 13.

Bell, A. (2000). Maori and Pakeha English. In A. Bell and K. Kuiper (eds.), *New Zealand English*. Wellington: Victoria University Press, pp. 221–224.

Bell, A. and Johnson, G. (1997). Towards a sociolinguistics of style. *University of Pennsylvania Working Papers in Linguistics*, 4, 1–21.

Bennett, J. (2010). My one-step course to temporarily bring you happiness. *The Press*, 1 September, p. A19.

Benton, R.A. (1966). *Research into the English Language Difficulties of Maori School Children 1963–1964*. Wellington: Maori Education Foundation.

Bernard, J.R.L. (1974). Strine's fine, but you'll pay the price. *Sydney Morning Herald*, 19 February, p. 12.

Besnier, N. (1989). Information withholding as a manipulative and collusive strategy in Nukulaelae gossip. *Language in Society*, 18, 315–341.

Beun, J. (2009). Pushing the limits: pursuing the ultimate high. *Leader Post*, 14 November, p. G3.

Biddulph, J. (1986). *A Short Grammar of Black Country*. Pontypridd: Languages Information Centre.

Boersma, P. and Weenink, D. (2014). Praat: doing phonetics by computer [Computer program]. Version 5.4, www.praat.org.

Bolinger, D. (1964). Intonation as a universal. In H.G. Lunt (ed.), *Proceedings of the Ninth International Congress of Linguists*. The Hague: Mouton, pp. 833–844.

(1972). Around the edge of language: intonation. In D. Bolinger (ed.), *Intonation*. Harmondsworth: Penguin, pp. 19–29.

(1978). Intonation across languages. In J.H. Greenberg (ed.), *Universals of Human Language 2: Phonology*. Stanford: Stanford University Press, pp. 471–524.

(1989). *Intonation and its Uses: Melody in Grammar and Discourse*. London: Edward Arnold.

Borgen, A.S. (2000). *High Rising Terminals in New Zealand*. BA(Honours) thesis, University of Auckland.

Bradford, B. (1996). Upspeak. *SpeakOut! The Newsletter of the IATEFL Pronunciation Special Interest Group*, 18, 22–24.

(1997). Upspeak in British English. *English Today*, 13(3), 29–36.

Bradshaw, P. (2010). Is this therapy? *The Guardian*, 2 December, p. 19.

Bramsen, P., Escobar-Molano, M., Patel, A. and Alonso, R. (2011). *Extracting Social Power Relationships from Natural Language*. Paper presented at 49th Annual Meeting of the Association for Computational Linguistics: Human Language Technologies, Stroudsburg, PA.

Brazil, D. (1997). *The Communicative Role of Intonation in English*. Cambridge: Cambridge University Press.

Brazil, D., Coulthart, M. and Johns, C. (1980). *Discourse Intonation and Language Teaching*. London: Longman.

Brend, R. (1975). Male–female intonation patterns in American English. In B. Thorne and N. Henley (eds.), *Language and Sex: Difference and Dominance*. Rowley, MA: Newberry House, pp. 84–87.

Brennan, S.E. and Williams, M. (1995). The feeling of another's knowing: prosody and filled pauses as cues to listeners about the metacognitive states of speakers. *Journal of Memory and Language*, 34(3), 383–398.

Briggs, B. (1994). Voice of America's youth rings out: uptalk intonation goes. *Denver Post*, 3 March.

Britain, D. (1992). Linguistic change in intonation: the use of high rising terminals in New Zealand English. *Language Variation and Change*, 4, 77–104.

(1998a). Linguistic change in intonation: the use of high-rising terminals in New Zealand English. In P. Trudgill and J. Cheshire (eds.), *The Sociolinguistics Reader, Vol. 1: Multilingualism and Variation*. London: Arnold, pp. 213–239.

(1998b). High rising terminals in New Zealand English: who uses them, when and why. *Essex Research Reports in Linguistics*, 21.

Britain, D. and Newman, J. (1992). High rising terminals in New Zealand English. *Journal of the International Phonetic Association*, 22(1–2), 1–11.

Brown, G., Currie, K.L. and Kenworthy, J. (1980). *Questions of Intonation*. London: Croom Helm.

Brown, P. and Levinson, S.C. (1978). Universals in language usage: politeness phenomena. In E.N. Goody (ed.), *Questions and Politeness*. Cambridge: Cambridge University Press, pp. 56–289.

Brown, R. (2000). *A study in HRTs*. Undergraduate dissertation, University of Auckland.

Bruce, G. (1977). *Swedish Word Accents in Sentence Perspective*. Lund: Gleerup.

Bruce, M. (2007). Like it or not. *Herald Sun*, 6 February, p. 33.

Bryant, P. (1980). *Australian Questioning Intonation: An Addition to Speakers' Response-Seeking Repertoire*. BA(Honours) thesis, Australian National University.

Buckman, A. (2002). Cautious Connie's demanding baby – good stories, but lose the fake sense of urgency. *New York Post*, 25 June, p. 76.

Burchfield, R. (1994). *Glossary of Linguistic Terms*. Cambridge: Cambridge University Press, pp. 554–567.

Burgess, O.N. (1973). Intonation patterns in Australian English. *Language & Speech*, 16(4), 314–326.

Burridge, K. and Mulder, J.G. (1998). *English in Australia and New Zealand: An Introduction to its History, Structure and Use*. Melbourne: Oxford University Press.

Calhoun, S. (forthcoming). The interaction of syntax and prosody in focus fronting in Samoan. *Lingua*.

Calhoun, S. and Schweitzer, A. (2012). Can intonation contours be lexicalised? Implications for discourse meanings. In G. Elordieta and P. Prieto (eds.), *Prosody and Meaning (Interface Explorations 25)*. Berlin: De Gruyter Mouton, pp. 271–327.

Calo, C. (1993). Like, uptalk? *New York Times*, 19 September, p. A18.

Cameron, D. (2001). *Working with Spoken Discourse*. London: Sage.

Carmichael, L.M. (2005). *Situation-Based Intonation Pattern Distribution in a Corpus of American English*. PhD thesis, University of Washington.

Cassidy, F.G. (1961). *Jamaica Talk: Three Hundred Years of the English Language in Jamaica*. London: Macmillan.

Cave, K. (1994). What's up? Culture: teens' distinctive speech pattern of lifting the end of their sentences is catching on in a big way – and parents hate it. *Orange County Register*, 14 July, p. E01.

Cernetig, M. (1997). Manning tunes his twang, consults image specialist: reform Leader's makeover efforts intensify as election nears. *The Globe and Mail*, 5 February, p. A4.

Chambers, J.K. (1998). TV makes people sound the same. In L. Bauer and P. Trudgill (eds.), *Language Myths*. London: Penguin Books, pp. 123–131.

Chaudron, C. (1982). Vocabulary elaboration in teachers' speech to L2 learners. *Studies in Second Language Acquisition*, 4(2), 170–180.

Cheng, W. and Warren, M. (2005). // / CAN i help you //: the use of rise and rise-fall tones in the Hong Kong Corpus of Spoken English. *International Journal of Corpus Linguistics*, 10(1), 85–107.

Cheshire, J. (2005). Syntactic variation and beyond: gender and social class variation in the use of discourse-new markers. *Journal of Sociolinguistics*, 9(4), 479–508.

Cheshire, J. and Williams, A. (2002). Information structure in male and female adolescent talk. *Journal of English Linguistics*, 30, 217–238.

Childs, B. and Wolfram, W. (2008). Bahamian English: phonology. In B. Kortmann and E. W. Schneider (eds.), *Varieties of English. Vol. 2: The Americas and the Caribbean*. Berlin: Mouton de Gruyter, pp. 239–255.

Ching, M.K.L. (1982). The question intonation in assertions. *American Speech*, 57(2), 95–107.

Cieri, C., Graff, D., Kimball, O., Miller, D. and Walker, K. (2004). *Fisher English Training Speech Part 1 Speech*. Philadelphia: Linguistic Data Consortium.

Clark, H. (1992). *Arenas of Language Use*. Chicago: University of Chicago Press. (1996). *Using Language*. Cambridge: Cambridge University Press.

Clark, H. and Wilkes-Gibbs, D. (1986). Referring as a collaborative process. *Cognition* 22, 1–39.

Clarke, D. (2005). A galaxy long, long in play. *The Irish Times*, 29 April, p. 8.

Clopper, C.G. and Smiljanic, R. (2011). Effects of gender and regional dialect on prosodic patterns in American English. *Journal of Phonetics*, 39(2), 237–245.

Collins, B. and Mees, I.M. (1990). The phonetics of Cardiff English. In N. Coupland and A.R. Thomas (eds.), *English in Wales: Diversity, Conflict and Change*. Clevedon: Multilingual Matters, pp. 87–103.

Collins, P. (1989). Sociolinguistics in Australia: a survey. In P. Collins and D. Blair (eds.), *Australian English. The Language of a New Society*. St Lucia, Queensland: University of Queensland Press, pp. 3–20.

Conley, J.M., O'Barr, W.M. and Lind, E.A. (1978). The power of language: presentational style in the courtroom. *Duke Law Journal*, 1978, 1375–1399.

Conn, J. (2006). Dialects in the mist (Portland, OR). In W. Wolfram and B. Ward (eds.), *American Voices: How Dialects Differ from Coast to Coast*. Malden, MA: Blackwell, pp. 149–155.

Conte, A. (2007). Stand up for yourself. *Seventeen*, 1 November, p. 84.

Corwin, A.I. (2009). Language and gender variance: constructing gender beyond the male/female binary. *Electronic Journal of Human Sexuality*, 12.

Coughlan, S. (2005). Uptalk becoming standard speech. *BBC News*, June 21. http://news.bbc.co.uk/2/hi/uk_news/education/4116788.stm.

Coupland, N.C.R. (1988). *Dialect in Use: Sociolinguistic Variation in Cardiff English*. Cardiff: University of Wales Press.

Courtney, N. (1996). The nature of Australian. *English Today*, 12(2), 23–29.

Cowherd, K. (1995). 'Uptalk'? It's, like, talking in queries? Drives you crazy? *The Commercial Appeal*, April 17, p. C1.

Cox, F. and Palethorpe, S. (2007). Australian English. *Journal of the International Phonetic Association*, 37(3), 341–350.

Cruttenden, A. (1981). Falls and rises: meanings and universals. *Journal of Linguistics*, 17, 77–91.

(1986). *Intonation*. Cambridge: Cambridge University Press.

(1995). Rises in English. In J.W. Lewis (ed.), *Studies in General and English Phonetics: Essays in Honour of Professor J.D. O'Connor*. London: Routledge, pp. 155–173.

(1997). *Intonation*, 2nd edn. Cambridge: Cambridge University Press.

(2007). Intonational diglossia: a case study of Glasgow. *Journal of the International Phonetic Association*, 37, 257–274.

Crystal, D. (1969). *Prosodic Systems and Intonation in English*. Cambridge: Cambridge University Press.

Crystal, D. and Davy, D. (1975). *Advanced Conversational English*. London: Longman.

Dalton, M. and Ní Chasaide, A. (2005). Tonal alignment in Irish dialects. *Language and Speech*, 48, 441–464.

Daly, N. and Warren, P. (2001). Pitching it differently in New Zealand English: Speaker sex and intonation patterns. *Journal of Sociolinguistics*, 5, 85–96.

Danesi, M. (1997). Investigating Italian adolescent talk: are there any implications for the teaching of Italian as a second language? *Italica*, 74(4), 455–465.

(2003). *My Son is an Alien: A Cultural Portrait of Today's Youth*. Lanham, MD: Rowman & Littlefield.

Daum, M. (2007). Little voices of distraction. *Los Angeles Times*, 7 July.

Davis, H. (2002). The Canuck uptalk epidemic. *Globe and Mail*, 3 January.

Deane, B. (2001). The first rule for radio talkback: get straight to the point. *Sydney Morning Herald*, 26 November, p. 15.

Delbridge, A. (1970). The recent study of spoken Australian English. In W.S. Ramson (ed.), *English Transported: Essays on Australasian English*. Canberra: Australian National University Press, pp. 15–31.

del Giudice, A. (2006). *High Rising Terminals in Declaratives and Polar Question Intonation of California English*. Manuscript. University of California, San Diego.

DeSimone, R.A. and Haman, E.A. (2005). *How To File For Divorce In Pennsylvania*. Naperville, IL: SphinxLegal.

Deterding, D. and Sharbawi, S. (2013). *Brunei English: A New Variety in a Multilingual Society*. Dordrecht: Springer.

Di Gioacchino, M. and Crook Jessop, L. (2010). Uptalk: towards a quantitative analysis. *Toronto Working Papers in Linguistics*, 33, 1–15.

Dineen, A. (1992). High rise tones and Australian English intonation: a descriptive problem. In T. Dutton, M. Ross and D. Tryon (eds.), *The Language Game: Papers in Memory of Donald C. Laycock*. Canberra: Department of Linguistics, Australian National University, pp. 115–124.

DiResta, D. (2001a). *Does Uptalk Make You Upchuck?* www.diresta.com/public-speaking-articles/article-uptalk.html.

(2001b). *'Uptalk' Invading the Workplace*. www.diresta.com/media-news/press-releases-uptalk-invading-the-workplace.html.

(2010). Ten ways women sabotage communication in the workplace. *Amaranth Womyn*. http://amaranthwomyn.com/factpage-2.php.

Dorrington, N. (2010a). *'Speaking Up': A Comparative Investigation into the Onset of Uptalk in General South African English*. BA(Honours) thesis, Rhodes University.

(2010b). *'Speaking Up': A Investigation into the Uptalk Phenomenon South Africa*. Paper presented at LSSA/SAALA/SAALT Conference, University of South Africa.

Dryer, M.S. (2013). Polar questions. In M.S. Dryer and M. Haspelmath (eds.), *The World Atlas of Language Structures Online*. Munich: Max Planck Digital Library, http://wals.info/chapter/116.

Du Steinberg, W. (2007). The ITA program: an academic bridging program for the changing demographics on North American campuses. *Journal of Continuing Higher Education*, 55(3), 31–37.

Dunn, J. (1999). The secret life of teenage girls. *Rolling Stone*, 11 November, p. 106.

Duranti, A. (1981). *The Samoan Fono: A Sociolinguistic Study*. Canberra: Australian National University, Department of Linguistics.

Eades, D. (1991). Communicative strategies in Aboriginal English. In S. Romaine (ed.), *Language in Australia*. Cambridge: Cambridge University Press, pp. 84–93.

Eckert, P. (1989). The whole woman: sex and gender differences in variation. *Language Variation and Change*, 1, 245–268.

(2008). Language and gender in adolescence. In J. Holmes and M. Meyerhoff (eds.), *The Handbook of Language and Gender*. Oxford: Blackwell, pp. 381–400.

Eckert, P. and McConnell-Ginet, S. (2003). *Language and Gender*. Cambridge: Cambridge University Press.

Edelsky, C. (1979). Question intonation and sex roles. *Language in Society*, 8, 15–32.

Edelstein, A. (1998). Fathering: from a handful to a mouthful. *Newsday*, 10 October, p. B03.

Edenson, J. (1996). *Business Voices*. Venture TV, Canadian Broadcasting Corporation.

Edwards, V. and Sienkewicz, T.J. (1990). *Oral Cultures Past and Present: Rappin' and Homer*. Oxford: Basil Blackwell.

Ellingsæter, C.M. (2014). *'I Sound So Posh Compared To You Lot': Phonological Variation and Change in the Surrey Accent*. Master of English Linguistics thesis, Bergen.

Elmes, S. (2005). *Talking for Britain: A Journey Through the Nation's Dialects*. London: Penguin Books.

English, P. (2011). Change of scene: Black Watch director John swaps Easterhouse for elite US uni. *Daily Record*, 5 March, p. 1819.

Fergus, J. (1997). The sky is falling. *Outdoor Life*, 31 March, p. 22.

Fergus, M.A. (1994). What's up dog? Chill and like read this. *Pantagraph*, 2 October, p. C1.

Feschuk, S. (2009). Ah, the perils of youth. *Maclean's*, 22 June, p. 2.

Finn, P. (2008). Cape Flats English: phonology. In R. Mesthrie (ed.), *Varieties of English. Vol 4: Africa, South and Southeast Asia*. Berlin: Mouton de Gruyter, pp. 200–222.

Fiorito, J. (2005). Relishing poetry with lots of mustard. *Toronto Star*, 6 June, p. B04.

Fisher, J.E. (1997). Questions, answers and answers that sound like questions. *The Salt Lake Tribune*, 29 June, p. J.8.

Fitzgibbon, G. (2007). Demonatory, actually. *The Press*, 3 November, p. A21.

Fletcher, J. (2005). *Compound Rises and 'Uptalk' in Spoken English*. Paper presented at Interspeech 2005, Lisbon, Portugal.

Fletcher, J. and Harrington, J. (2001). High-rising terminals and fall-rise tunes in Australian English. *Phonetica*, 58(4), 215–229.

Fletcher, J. and Loakes, D. (2006). Patterns of rising and falling in Australian English. In P. Warren and C.I. Watson (eds.), *Proceedings of the Eleventh Australasian Conference on Speech Science and Technology*. Canberra: Australasian Speech Science and Technology Association, pp. 42–47.

   (2010). *Interpreting rising intonation in Australian English*. Paper presented at Speech Prosody 2010.

Fletcher, J., Stirling, L., Mushin, I. and Wales, R. (2002a). Intonational rises and dialog acts in the Australian English map task. *Language and Speech*, 45(3), 229–253.

Fletcher, J., Wales, R.J., Stirling, L.F. and Mushin, I.M. (2002b). A dialogue act analysis of rises in Australian English map task dialogues. In B. Bel and I. Marlien (eds.), *Proceedings of Speech Prosody 2002*. Aix-en-Provence: Universite de Provence, pp. 299–302.

Fletcher, J., Grabe, E. and Warren, P. (2005). Intonational variation in four dialects of English: the high rising tone. In S.-A. Jun (ed.), *Prosodic Typology: The Phonology of Intonation and Phrasing*. Oxford: Oxford University Press, pp. 390–409.

Fodor, J.D. (2002). Prosodic disambiguation in silent reading. In M. Hirotani (ed.), *Proceedings of NELS 32*. Amherst, MA: GLSA, University of Massachusetts.

Forman, R. (2009). Review of *Intonation in the Grammar of English*, by M.A.K. Halliday and W. Greaves. *Australian Review of Applied Linguistics*, 32, 17.

Fought, C. (2003). *Chicano English in Context*. Basingstoke: Palgrave Macmillan.

   (2005). Do you speak American? *PBS Online*, www.pbs.org/speak/seatosea/ americanvarieties/tv.

   (2006). Talkin' with mi Gente (Chicano English). In W. Wolfram and B. Ward (eds.), *American Voices: How Dialects Differ from Coast to Coast*. Malden, MA: Blackwell, pp. 233–237.

Foulkes, P. and Barron, A. (2000). Telephone speaker recognition amongst members of a close social network. *Forensic Linguistics*, 7(2), 180–198.

Foulkes, P. and Docherty, G. (2006). The social life of phonetics and phonology. *Journal of Phonetics*, 34, 409–438.

   (2007). Phonological variation in England. In D. Britain (ed.), *Language in the British Isles*. Cambridge: Cambridge University Press, pp. 52–74.

Francis, D. (1988). *The Edge*. New York: Fawcett Crest.

Freedland, J. (2002). In dysfunctional Britain, the office is now our home: our everyday insecurities are laid bare in TV's latest comedy hit. *The Guardian*, 17 October, p. 24.

Freeman, J.B. and Ambady, N. (2010). MouseTracker: software for studying real-time mental processing using a computer mouse-tracking method. *Behavior Research Methods*, 42(1), 226–241.

Fry, S. (2001). *Room 101*. Episode 6x10. Broadcast on 3 December.

Fulford, R. (1995). What's uptalk? An unsettling talk tic? *The Globe and Mail*, 25 January, p. C1.

Geenberg, K. (2009). *'He's So Smart!' Testing Listener Perceptions of Phrase-Final Pauses and Speaker Style in University Discourse*. Paper presented at NWAV38, University of Ottawa.

Geluykens, R. (1987). Intonation and speech act type: an experimental approach to rising intonation in queclaratives. *Journal of Pragmatics*, 11(4), 483–494.

   (1989). R(a)ising questions: question intonation revisited: a reply to Batliner and Oppenrieder. *Journal of Pragmatics*, 13(4), 567–575.

Gernsbacher, M.A. and Jescheniak, J.D. (1995). Cataphoric devices in spoken discourse. *Cognitive Psychology*, 29(1), 24–58.

Gerstel, J. (2006). Watch your language: the words you choose create an impression, regardless of the ideas you are trying to convey. If you're old- fashioned, too bad. The young speak the English of the future. *Toronto Star*, 8 July, p. L01.

Gimson, A.C. (1962). *An Introduction to the Pronunciation of English*. London: Arnold.

Goldsmith, J. (1990). *Autosegmental and Metrical Phonology*. Oxford: Blackwell.

Gordon, E. (1998). Embryonic variants in New Zealand English sound changes. *Te Reo*, 41, 62–68.

(2010). You know, they don't seem to know that we exist? *The Press*, 21 August, p. C7.

Gordon, E. and Trudgill, P. (1999). Shades of things to come: embryonic variants in New Zealand English sound changes. *English World-Wide*, 20(1), 111–124.

Gorman, J. (1993a). Like, uptalk? *New York Times Magazine*, 15 August, p. 614.

(1993b). The lowdown on uptalk. *San Francisco Chronicle*, 22 August, p. 15Z13.

Grabe, E. (1998). Pitch accent realisation in English and German. *Journal of Phonetics*, 26, 129–144.

(2002). Variation adds to prosodic typology. In B. Bel and I. Marlien (eds.), *Proceedings of Speech Prosody 2002*. Aix-en-Provence: Laboratoire Parole et Langage, pp. 127–132.

(2004). Intonational variation in urban dialects of English spoken in the British Isles. In P. Gilles and J. Peters (eds.), *Regional Variation in Intonation*. Tuebingen: Linguistische Arbeiten, pp. 9–31.

Grabe, E. and Post, B. (2002). Intonational variation in English. In B. Bel and I. Marlien (eds.), *Proceedings of Speech Prosody 2002*. Aix-en-Provence: Laboratoire Parole et Langage, pp. 343–346.

Grabe, E., Kochanski, G. and Coleman, J. (2005). The intonation of native accent varieties in the British Isles: potential for miscommunication? In K. Dziubalskakolaczyk and J. Przedlacka (eds.), *English Pronunciation Models: A Changing Scene*. Bern: Peter Lang, pp. 311–337.

Grabe, E., Coleman, J. and Kochanski, G. (2007). Connecting intonation labels to mathematical descriptions of fundamental frequency. *Language and Speech*, 50(3), 281–310.

Graham, B. and Reidy, M. (2009). *Working World 101: The New Grad's Guide To Getting a Job*. Avon, MA: Adams Media.

Granello, D.H. (2010). A suicide crisis intervention model with 25 practical strategies for implementation. *Journal of Mental Health Counseling*, 32(3), 218–235.

Grant, A.D. and Taylor, A. (2014). Communication essentials for female executives to develop leadership presence: getting beyond the barriers of understating accomplishment. *Business Horizons*, 57(1), 73–83.

Gravano, A., Benus, S., Hirschberg, J., Sneed German, E. and Ward, G. (2008). The effect of contour type and epistemic modality on the assessment of speaker certainty. *Speech Prosody 2008*. Brazil: Campinas, pp. 401–404.

Gray, J. (2007). Young, old and in-between: can we all get along? *The Globe and Mail*, 28 September, p. C1.

Gregory, G. (2011). Teaching and learning about language change (part two). *Changing English*, 18(2), 199–218.

Grescoe, T. (2002). A maple leaf ragging. *Maclean's*, 28 January, p. 60.

Grice, H.P. (1975). Logic and communication. In P. Cole and J. Morgan (eds.), *Syntax and Semantics 3: Speech Acts*. New York: Academic Press, pp. 41–58.

Grice, M. and Baumann, S. (2002). Deutsche Intonation und GToBI. *Linguistische Berichte*, 191, 267–298.

Grice, M., Ladd, D.R. and Arvaniti, A. (2000). On the place of phrase accents in intonational phonology. *Phonology*, 17, 143–185.

Grieve, A. (2010). 'Aber ganz ehrlich': differences in episodic structure, apologies and truth-orientation in German and Australian workplace telephone discourse. *Journal of Pragmatics*, 42(1), 190–219.

Guffey, M.E. (2006). *Mary Ellen Guffey's Essentials of Business Communication*. Mason, OH: Thomson South-Western.

Guffey, M.E. and Almonte, R. (2009). *Essentials of Business Communication*. Cengage Learning.

Gunlogson, C. (2001). *True to Form: Rising and Falling Declaratives as Questions in English*. PhD thesis, University of California Santa Cruz.

(2002). Declarative questions. In B. Jackson (ed.), *SALT XII*. Ithaca, NY: Cornell University, pp. 124–143.

Gussenhoven, C. (1984). A semantic analysis of the nuclear tones of English. In C. Gussenhoven (ed.), *On the Grammar and Semantics of Sentence Accents*. Dordrecht: Foris, pp. 193–265.

(2002). Intonation and interpretation: phonetics and phonology. In B. Bel and I. Marlien (eds.), *Proceedings of Speech Prosody 2002*. Aix-en-Provence: Laboratoire Parole et Langage, pp. 47–57.

Guy, G. and Vonwiller, J. (1984). The meaning of an intonation in Australian English. *Australian Journal of Linguistics*, 4(1), 1–17.

(1989). The high rising tone in Australian English. In P. Collins and D. Blair (eds.), *Australian English: The Language of a New Society*. St Lucia, Queensland: University of Queensland Press, pp. 21–34.

Guy, G., Horvath, B., Vonwiller, J., Daisley, E. and Rogers, I. (1986). An intonational change in progress in Australian English. *Language in Society*, 15(1), 23–51.

Haan, J. (2002). *Speaking of Questions: An Exploration of Dutch Question Intonation*. PhD thesis, University of Nijmegen.

Hadding-Koch, K. and Studdert-Kennedy, M. (1964). An experimental study of some intonation contours. *Phonetica*, 11, 175–185.

Halford, B.K. (2007). Adolescent intonation in Canada: talk units in in-group conversations. *Anglia: Zeitschrift für englische Philologie*, 125(1), 4–30.

Halliday, M.A.K. (1966). Intonation systems in English. In A. McIntosh and M.A.K. Halliday (eds.), *Patterns of Language: Papers in General, Descriptive, and Applied Linguistics*. London: Longman, pp. 111–133.

(1967). *Intonation and Grammar in British English*. Berlin: Mouton.

Halliday, M.A.K. and Greaves, W. (2008). *Intonation in the Grammar of English*. London: Equinox.

Hancock, A., Colton, L. and Douglas, F. (2014). Intonation and gender perception: applications for transgender speakers. *Journal of Voice*, 28(2), 203–209.

Hawkins, R. (2004). Thesaurus Rex. *The Globe and Mail*, 1 June, p. A20.

Hayes, D. (2008). *Anytime Playdate: Inside the Preschool Entertainment Boom, Or, How Television Became My Baby's Best Friend*. New York: Simon and Schuster.

Hazenberg, E. (2012). *Language and Identity Practice: A Sociolinguistic Study of Gender in Ottawa, Ontario.* MA thesis, Memorial University of Newfoundland, St John's, NL.

(2013). *"Is This It?" Stance and Indexicality in Transsexual Speech.* Paper presented at the 4th New Zealand Discourse Conference, Auckland University of Technology.

Heffernan, V. (2004). Who needs money when you've got a lot of nerve? *New York Times*, 16 June, p. E3.

Henning, C. (1996). Our soaps are sizzling in the UK: the *Neighbours* invasion. *Sydney Morning Herald*, 30 November, p. 26.

Henton, C.G. (1989). Fact and fiction in the description of female and male speech. *Language and Communication*, 9, 299–311.

(1995). Pitch dynamism in female and male speech. *Language and Communication*, 15, 43–61.

Hermes, D.J. and van Gestel, J.C. (1991). The frequency scale of speech intonation. *Journal of the Acoustical Society of America*, 90, 97–103.

Hickey, R. (2008). Irish English: phonology. In B. Kortmann and C. Upton (eds.), *Varieties of English. Vol 1: The British Isles.* Berlin: Mouton de Gruyter, pp. 71–104.

Hincks, R. (2005). Measures and perceptions of liveliness in student oral presentation speech: a proposal for an automatic feedback mechanism. *System*, 33(4), 575–591.

Hirschberg, J. (2002). The pragmatics of intonational meaning. In B. Bel and I. Marlien (eds.), *Proceedings of Speech Prosody 2002.* Aix-en-Provence: Laboratoire Parole et Langage, pp. 65–68.

Hirschberg, J. and Ward, G. (1995). The interpretation of the high-rise question contour in English. *Journal of Pragmatics*, 24, 407–412.

Hoad, P. (2005). Dark star. *The Observer*, 5 June, p. 26.

Hobbs, J.R. (1990). The Pierrehumbert–Hirschberg theory of intonational meaning made simple: comments on Pierrehumbert and Hirschberg. In P.R. Cohen, J.L. Morgan and M.E. Pollack (eds.), *Intentions in Communication*, Cambridge, MA: MIT Press, pp. 313–323.

Hoff, M.A. (2014). *Ethnic Identity and Accent: Exploring Phonological Acquisition for International Students from China.* MA thesis, Bowling Green State University.

Hogan, C.A. (2010). *Conclave Vol 2.* Manuscript. CD sleeve notes: All About Jazz, Jazz Review, *Down Beat*.

Holmes, J. (1982). The functions of tag questions. *English Language Journal*, 3, 40–65.

(1984). Modifying illocutionary force. *Journal of Pragmatics*, 8(3), 345–365.

(1986). Functions of *you know* in women's and men's speech. *Language in Society*, 15(1), 1–21.

(1995). *Women, Men and Politeness.* London: Longman.

(2002). Politeness strategies in New Zealand women's speech. In A. Bell and J. Holmes (eds.), *New Zealand Ways of Speaking English.* Clevedon: Multilingual Matters, pp. 252–275.

(2005). Using Maori English in New Zealand. *International Journal of the Sociology of Language*, 172, 91–115.

Holmes, J. and Bell, A. (1988). Learning by experience: notes for New Zealand social dialectologists. *Te Reo*, 31, 19–49.

(1990). Attitudes, varieties, discourse: an introduction to the sociolinguistics of New Zealand English. In A. Bell and J. Holmes (eds.), *New Zealand Ways of Speaking English*. Clevedon: Multilingual Matters, pp. 1–28.

(1996). Maori English (New Zealand). In S.A. Wurm, P. Mühlhäusler and D.T. Tryon (eds.), *Atlas of Languages of Intercultural Communication in the Pacific, Asia, and the Americas: Texts, Volume 2*, New York: Mouton de Gruyter, pp. 177–181.

Holmes, J. and Schnurr, S. (2006). 'Doing femininity' at work: more than just relational practice. *Journal of Sociolinguistics*, 10(1), 31–51.

Holmes, J., Bell, A. and Boyce, M. (1991). *Variation and Change in New Zealand English: A Social Dialect Investigation*. Project Report to the Social Sciences Committee of the Foundation for Research, Science and Technology. Wellington: Department of Linguistics, Victoria University of Wellington.

Horowitz, J. (2006). City girl squawk: it's like so bad, It. Really. Sucks? *The New York Observer*, 27 March, p. 1.

Horvath, B. (1985). *Variation in Australian English: The Sociolects of Sydney*. Cambridge: Cambridge University Press.

(2004). Australian English: phonology. In B. Kortmann, E.W. Schneider, K. Burridge, R. Mesthrie and C. Upton (eds.), *A Handbook of Varieties of English: A Multimedia Reference Tool*, Vol. 1. Berlin: Mouton de Gruyter, pp. 625–644.

House, J. (2006). Constructing a context with intonation. *Journal of Pragmatics*, 38(10), 1542–1558.

(2007). The role of prosody in constraining context selection: a procedural approach. *Nouveux cahiers de linguistique française*, 28, 369–383.

Howard, P. (2001). Hello, can you speak up? I can't hear your uptalk, I'm on the train. *The Times*, 7 September, p. 16.

Hustad, M. (2008). *How to Be Useful: A Beginner's Guide to Not Hating Work*. New York: Houghton Mifflin.

Innes, B. (2007). 'Everything happened so quickly?' HRT intonation in New Zealand courtrooms. *Research on Language and Social Interaction*, 40(2–3), 227–254.

Inoue, F. (1997). Intoneshon no Shakaisei. In M. Sugito, T. Kunihiro, H. Hirose and M. Kono (eds.), *Nihongo Onsei 2 Akusento, Intoneshon, Rizumu to Pozu*. Tokyo: Sanseido, pp. 143–168.

(1998). Sociolinguistics of intonational change in progress in Tokyo. *Area and Culture Studies*, 56, 11–24.

(1999). Trends of linguistic variations in modern Japan. *Area and Culture Studies*, 58, 39–46.

(2006). Sociolinguistic characteristics of intonation. In Y. Kawaguchi, I. Fónagy and T. Moriguchi (eds.), *Prosody and Syntax: Cross-Linguistic Perspective*. Amsterdam: John Benjamins, pp. 197–222.

Inoue, M. (2006). *Vicarious Language: Gender and Linguistic Modernity in Japan*. Berkeley, CA: University of California Press.

International Dialects of English Archive (2000). Audio sample *Scotland 3*, www.dialectsarchive.com/scotland-3.

International Dialects of English Archive (2013). Audio sample *British Columbia 1*, www.dialectsarchive.com/british-columbia-1.

Iowa Center for the Arts (2008). University of Iowa theater alumnus Bruce Shapiro is dialect Wizard of Oz. *US Fed News Service*, 28 July.

Irvine, J.T. and Gal, S. (2000). Language ideology and linguistic differentiation. In P.V. Kroskrity (ed.), *Regimes of Language: Ideologies, Polities, and Identities*. Santa Fe, NM: School of American Research Press, pp. 35–83.

Jacobs, A. (2004). Zooey at the Zoo: Sundance report. *The New York Observer*, 2 February, p. 22.

(2005). The sexiest woman alive. *Esquire*, 30 November, p. 154.

James, E., Mahut, C. and Latkiewitcz, G. (1989). The investigation of an apparently new intonation pattern in Toronto English. *Information Communication*, 10, 11–17.

Jarman, E. and Cruttenden, A. (1976). Belfast intonation and the myth of the fall. *Journal of the International Phonetic Association*, 61, 4–12.

Jenkins, J. (2004). Research in teaching pronunciation and intonation. *Annual Review of Applied Linguistics*, 24, 109–125.

Jespersen, A. (2014). *The Effect of Speaker Roles and Speech Style on the Use of HRTs in Aboriginal English*. Paper presented at the BAAP 2014, Oxford, UK.

Johnson, P. (2002). Stewart: 'I want to focus on my salad'. *USA Today*, 26 June, p. D03.

Johnstone, B. (2003). Conversation, text, and discourse. In D.R. Preston (ed.), *Needed Research in American Dialects*. Durham: Duke University Press for the American Dialect Society, pp. 75–98.

Jones, C.J.J. and Roux, J.C. (2003). Acoustic and perceptual qualities of queclaratives in Xhosa. *South African Journal of African Languages*, 23(4), 223–236.

Jun, S.-A. (ed.) (2005). *Prosodic Typology: The Phonology of Intonation and Phrasing*. Oxford: Oxford University Press.

(ed.). (2014). *Prosodic Typology II: The Phonology of Intonation and Phrasing*. Oxford: Oxford University Press.

Junod, T. (2007). The Isaac Newton of biology. *Esquire*, 1 December, p. 184.

Jurafsky, D., Schriberg, L. and Biasca, D. (1997). *Switchboard SWBD-DAMSL Shallow-Discourse-Function-Annotation Coder's Manual, Draft 13*. Technical Report TR 97–02. University of Colorado at Boulder, Institute for Cognitive Science.

Kachru, B.B. (1992). *The Other Tongue: English Across Cultures*, 2nd edn. Urbana, IL: University of Illinois Press.

Kaiser, J., Munrow, A., Pidwell, R., Tubby, J. and White, J. (1987). *Final High-Rising Tones in Declarative Utterances*. Unpublished research project. Auckland: University of Auckland.

Kaldor, S. and Malcolm, I.G. (1991). Aboriginal English: an overview. In S. Romaine (ed.), *Language in Australia*. Cambridge: Cambridge University Press, pp. 67–83.

Kang, O., Rubin, D.O.N. and Pickering, L. (2010). Suprasegmental measures of accentedness and judgments of language learner proficiency in oral English. *The Modern Language Journal*, 94(4), 554–566.

Kapos, S. (2004). Gauging grads' prospects: patience, professionalism recommended for women entering jittery job market. *Chicago Tribune*, 2 June, p. 3.

Kennedy, D. (1996). Soap opera Australian-speak raises the tone. *The Times*, 19 March, p. 1.

Kenny, M. (2007). It is a paradox that as people become more prosperous they may become more unhappy. *Irish Independent*, 17 November, p. 1.

Kerwin, R. (1997). Backward caps? Backward brains. *The San Francisco Examiner*, 13 August, p. A19.

Kiesling, S.F. (2005). Variation, stance and style: word-final –er, high rising tone, and ethnicity in Australian English. *English World-Wide*, 26(1), 1–42.

(2006). English in Australia and New Zealand. In B.B. Kachru, Y. Kachru and C.L. Nelson (eds.), *The Handbook of World Englishes*. Oxford: Blackwell, pp. 74–89.

Kill, S.M.J. (2001). Blame the Canadians? *The Guardian*, 24 September, p. 19.

Knowles, G. (1975). *Scouse: The Urban Dialect of Liverpool*. PhD thesis, University of Leeds.

(1981). Variable strategies in intonation. In D. Gibbon and H. Richter (eds.), *Intonation, Accent and Rhythm*. Berlin: de Gruyter, pp. 226–242.

Koch, C. (2012). Say what? OMG, we're speaking a whole e new language. But is it a bit t n ridic. *Sunday Times*, 15 January, p. 21.

Kopun, F. (2009). Long hours, lots of travel and sharing a loo with 16 girls. *The Spectator*, 17 November, p. G9.

Kortenhoven, A. (1998). *Rising Intonation in Children's Narratives*. Manuscript.

Kotyk, B. (2008). How … is that? *The Globe and Mail*, 9 June, p. A14.

Kroch, A.S. (1978). Toward a theory of social dialect variation. *Language in Society*, 7(1), 17–36.

Kyff, R. (1995). 1994 gets in last word on language. *Austin American Statesman*, 2 January, p. B6.

(1998). This just in from the front lines. *Hartford Courant*, 29 April, p. F2.

(2004). On girly growls and yaks for rent. *Hartford Courant*, 27 August, p. D2.

Labov, W. (1966). *The Social Stratification of English in New York City*. Washington, DC: Center for Applied Linguistics.

(1980). The social origins of sound change. In W. Labov (ed.), *Locating Language in Time and Space*. New York: Academic Press, pp. 251–265.

(1982). *Sociolinguistic patterns*. Philadelphia: University of Pennsylvania Press.

Labov, W. and Waletzky, J. (1967). Narrative analysis. In J. Helm (ed.), *Essays on the Verbal Skills and Visual Arts*. Seattle: University of Washington Press, pp. 12–44.

Lacey, C., Rampersaud, S. and Tennant, J. (1997). Observations sur les finales à montée élevée dans les phrases déclaratives en anglais canadien. In H. Gezundhajt and P. Martin (eds.), *Promenades phonétiques*. Toronto: Éditions Mélodie, pp. 131–143.

Ladd, D.R. (1980). *The Structure of Intonational Meaning: Evidence from English*. Bloomington: Indiana University Press.

(1996). *Intonational Phonology*. Cambridge: Cambridge University Press.

(2008). *Intonational Phonology*, 2nd edn. Cambridge: Cambridge University Press.

Lakoff, R. (1973). Language and woman's place. *Language in Society*, 2, 45–79.

(1975). *Language and Woman's Place*. New York: Harper & Row.

Lanham, L. (1967). *The Pronunciation of South African English: A Phonetic-Phonemic Introduction*. Amsterdam: Balkema.

(1982). English in South Africa. In R.W. Bailey and M. Görlach (eds.), *English as a World Language*. Ann Arbor: University of Michigan Press, pp. 324–352.

Laver, J. (1994). *Principles of Phonetics*. Cambridge: Cambridge University Press.

Lawson, M. (1998). TV is the perp. *The Guardian*, 21 March, p. 25.

Leach, H. (2008). *The Pavlova Story: A Slice of New Zealand's Culinary History*. Dunedin: Otago University Press.

Leeman, A. (2009). Intonational variation in Swiss German. In S. Tsiplakou, M. Karyolemou and P.Y. Pavlou (eds.), *Language Variation – European Perspectives II: Selected Papers from the 4th International Conference on Language Variation in Europe (ICLaVE 4), Nicosia, June 2007*. Amsterdam: John Benjamins, pp. 135–143.

Leitner, G. (2004). *Australia's Many Voices: Australian English – the National Language*, Vol. 90.1. New York: Mouton de Gruyter.

Levis, J.M. (1996). *An Experimental Study of the Status of Two Low-Rising Intonation Contours in American English*. PhD thesis, University of Illinois at Urbana-Champaign.

(1999). Intonation in theory and practice, revisited. *TESOL Quarterly*, 33(1), 37–63.

Liberman, M. (2005a). This is, like, such total crap? *Language Log*, http://158.130.17.5/~myl/languagelog/archives/002708.html.

(2005b). Uptalk uptick? *Language Log*, http://itre.cis.upenn.edu/~myl/languagelog/archives/002708.html.

(2006a). Angry rises. *Language Log*, http://itre.cis.upenn.edu/~myl/languagelog/archives/002967.html.

(2006b). Uptalk is not HRT. *Language Log*, http://itre.cis.upenn.edu/~myl/languagelog/archives/002967.html.

(2008a). Uptalk anxiety. *Language Log*, http://languagelog.ldc.upenn.edu/nll/?p=568.

(2008b). The phonetics of uptalk. *Language Log*, http://languagelog.ldc.upenn.edu/nll/?p=586.

(2008c). Word (in)constancy. *Language Log*, http://languagelog.ldc.upenn.edu/nll/?p=600.

(2008d). Uptalk v. UNBI again. *Language Log*, http://languagelog.ldc.upenn.edu/nll/?p=863.

(2008e). Elementary-school uptalk. *Language Log*, http://languagelog.ldc.upenn.edu/nll/?p=874.

(2008f). Medical uptalk. *Language Log*, http://languagelog.ldc.upenn.edu/nll/?p=948.

(2010). Annals of uptalk: the python wrestler. *Language Log*, http://languagelog.ldc.upenn.edu/nll/?p=2163.

(2013a). Uptalk awakening. *Language Log*, http://languagelog.ldc.upenn.edu/nll/?p=7406.

(2013b). Okie uptalk. *Language Log*, http://languagelog.ldc.upenn.edu/nll/?p=8373.

Lippi-Green, R. (2012). *English with an Accent*, 2nd edn. Abingdon: Routledge.

Local, J. (1986). Patterns and problems in a study of Tyneside intonation. In C. Johns-Lewis (ed.), *Intonation in Discourse*. London: Croom Helm, pp. 181–197.

Local, J., Kelly, J. and Wells, W.H.G. (1986). Towards a phonology of conversation: turn-taking in Tyneside English. *Journal of Linguistics*, 22(2), 411–437.

Lodge, D. (1991). *Paradise News*. Harmondsworth: Penguin.

Loviglio, J. (2008). Sound effects: gender, voice and the cultural work of NPR. *Radio Journal: International Studies in Broadcast & Audio Media*, 5(2–3), 67–81.

Lowry, O. (2002). The stylistic variation of nuclear patterns in Belfast English. *Journal of the International Phonetic Association*, 32(1), 33.

(2011). Belfast intonation and speaker gender. *Journal of English Linguistics*, 39(3), 209–232.

Lusher, T. (2010). Uptalking is, like, totally cool again? *The Guardian*, 3 May, p. G2.

MacAfee, C. (1983). *Glasgow*. Amsterdam: John Benjamins.

MacNeil, R. and Cran, W. (2005). *Do You Speak American? A Companion to the PBS Television Series*. New York: Nan A. Talese/Doubleday.

Maekawa, K. (2011). *Discrimination of Speech Registers by Prosody*. Paper presented at ICPhS XVII, Hong Kong.

(2012). *Prediction of Non-Linguistic Information of Spontaneous Speech from the Prosodic Annotation: Evaluation of the X-JToBI System*. Paper presented at Eighth International Conference on Language Resources and Evaluation (LREC).

Maidment, J.A. (1994). *Estuary English: Hybrid or Hype?* Paper presented at the 4th New Zealand Conference on Language & Society, Lincoln University, New Zealand.

MailOnline (2014). Want a promotion? Don't speak like an Aussie: rising in pitch at the end of sentences make you sound 'insecure'. *MailOnline*, 13 January, www.dailymail.co.uk/sciencetech/article-2538554/Want-promotion-D ont-speak-like-AUSSIE-Rising-pitch-end-sentences-make-sound-insecure. html#ixzz3E5PJ6rAX.

Malan, K. (1996). Cape Flats English. In V. De Klerk (ed.), *Focus on South Africa*. Amsterdam: John Benjamin, pp. 125–148.

Mali, T. (2000). *What Teachers Make* [poem], www.youtube.com/watch?v=0xuFnP5N2uA.

(2005). *Totally Like Whatever* [poem], www.npr.org/templates/story/story. php?storyId=4608329.

Marsh, S. (2006). The rise of the interrogatory statement. *The Times*, 28 March, p. 7.

Mason, J. (2007). A grande idea. *The Ottawa Citizen*, 25 March, p. B8.

Matluck, J. (1952). La pronunciación del español en el valle de México. *Nueva Revista de Filología Hispánica*, 6(2), 109–120.

Matthews, P.H. (2007). *The Concise Oxford Dictionary of Linguistics*, 2nd edn. Oxford: Oxford University Press.

McCarthy, G. (2001). Soul music. *Sunday Times*, 7 October, p. 13.

McConnell-Ginet, S. (1975). Our father tongue: essays in linguistic politics. Review of: *Language and Woman's Place* by Robin Lakoff. *Diacritics*, 5(4), 44–50.

(1978). Intonation in a man's world. *Signs*, 3(3), 541–559.

(1983). Intonation in a man's world. In B. Thorne, C. Kramarae and N. Henley (eds.), *Language, Gender, and Society*. Rowley, MA: Newbury House, pp. 69–88.

McDonough, K. (2000). Tune in tonight. *The Charleston Daily Mail*, 5 August, p. 7B.

(2001). 'Undeclared' gets an A; skip 'Philly' cheese: college life rules new series; trial show is out of order. *The Charleston Daily Mail*, 18 September, p. 5D.

McElholm, D.D. (1986). Intonation in Derry English. In H. Kirkwood (ed.), *Studies in Intonation*. Coleraine: New University of Ulster, pp. 1–58.

McGillivray, D. (1994). On the hunt for new words, we... *Postmedia News*, 15 November, p. 1.

McGregor, J. (2005). *High Rising Tunes in Australian English*. PhD thesis, Macquarie University, Sydney, Australia.

McGregor, J. and Palethorpe, S. (2008). High rising tunes in Australian English: the communicative function of L* and H* pitch accent onsets. *Australian Journal of Linguistics*, 28(2), 171–193.

McGregor, R.L. (1979). *High-Rising Tone in Non-Question Forms in Sydney Australian English*. MA Thesis, Macquarie University.

(1980). The social distribution of an Australian English intonation contour. *Working Papers of the Speech and Language Research Centre, Macquarie University*, 2(6), 1–26.

McKerras, R. (2010). Letter. *The Press*, 4 September, p. A20.

McLean, G. (2002). Television: TV review: *In For the Kill*. *The Guardian*, 6 August, p. 26.

McLemore, C. (1991). *The Pragmatic Interpretation of English Intonation: Sorority Speech*. PhD thesis, University of Texas, Austin, TX.

McNally, F. (2005). 100% natural upspeak. *The Irish Times*, 12 November, p. 16.

McQuillan, D. (2004). One-woman brand. *The Irish Times*, 31 January, p. 80.

Mees, I.M. and Collins, B. (1999). Cardiff: a real time study of glottalisation. In P. Foulkes and G. Docherty (eds.), *Urban Voices: Accent Studies in the British Isles*. London: Arnold, pp. 185–202.

Megenney, W. (1982). Elementos subsaháricos en el español dominicano. In O. Alba (ed.), *El español del Caribe*. Santiago de los Caballeros: Universidad Católica Madre y Maestra, pp. 183–201.

Mellow Monk (2006). Japanese teens? Are, like, uptalking, too? *Mellow Monk's Green Tea Blog*, http://blog.mellowmonk.com/2006/03/japanese-teens-are-like-uptalking-too.html.

Mendelsohn, J. (1993). Talking? About a new way of talking? *USA Today*, 2 November, p. 01D.

Merin, A. (1994). Algebra of elementary social acts. In S.L. Tsohatzidis (ed.), *Foundations of Speech Act Theory*. London: Routledge, pp. 234–263.

Mesner, S. (2001). Strewth! Currys' new slogan is a bit crook, mate. *Marketing*, 6 September, p. 60.

Metcalf, A.A. (1974). The study of California Chicano English. *International Journal of the Sociology of Language*, 1(2), 53–58.

Meyerhoff, M. (1991). *Grounding and Overcoming Obstacles: The Positive Politeness Motivations of High Rising Terminals*. Manuscript.

    (1992). High rising terminal declarative, eh? *New York Times*, 19 January.

    (1996). Dealing with gender identity as a sociolinguistic variable. In V.L. Bergvall, J.M. Bing and A.F. Freed (eds.), *Rethinking Language and Gender Research: Theory and Practice*. London: Longman, pp. 202–227.

Michaels, S. (1984). Listening and responding: hearing the logic in children's classroom narratives. *Theory into Practice*, 23(3), 218–224.

Millar, J.B., Vonwiller, J.P., Harrington, J.M. and Dermody, P.J. (1994). *Proceedings of ICASSP-94, Adelaide*, 1, 97–100.

Miller, J. (2004). Scottish English: morphology and syntax. In B. Kortmann, E.W. Schneider, K. Burridge, R. Mesthrie and C. Upton (eds.), *A Handbook of Varieties of English: A Multimedia Reference Tool*, Vol. 2. Berlin: Mouton de Gruyter, pp. 47–72.

Milroy, J. and Milroy, L. (1999). *Authority in Language: Investigating Standard English*, 3rd edn. London: Routledge.

Miskin, R. (2008). Why do so many younger people now speak with a raised inflection at the end of sentences? *The Times*, 25 January, p. 75.

Mitchell, A.G. and Delbridge, A. (1965). *The Speech of Australian Adolescents*. Sydney: Angus & Robertson.

Moore, B. (2008). *Speaking Our Language: The Story of Australian English*. Sydney: Oxford University Press.

Morales-Muñoz, K., Rodríguez, Z.S., Román, M.C.V. and Faraclas, N. (2009). A comparison of intonation in St Croix English Lexifier Creole and Puerto Rican

Spanish: West African influences on intonation patterns in the Eastern Caribbean. *Cuadernos de Lingüística/UPR Working Papers*, 2(1), 34–54.

Morris, V. (1998). Hear at last: the Monica-Linda tapes. *New York Post*, 18 November, p. 5.

Mullaney, A. (2010). Can you tell why they made it yet? *The Scotsman*, 30 December, p. 40.

Nilsenová, M. (2002). A game-theoretical approach to the meaning of intonation in rising declaratives and negative polar questions. In B. Bel and I. Marlien (eds.), *Proceedings of Speech Prosody 2002*. Aix-en-Provence: Laboratoire Parole et Langage, pp. 535–538.

Norman, P. (2001). What would 'Enry 'Iggins make of our Slop English? *Daily Mail*, 2 March.

Nussbaum, E. (2007). I'm naked on the internet. *The Australian*, 24 March, p. 1.

O'Barr, W.M. and Atkins, B. (1980). 'Women's language' or 'powerless language'? In S. McConnell-Ginet, R. Borker and N. Furman (eds.), *Women and Language in Literature and Society*. New York: Praeger, pp. 93–110.

O'Connor, J.D. and Arnold, G.F. (1961). *The Intonation of Colloquial English*. London: Longman.

Ogden, R. and Routarinne, S. (2005). The communicative functions of final rises in Finnish intonation. *Phonetica*, 62(2–4), 160–175.

Ohala, J.J. (1983). Cross-language use of pitch: an ethological view. *Phonetica*, 40, 1–18.

Orange County Register (1993). What's up, Talk? *Orange County Register*, 21 October, p. B08.

Orlando Sentinel (1995). Reap respect by changing your wimpy speech patterns. *Orlando Sentinel*, 1 November, p. E3.

Paddock, H. (1981). *A dialect survey of Carbonear, Newfoundland*, Vol. 68. Urbana, IL: American Dialect Society.

Page, J. (1996). Once more on pregnancy. *The Record*, 11 March, p. a03.

Palmer, G. (2003). *Grumpy Old Men*. Episode 1, BBC. Broadcast on 10 October.

Park, M.W. (2011). *Teaching Intonation Patterns through Reading Aloud*. MA(TESOL) thesis, Portland State University.

Parkin, J. (2005). Why I won't be seen dead in Primark; because cheap chic makes me look more hobo than boho. *Daily Mail*, 14 July, p. 52.

(2006). Stomach-churning gossip about the school loos. Slang that's, like, totally infuriating. Oh, the joys (and, yes, benefits) of family mealtimes. *Daily Mail*, 29 June, p. 49.

(2008). I lust after Monty Don, look like a walrus at the swimming pool, and I'm addicted to National Trust shops. Help! I'm finally turning 50. *Daily Mail*, 14 February, p. 59.

Parr, J. (1995). Uptalk, eh? *The Globe and Mail*, 1 February, p. A18.

Pearson, B. (2001). Blame the Canadians? *The Guardian*, 24 September, p. 19.

Pellowe, J. and Jones, V. (1978). On intonational variability in Tyneside speech. In P. Trudgill (ed.), *Sociolinguistic Patterns in British Speech*. London: Edward Arnold, pp. 101–121.

Penfield, J. (1984). Prosodic patterns: some hypotheses and findings from fieldwork. In J. Ornstein-Galicia (ed.), *Form and Function in Chicano English*. Rowley, MA: Newbury House, pp. 71–82).

Pennington, M.C., Lau, L. and Sachdev, I. (2011). Diversity in adoption of linguistic features of London English by Chinese and Bangladeshi adolescents. *Language Learning Journal*, 39(2), 177–199.

Perry, W. (2005). A 'strap-on party' for the people. *The Gay & Lesbian Review Worldwide*, 31 August, p. 28.

Peters, J. (2005). Intonation. In *Duden, Vol. 4: Die Grammatik*. Mannheim: Bibliographisches Institut.

    (2007). *Uptalk. Ein prosodisches Merkmal der politischen Reden Franz Müntentierings und seine Verwendung als Stilmittel in der Satire*. Presentation at University of Paderborn.

Pierrehumbert, J. (1980). *The Phonology and Phonetics of English Intonation*. PhD thesis, Massachusetts Institute of Technology.

    (2000). Tonal elements and their alignment. In M. Horne (ed.), *Prosody: Theory and Experiment. Studies Presented to Gösta Bruce*. Dordrecht: Kluwer, pp. 11–36.

Pierrehumbert, J. and Hirschberg, J. (1990). The meaning of intonational contours in the interpretation of discourse. In P.R. Cohen, J. Morgan and M.E. Pollack (eds.), *Intentions in Communication*. Cambridge, MA: MIT Press, pp. 271–311.

Pike, K.L. (1945). *The Intonation of American English*. Ann Arbor, MI: University of Michigan Press.

Pilch, H. (1983/1984). The structure of Welsh tonality. *Studia Celtica*, 18/19, 234–252.

Pinker, S. (2000). Won't extinguish others: English might not be the language of the next century after all. *Morning Star*, 2 January, p. 9E.

Podesva, R.J. (2011). Salience and the social meaning of declarative contours: three case studies of gay professionals. *Journal of English Linguistics*, 39(3), 233–264.

Post, B. (2000). *Tonal and Phrasal Structures in French Intonation*. PhD Thesis, University of Nijmegen.

Pratt-Johnson, Y. (2005). *The Growing Use of Uptalk in the United States: Language Trend or Shift?* Paper presented at the Language and Global Communication Conference, Cardiff University, Wales, www.cardiff.ac.uk/encap/projects/globalcomm/lgc2005/details.asp_id=66.html.

    (2006). *The Use of Uptalk Among African American High School Students and Young Adults in the United States*. Paper presented at the Sociolinguistics Symposium, University of Limerick, Ireland.

Price, S. (2010). Comedy. *The Independent on Sunday*, 28 November, p. 58.

Prieto, P. and Roseano, P. (eds.) (2010). *Transcription of Intonation of the Spanish Language*. Munich: Lincom Europa.

Pullum, G.K. (2006). Intonation contours and polonium poisoning. *Language Log*, http://itre.cis.upenn.edu/~myl/languagelog/archives/003920.html.

Rahilly, J. (1997). Aspects of prosody in Hiberno-English: the case of Belfast. In J.L. Kallen (ed.), *Focus on Ireland*. Amsterdam: John Benjamins, pp. 109–132.

Raithel, V. (2005). *The Perception of Intonation Contours and Focus by Aphasic and Healthy Individuals*. Tübingen: Gunter Narr Verlag.

Ramisch, H. (2008). Channel Island English: phonology. In B. Kortmann and C. Upton (eds.), *Varieties of English. Vol 1: The British Isles*. Berlin: Mouton de Gruyter, pp. 223–236.

Rau, E. (1996). Shed that passive image. *Providence Journal*, 14 March, p. H08.

Redbook (2007). Are your words holding you back? *Redbook*, 31 October, p. 184.

Rehner, K. and Legate, J.A. (1996). *A Study of High Rising Terminal Contours in Declaratives*. Manuscript.

Richardson, D.C., Dale, R. and Tomlinson, J.M. (2009). Conversation, gaze coordination and beliefs about visual context. *Cognitive Science*, 33, 1468–1482.

Ritchart, A. and Arvaniti, A. (2014). The form and use of uptalk in Southern Californian English. *Proceedings of Meetings on Acoustics*, 20.

Robinson, H. (2010). Let's, like, banish moronic interrogatives from class? Answer the question. Letter in response to Chris Woodhead's column. *Sunday Times*, 2 May, p. 9.

Room, A. (2002). Letter in response to: why do many young people, from all social backgrounds, intersperse their speech with the word 'like' after every few words of conversation? *The Times*, 29 May, p. 32.

Rosewarne, D. (2009). How Estuary English won the world over. *The Times Educational Supplement*, 13 November, p. 37.

Sachs, J., Brown, R. and Salerno, R.A. (1976). Adults' speech to children. In W. von Raffler-Engel and Y. Lebrun (eds.), *Baby Talk and Infant Speech*. Lisse, Netherlands: Swets & Zeitlinger, pp. 240–245.

Sacks, H. and Schegloff, E.A. (1979). Two preferences in the organization of reference to persons in conversation and their interaction. In G. Psathas (ed.), *Everyday Language: Studies in ethnomethodology*. New York: Irvington Publishers, pp. 15–21.

Sadock, J.M. (1971). Queclaratives. In D. Adams, M.A. Cambell, V. Cohen, J. Levins, E. Maxwell, C. Nygren and J. Reighard (eds.), *Papers from the 7th Regional Meeting of the Chicago Linguistics Society*. Chicago: Chicago Linguistics Society, pp. 223–232.

 (1974). *Toward a Linguistic Theory of Speech Acts*. New York: Academic Press.

Šafářová, M. (2006). *Rises and Falls: Studies in the Semantics and Pragmatics of Intonation*. PhD thesis, University of Amsterdam.

Šafářová, M., Muller, P. and Prévot, L. (2005). *The Discourse Function of Final Rises in French Dialogues*. Paper presented at the DIALIR'05, Ninth workshop on the semantics and pragmatics of dialogue (SEMDIAL), Nancy, France.

Salazar, M. L. (2009). *The Role of /Overlaps\ in Intercultural Workplace Interaction*. MA thesis, Victoria University of Wellington.

Santa Ana, O. and Bayley, R. (2008). Chicano English: phonology. In B. Kortmann and E.W. Schneider (eds.), *Varieties of English, Vol. 2: The Americas and the Caribbean*. Berlin: Mouton de Gruyter, pp. 219–238.

Scherer, K.R., Ladd, D.R. and Silverman, K.E.A. (1984). Vocal cues to speaker affect: testing two models. *The Journal of the Acoustical Society of America*, 76(5), 1346–1356.

Schneider, E.W. (2004). Global synopsis: phonetic and phonological variation in English world-wide. In B. Kortmann, E.W. Schneider, K. Burridge, R. Mesthrie and C. Upton (eds.), *A Handbook of Varieties of English: A Multimedia Reference Tool*, Vol. 4. Berlin: Mouton, pp. 1111–1137.

 (2008). Synopsis: phonological variation in the Americas and the Caribbean. In B. Kortmann and E.W. Schneider (eds.), *Varieties of English, Vol. 2: The Americas and the Caribbean*. Berlin: Mouton de Gruyter, pp. 383–398.

Schweitzer, K., Calhoun, S., Schütze, H., Schweitzer, A. and Walsh, M. (2010). Relative frequency affects pitch accent realisation: evidence for exemplar storage of prosody. In M. Tabain, J. Fletcher, D. Grayden, J. Hajek and A. Butcher (eds.), *Proceedings of the 13th Australasian International Conference on Speech Science and Technology*. Melbourne: Causal Productions, pp. 62–65.

Seabrook, J. (2008). Hello, HAL: Annals of Technology. *The New Yorker*, 23 June, p. 38.

Seaton, M. (2001). Word up. *The Guardian*, 21 September, p. 1.

Séguinot, C. (1979). The intonation of yes–no questions. In P. Léon and P. Martin (eds.), *Toronto English, Studia Phonetica 14*. Paris: Didier, pp. 129–141.

Shepherd, M.A. (2011). Functional significance of rising-intonation declaratives in settings with special discursive norms. *Linguistic Society of America Annual Meeting Extended Abstracts*, www.sciary.com/journal-scientific-lsaabstracts-article-287596.

Shobbrook, K. and House, J. (2003). High rising tones in Southern British English. In M.J. Solé, D. Recasens and J. Romero (eds.), *15th International Congress of Phonetic Sciences*. Barcelona: Universitat Autonoma de Barcelona, pp. 1273–1276.

Shokeir, V. (2007). *Uptalk in Southern Ontario English*. Paper presented at NWAV 36, University of Pennsylvania.

    (2008). Evidence for the stable use of uptalk in South Ontario English. *University of Pennsylvania Working Papers in Linguistics*, 14(2), 16–24.

Silverman, K., Beckman, M.E., Pitrelli, J., Ostendorf, M., Wightman, C., Price, P., Pierrehumbert, J. and Hirschberg, J. (1992). ToBI: a standard for labeling English prosody. *Proceedings of the Second International Conference on Spoken Language Processing*, pp. 867–870.

Smets, B. (2000). It's like, the way Torontonians talk? Like this? My daughter caught it? *National Post*, 15 July, p. G4.

Smith, J.J. (2011). *NorCal vs. SoCal: Culture Communication*. BA thesis, California Polytechnic State University.

Smith, V.L. and Clark, H.H. (1993). On the course of answering questions. *Journal of Memory and Language*, 32(1), 25–38.

Smith, Z. (2006). Cinema. *Sunday Telegraph*, 12 February, p. 24.

Southern, T. (1963). Twirling at Ole Miss. *Esquire*, February, pp. 100–105, 121.

    ([1963] 1990). Twirling at Ole Miss. In *Red-Dirt Marijuana*. New York: Citadel Press, pp. 145–157.

Speer, S.R., Warren, P. and Schafer, A.J. (2011). Situationally independent prosodic phrasing. *Laboratory Phonology*, 2(1), 35–98.

Spindler, J. M. (2003). *Was That a Question? A Study of High-Rise Terminals*. MA thesis, South Dakota State University.

Stanton, K. (2006). *A Study of High Rising Terminals in Various Dialects of English*. Undergraduate project, University of Canterbury.

Starks, D., Christie, J. and Thompson, L. (2007). Niuean English: initial insights into an emerging variety. *English World-Wide*, 28(2), 133–146.

Steele, P. (1995). *Social Perceptions of High Rising Tone in the Australian Speech Community: A Sociolinguistic Replication Study Based on Guy and Vonwiller's 1984 Subjective Reaction Matched Guise Test*. Manuscript. Department of Linguistics, Australian National University, Canberra.

    (1996). *A Discourse Approach to the Function of Australian High Rising Tone in Narrative*. BA(Honours) thesis, Australian National University, Canberra.

Stevenson, J. (1995). Punch in ribs fast lesson in the power of speech. *Edmonton Journal*, 10 June, p. G8.

Stirling, L. and Manderson, L. (2011). About you: empathy, objectivity and authority. *Journal of Pragmatics*, 43(6), 1581–1602.

Stirling, L., Fletcher, J., Mushin, I. and Wales, R. (2001). Representational issues in annotation: using the Australian map task corpus to relate prosody and discourse structure. *Speech Communication*, 13, 113–134.

Stokel-Walker, C. (2014). The unstoppable march of the upward inflection? *BBC News Magazine*, 11 August, www.bbc.com/news/magazine-28708526.

Strang, B. (1964). Comments on D.L. Bolinger, intonation as a universal. In H.G. Lunt (ed.), *Proceedings of the Ninth International Congress of Linguists*. The Hague: Mouton.

Stuart-Smith, J. (1999). Glasgow: accent and voice quality. In P. Foulkes and G. Docherty (eds.), *Urban Voices: Accent Studies in the British Isles*. London: Arnold, pp. 203–222.

   (2008). Scottish English: phonology. In B. Kortmann and C. Upton (eds.), *Varieties of English. Vol 1: The British Isles*. Berlin: Mouton de Gruyter, pp. 48–70.

Stubbe, M. (1998). Are you listening? Cultural influences on the use of supportive verbal feedback in conversation. *Journal of Pragmatics*, 29(3), 257–289.

Sucharov, M. (2002). Down with 'uptalk'. *The Globe and Mail*, 5 January, p. A12.

Sudbury, A. (2001). Falkland Islands English: a southern hemisphere variety? *English World-Wide*, 22(1), 55–80.

Sullivan, J. (2009). *Exploring Intonational Change: Could a Final Rise be Derived from a Final Fall?* Paper presented at Language at the University of Essex (LangUE).

   (2010). *Belfast and Glasgow English 'Rises': Are There Phonological Distinctions Between Them?* Paper presented at the the Eighteenth Manchester Phonology Meeting, University of Manchester.

   (2011). *Approaching Intonational Distance and Change*. PhD thesis, University of Edinburgh.

Sussex, R. (2010). Word limit. *The Courier-Mail*, 14 August, p. 25.

Sutcliffe, D. (2003). Eastern Caribbean suprasegmental systems: a comparative view, with particular reference to Barbadian, Trinidadian, and Guyanese. In M. Aceto and J.P. Williams (eds.), *Contact Englishes of the Eastern Caribbean*. Amsterdam: John Benjamins, pp. 265–296.

Szakay, A. (2007). *Identifying Maori English and Pakeha English from Suprasegmental Cues: A Study Based on Speech Resynthesis*. MA thesis, University of Canterbury, Christchurch.

   (2008). Suprasegmentals and ethnic stereotypes in New Zealand. In P. Warren (ed.), *Laboratory Phonology 11 Book of Abstracts*. Wellington: Victoria University of Wellington, pp. 135–136.

   (2012). Voice quality as a marker of ethnicity in New Zealand: from acoustics to perception. *Journal of Sociolinguistics*, 16(3), 382–397.

Talla Sando, Y. (2009). *Upspeak Across Canadian English Accents: Acoustic and Sociophonetic Evidence*. Actes du congrès annuel de l'Association canadienne de linguistique 2009.

Tarone, E. (1973). Aspects of intonation in black English. *American Speech*, 48, 29–36.

Tartt, D. (2013). *The Goldfinch*. New York: Little, Brown and Company.

Tench, P. (1990). The pronunciation of English in Abercrave. In N. Coupland and A.R. Thomas (eds.), *English in Wales: Diversity, Conflict and Change*. Clevedon: Multilingual Matters, pp. 130–141.

   (1996). A new tone – for routine listing. *SpeakOut! The Newsletter of the IATEFL Pronunciation Special Interest Group*, 18, 26–32.

   (1997). Intonation innovations. *IATEFL Newsletter*, 140, 17–18.

   (2003). Processes of semogenesis in English intonation. *Functions of Language*, 10(2), 209–234.

(2014). A systemic functional model of the intonation of clauses in English. In M.I. Arboleda-Guirao (ed.), *Readings in English Phonetics and Phonology.* Valencia: Universitat de Valencia, pp. 261–296.

Tennant, J. and Rampersaud, S. (2000). *Language Contact and Intonational Variability: High Rising Terminals in Ontario French.* Paper presented at NWAV-29, Michigan State University.

Tent, J. and Mugler, F. (2008). Fiji English: phonology. In B. Kortmann and E.W. Schneider (eds.), *Varieties of English, Vol. 3: The Pacific and Australasia.* Berlin: Mouton de Gruyter, pp. 234–266.

terHorst, C. (2014). Being more like you. *EcoEvoLab blog,* www.ecoevolab.com/being-more-like-you.

Terraschke, A. and Holmes, J. (2007). Und tralala: vagueness and general extenders in German and New Zealand English. In J. Cutting (ed.), *Vague Language Explored,* London: Palgrave Macmillan.

Themistocleous, C. (2012). *'You Sound Nicosian': Speech Melody as an Urban Identity Marker.* Paper presented at Sociolinguistics Symposium 19, Freie Universität Berlin.

Theodoropoulou, I. (2008). Football register formation: the case of Greece's triumph in Euro 2004. In E. Lavric, G. Pisek, A. Skinner and W. Stadler (eds.), *The Linguistics of Football,* Tübingen: Gunter Narr Verlag, pp. 333–342.

Thielmann, J. (2005). 10 Four. *Edmonton Journal,* 5 March, p. D10.

Thomas, E.R. and Ericson, H.A. (2007). Intonational distinctiveness of Mexican American English. *University of Pennsylvania Working Papers in Linguistics,* 13(2), 193–205.

Thomas, H. (2000). Making the band. *Rolling Stone,* 27 April, p. 77.

Thomas, R.A. (1994). English in Wales. In R. Burchfield (ed.), *The Cambridge History of the English Language Vol. 5: English in Britain and Overseas: Origins and Development.* Cambridge: Cambridge University Press, pp. 94–147.

Times Q&A (2002). What has caused the popularity of upspeak? *The Times,* 10 May, p. 39.

Today (2006). BBC Radio 4. Broadcast on 21 November.

Tomkins, R. (2004). Why a vote for Tomkins is a vote for human freedom. *Financial Times,* 22 October, p. 11.

(2005). A dearth of manners will not bring civilisation to its knees. *Financial Times,* 13 September, p. 14.

Tomlinson, J.M. (2009). *Talking it Up: The Role of Temporal Context in the Interpretation of Uptalk.* PhD thesis, University of California, Santa Cruz.

Tomlinson, J.M. and Fox Tree, J.E. (2011). Listeners' comprehension of uptalk in spontaneous speech. *Cognition,* 119(1), 58–69.

Tomlinson, J.M. and Richardson, D.C. (2007). Do you believe what eye believe? In B.N. Kokinov, D.C. Richardson, T. Roth-Berghofer and L. Vieu (eds.), *Modeling and Using Context. Lecture Notes in Computer Science (Lecture Notes in Artificial Intelligence),* Vol. 4635. Berlin: Springer Verlag, pp. 482–492.

Toon, T.E. (1982). Variation in contemporary American English. In R.W. Bailey and M. Görlach (eds.), *English as a World Language.* Ann Arbor: University of Michigan Press, pp. 210–250.

Tottie, G. and Hoffmann, S. (2006). Tag questions in British and American English. *Journal of English Linguistics*, 34(4), 283–311.

Trager, G. and Smith, H. (1951). *An Outline of English Structure*. Washington: American Council of Learned Societies.

Trudgill, P. (2008). The dialect of East Anglia: phonology. In B. Kortmann and C. Upton (eds.), *Varieties of English. Vol 1: The British Isles*. Berlin: Mouton de Gruyter, pp. 178–193.

Tsiplakou, S. (2012). *Charting Nicosian: Properties and Perceptions of an Emergent Urban Dialect Variety*. Paper presented at the Sociolinguistics Symposium 19, Freie Universität Berlin, http://neon.niederlandistik.fu-berlin.de/ss19/paper/726.

Ueki, K. (2005). High rising terminals in Japanese discourse. *University of Hawai'i Working Papers in Linguistics*, 36(7), 1–16.

 (2011). *Prosody and intonation of Western Cham*. PhD thesis, University of Hawai'i at Manoa.

Uldall, E. (1961). Ambiguity: question or statement – 'are you asking me or telling me?' In A. Sovijarvi and P. Aalto (eds.), *Proceedings of the Fourth International Congress of Phonetic Sciences*. The Hague: Mouton, pp. 779–783.

 (1964). Dimensions of meaning in intonation. In D. Abercrombie, D.B. Fry, P.A.D. MacCarthy, N.D. Scott and J.L.M. Trim (eds.), *In Honour of Daniel Jones: Papers Contributed on the Occasion of his Eightieth Birthday*. London: Longman, pp. 271–279.

Updike, J. (1976). *Marry Me*. New York: Alfred A. Knopf.

Upton, C. (2008). Synopsis: phonological variation in the British Isles. In B. Kortmann and C. Upton (eds.), *Varieties of English. Vol 1: The British Isles*. Berlin: Mouton de Gruyter, pp. 269–282.

Venditti, J. J. (2005). The J_ToBI model of Japanese intonation. In S.-A. Jun (ed.), *Prosodic Typology: The Phonology of Intonation and Phrasing*. Oxford: Oxford University Press, pp. 172–200.

VoicetowordBlog (2011). Intonation – Uptalk! *VoicetowordBlog*, http://voicetoword.ca/blog/http:/voicetoword.ca/accent-modification/intonation-%E2%80%93-uptalk-from-voice-to-word.

Walters, J.R. (2003a). 'Celtic English': influences on a South Wales valleys accent. *English World-Wide*, 24, 63–87.

 (2003b). On the intonation of a South Wales Valleys accent of English. *Journal of the International Phonetic Association*, 33(2), 211–238.

Warner, M.P. (1967). *Language in Trinidad, with special reference to English*. MPhil thesis, University of York.

Warren, J. (1999). 'Wogspeak': transformations of Australian English. *Journal of Australian Studies*, 23(62), 85–94.

Warren, P. (2002). NZSED: building and using a speech database for New Zealand English *New Zealand English Journal*, 16, 53–58.

 (2005a). Issues in the study of intonation in language varieties. *Language and Speech*, 48(4), 345–358.

 (2005b). Patterns of late rising in New Zealand English: intonation variation or intonational change? *Language Variation and Change*, 17, 209–230.

(2006). Word recognition and sound merger. In J. Luchjenbroers (ed.), *Cognitive Linguistic Investigations Across Languages, Fields, and Philosophical Boundaries.* Amsterdam: John Benjamins, pp. 169–186.

(2014a). Sociophonetic and prosodic influences on judgements of sentence type. In J. Hay and E. Parnell (eds.), *Proceedings of the 15th Australasian International Conference on Speech Science and Technology.* Christchurch: ASSTA, pp. 185–188.

(2014b). Uncertainty in the origins of uptalk. *New Zealand English Journal*, 27, 1–9.

Warren, P. and Bauer, L. (2004). Maori English: phonology. In B. Kortmann, E.W. Schneider, K. Burridge, R. Mesthrie and C. Upton (eds.), *A Handbook of Varieties of English: A Multimedia Reference Tool*, Vol. 1. Berlin: Mouton de Gruyter, pp. 614–624.

Warren, P. and Britain, D. (2000). Intonation and prosody in New Zealand English. In A. Bell and K. Kuiper (eds.), *New Zealand English.* Wellington: Victoria University Press, pp. 146–172.

Warren, P. and Daly, N. (2000). Sex as a factor in rises in New Zealand English. In J. Holmes (ed.), *Gendered Speech in Social Context: Perspectives from Gown and Town.* Wellington: Victoria University Press, pp. 99–115.

(2005). Characterising New Zealand intonation: broad and narrow analysis. In A. Bell, R. Harlow and D. Starks (eds.), *Languages of New Zealand.* Wellington: Victoria University Press.

Waterhouse, K. (2000). Curtains for the snivelling coalman. *Daily Mail*, 13 July, p. 14.

Watson, D. (2003). *Death Sentence: The Decay of Public Language*, New York: Random House.

Watson, W. (2000). Do we really all dislike westerners? *The Ottawa Citizen*, 3 December, p. A16.

Watt, D.L.E. (1994). *The Phonology and Semology of Intonation in English: An Instrumental and Systemic Perspective.* Bloomington: Indiana University Linguistics Club.

Webb, K. (2008). *High Rising Terminals in Australian English: Form and Function.* BA(Honours) thesis, University of Melbourne, Melbourne.

Weldon, T.L. (2008). Gullah: phonology. In B. Kortmann and E.W. Schneider (eds.), *Varieties of English. Vol. 2: The Americas and the Caribbean.* Berlin: Mouton de Gruyter, pp. 192–207.

Wells, B. and Peppé, S. (1996). Ending up in Ulster: prosody and turn-taking in English dialects. In E. Couper-Kuhlen and M. Selting (eds.), *Prosody in Conversation.* Cambridge: Cambridge University Press, pp. 101–130.

Wells, J.C. (1982). *Accents of English.* Cambridge: Cambridge University Press.

(2006). *English Intonation: An Introduction.* Cambridge: Cambridge University Press.

White, C. (2007). Letters. *New York Times Magazine*, 22 July, p. 10.

White, D. (1995). It's not OK, OK? *Boston Globe*, 6 July, p. 61.

Whittaker, T. (1999). Lost between houses by David Gilmour. *Canadian Review of Books*, 28, 47.

Wichmann, A. (2011). Prosody and pragmatic effects. In G. Andersen and K. Aijmer (eds.), *Pragmatics of Society.* Berlin: De Gruyter Mouton, pp. 181–213.

Wichmann, A. and Caspers, J. (2001). *Melodic Cues to Turn-Taking in English: Evidence from Perception.* Paper presented at Second SIGdial Workshop on Discourse and Dialogue.

References

Wilhelm, S. (2015).

Wilhelm, S. (2015). *Word Up! The Rise of Rising Tones in Several Varieties of Contemporary English*. Paper presented at 17th Conference on Oral English/17th Colloque sur l'anglais oral de Villetaneuse, Spoken English and the Media, 4–5 April 2014.

Willis, E.W. (2010). Dominican Spanish Intonation. In P. Prieto and P. Roseano (eds.), *Transcription of Intonation of the Spanish Language*. Munich: Lincom Europa, pp. 123–153.

Wilson, F. (1995). 'Piano' composer joining Relache for 2 concerts. *Philadelphia Inquirer*, 29 September, p. 39.

Wolff, R.A. (2000). *Portland Dialect Study: High Rising Terminal Contours (HRTS) in Portland Speech*. MA thesis, Portland State University.

Wolfram, W. and Fasold, R.W. (1974). *The Study of Social Dialects in American English*. Englewood Cliffs, NJ: Prentice-Hall.

Wolfram, W. and Schilling-Estes, N. (2006). *American English: Dialects and Variation*. Malden, MA: Blackwell

Wolfram, W., Childs, B., Reaser, J. and Torbert, B. (2006). Islands of diversity (Bahamas). In W. Wolfram and B. Ward (eds.), *American Voices: How Dialects Differ from Coast to Coast*. Malden, MA: Blackwell, pp. 183–188.

Wollaston, S. (2005). He claims to prefer the written word, but Alan Bennett has plenty of stories to tell – and listening to him is a joy. *The Guardian*, 10 October, p. 32.

(2009). She's the boss of US *Marie Claire*. But I'll always know her as my old workmate Colesy. *The Guardian*, 16 September, p. 25.

Wood, A. (2002). What has caused the popularity of upspeak? *The Times*, 10 May, p. 39.

Word4Word (2005). *Friends, Neighbours and Big Brothers*, www.bbc.co.uk/radio4/factual/word4word_20050907.shtml.

Young, C. (2014). In a world … of uptalk, sexy babies, and God. *Cacophony: Communication Across the Curriculum*, http://cac.ophony.org/2014/01/31/in-a-world-of-uptalk-sexy-babies-and-god.

Youssef, V. and James, W. (2008). The creoles of Trinidad and Tobago: phonology. In B. Kortmann and E.W. Schneider (eds.), *Varieties of English, Vol. 2: The Americas and the Caribbean*. Berlin: Mouton de Gruyter pp. 320–338.

Zielinski, D. (1998). The gender gap. *Presentations*, 31 August, p. 36.

Zimmer, B. (2006). Further thoughts on 'The Affect'. *Language Log*, http://itre.cis.upenn.edu/~myl/languagelog/archives/002949.html.

Zwartz, J. and Warren, P. (2003). This is a statement? Lateness of rise as a factor in listener interpretation of HRTs. *Wellington Working Papers in Linguistics*, 15, 51–62.

Index

Warren, P., 28, 31–32, 37–38, 64, 75, 76, 86, 114, 117, 126, 152, 154, 184
Western Cham, 168
WHQ (wh-question). *See* questions

women. *See* social factors in uptalk use: sex

YNQ (yes–no question). *See* questions